LIFE PRINCIPLES FROM THE NEW TESTAMENT

AMG PUBLISHERS

Following God through the BIBLE

Cease Striving

BOOK 2

Mendy Clark, D.Ed.Min.

Following God

CEASE STRIVING
BOOK 2

© 2022 by Mendy Clark

Published by AMG Publishers. All Rights Reserved.
No part of this publication, including the artwork, may be reproduced, stored in a retrieval system, or transmitted in any form or by any means, electronic, mechanical, photocopying, recording, or otherwise—except for brief quotations in printed reviews, without the prior written permission of the publisher.

ISBN 13: 978-1-61715-528-4

Unless otherwise noted,
Scripture is taken from the *New American Standard Bible*®. Copyright © 1960, 1962, 1963, 1968, 1971, 1972, 1973, 1975, 1977, 1995, by The Lockman Foundation. Used by permission.
(www.Lockman.org)

Portions appear from *The Complete Word Study Old Testament*
Copyright © 1994 by AMG Publishers.
Used by permission.

Manuscript editing, text design, and layout by Rick Steele Editorial Services
http://steeleeditorialservices.myportfolio.com

Cover illustration by Daryle Beam/Bright Boy Design

Printed in the United States of America
2022 First Edition

Cease Striving is dedicated to those most profoundly and daily affected by my ignorance of God's sanctifying grace (Gal. 3:3):

To my dear husband Stan, and our four precious gifts from the Lord, Lindsey, Jenna, Maegan, and Tyler.

May the God of all grace continue to revive and restore the years the locust has eaten. I love you all more than words!

Acknowledgments

I would like to acknowledge the precious women on the Transforming the Heart Ministry Team, the Women's Bible Study groups at Chaffee Crossing Baptist Church in Fort Smith, Arkansas, and Charlottesville Community Church in Charlottesville, Virginia, for their participation, helpful comments and prayerful suggestions as they participated in the pilot study of this workbook.

Mendy Clark

MENDY CLARK (DEd Min, Southwestern Baptist Theological Seminary) is a Bible teacher, author, retreat speaker, educator and discipler of women. She is the founder, executive officer and lead teacher of Transforming the Heart Ministries. Transforming the Heart is a ministry dedicated to making disciples by equipping and training them using the biblical framework established in the all-sufficient Word of God.

Preface

"Cease striving and know that I am God."

Psalm 46:10

More than likely, if you've picked up this workbook, something in the title caught your attention. Maybe deep down, you are willing to admit that there is a striver within, and you seek rest for your soul.

Perhaps it's more than that. Maybe you have reached the end of yourself and have been crying out to the Lord for help. Striving to live the Christian life has made you anxious, joyless, and weary even to the point of exhaustion. If this is where you are, I understand entirely. It's what I call the "white-flag moment," when all of the sudden, in my head, a white flag goes up in frustration and exhaustion, and all I want to do is quit!

How do I know so much about striving? Let's just say the Lord, in His grace, has been rescuing me, from me, my entire life! Unknowingly, I spent the first twenty-five years of my walk, striving to live the Christian life in my flesh and failing miserably.

If this describes where you are, one thing is sure; the grace of God has placed this workbook in your hand. Notice I mentioned the grace of God explicitly because God's work of grace is the exact opposite of man's striving! Basically, this workbook is about two things:

God's Grace

and

Man's Striving

Be prepared as you walk through this study in Galatians, to see how Paul addresses and answers where man strives to be like god regarding salvation. You will see these areas specifically addressed in the questions Paul asks the Galatian believers, namely:

- Did you receive the Spirit by the works of the Law, or by hearing with faith (3:2)?
- Having begun by the Spirit, are you now being perfected by the flesh (3:3)?

If you consider Paul's first question, you will see that he is referring to man's salvation, in particular, justification. And in the second question, Paul is clearly referring to sanctification. Let's face it: there is an inherent desire to be "savior" in each of us, and it entered the human race at the Fall.

In this workbook, you will discover why people strive, where it enters into the heart of humanity, what and whom people strive to be, and how it manifests itself in our relationship with both God and humanity. You will also discover that God's work of grace through the Gospel of Jesus Christ is the only remedy for such striving.

Throughout the Book of Galatians, Paul admonishes believers who are struggling because false teachers have come in with the lie that man can be justified in religion and sanctified through his work of religious activity. In other words, the message of the false teacher is that salvation, whether referring to man's justification or sanctification, is achieved by Christ's work plus man's work. Paul warns that adding anything to God's work of grace, whether it is Christ's finished work on the cross, or the work of grace now by His Spirit through His Word, is a different gospel.

This workbook has been written:

- To those brave enough to admit that they love themselves more than God and others in far too many areas of their heart.
- To those who are willing to acknowledge that they are in desperate need of a Savior!
- To those who are ready to wave the white flag of surrender in their heart and willingly allow God be God in their life.

If this description fits you, this is a divine appointment with the one true God. I am convinced, once you truly see God's grace, you will cease striving!

My prayer as you proceed through the study is, "Save us, O Lord, from striving to accomplish Your kingdom work in the flesh, rather than simply yieldingly and obediently allowing You to do Your kingdom work through us."

Final Note: To be able to fill in all blanks in this workbook, you will need access to the New American Standard Bible (1995 edition).

Mendy Clark

CONTENTS

Lesson 1

The Only Thing I Want to Find Out

GALATIANS 3:1–5

In this lesson, we find a shift of focus in the letter. In chapter one, Paul expresses amazement that the churches in Galatia were so quickly deserting God who had called them by the grace of Christ (v. 6). In his state of shock, Paul acknowledges their disturbed state and addresses the reason that their minds had become agitated. He identifies the source, the false brethren known as the Judaizers, who had *sneaked in* to spy out their liberty in Christ (Gal. 2:4). Paul called the message they were preaching a different and distorted gospel (Gal. 1:6-7). To Paul, their agenda was clear. Their plan was an attempt to bring the churches in Galatia back into bondage (Gal. 2:4), whereby rendering them useless.

By giving his testimony, Paul explains the meaning of grace through faith in Christ Jesus. He begins with his former manner of life *in Judaism*, which had proven exhaustingly futile regarding salvation. In essence, Paul's testimony is a great illustration of God's grace, and his life was now mercifully *in Christ*.

As with grace, God had done everything, and the only thing Paul could bring to the table was his sin and desperate need for a Savior. Paul's flesh and hard work had accomplished nothing. The Lord Jesus had been the Initiator, and Paul was merely the recipient of a kind and gracious God. In short, it had been the kindness of God that had led Paul to repentance (Rom. 2:4), and Paul knew it. He refused to take any credit. The glory belonged to God alone. He also could not just stand idly by while the false brethren wreaked havoc among his spiritual children.

Now, in chapter 3, Paul, directly addresses the Galatians. Notice, Paul never addresses the false brethren. It is not his responsibility to try to change their hearts. They are not asking for help. Only God could open their blind eyes and rescue them from eternal damnation. Herein lies a lesson for us today. Our job is not to address or confront the false brethren. Paul wastes no time on them. God was not at work drawing their hearts. He was concerned with those who were being led astray by their false message. Therefore, let's begin this lesson by looking at Paul's direct message to the Galatian believers.

1. First note what Paul called them in verse 1?

At first impression, it appears that Paul is being offensive and calling them names. However, the more I thought about it, the more I realized why he might have resorted to this name.

2. In order to understand why Paul addresses them as such, let's look at Psalm 14:1, where the fool is described and answer the following questions:

a. What is the fool saying? ____

b. Notice where this conversation is occurring? ______________________________

Note: In the literal translation of the Hebrew language, the verse reads, "The fool has said in his heart, 'No God for me!' "

c. Now, look at Isaiah 14:13–14. Notice the context of these verses address Lucifer's rebellion and subsequent fall. Answer the following questions using these verses:

Note where his conversation is occurring (v. 13). _______________

What is he saying in his heart? Record the five "I will" statements:

I will ____

I will ____

I will ____

I will ____

And finally, I will ____

Do you see where the fool originated?

What is the difference in your heart (mind, will, and emotions) between saying, "There is no God" versus "No God for me!" Explain your answer.

So, who is behind the heart that says, "No God for me?" __________________

3. Now let's look back at what Paul calls the Galatians in verse 1. What is Paul saying about them by calling them foolish?

4. What question does Paul ask them in verse 1?

First, the word "bewitched" is an interesting choice of word. It comes from the Greek word, *baskaino*, and it means to "utter foolish babble, i.e., to mislead by pretenses as if by magic arts."[1]

---

1. Spiros Zodhiates, *The Complete Word Study Dictionary New Testament* (Chattanooga, TN: AMG Publishers,1993), 328.

Further defining the word, Dr. John MacArthur states, "The word, *baskaino*, means to charm or fascinate in a misleading way, as by flattery, false promises, or occultic power, and clearly suggests the use of feeling over fact, emotion over clear understanding of truth."[2]

Secondly, the word "bewitched," is translated from an aorist indicative passive verb. The aorist tense indicates a punctiliar action at a point in time (as opposed to the present tense, which means continuous action). The indicative mood is a statement of fact. Interestingly, the passive voice is used here meaning that the subject(s) (the believers in Galatia) were being acted upon. In other words, they were not choosing to be bewitched. It was something that was happening to them.

In other words, when you look at the question, "*Who* has bewitched you? The subject is "*Who*," and in this case, the false teachers were the ones actively responsible for bewitching the believers in Galatia. However, what Paul wants the church to know is that behind the false teacher lies the true source of foolishness and bewitching—the Enemy himself. In fact, not only was the Enemy trying to bewitch the believers; the false teachers were also under his spell. The warning here is that any time, we as believers, choose not to surrender our will and obey His Word we become vulnerable for playing the fool and being bewitched as well.

Furthermore, as I look at MacArthur's definition, my mind goes immediately to the illustration of the upside-down heart:

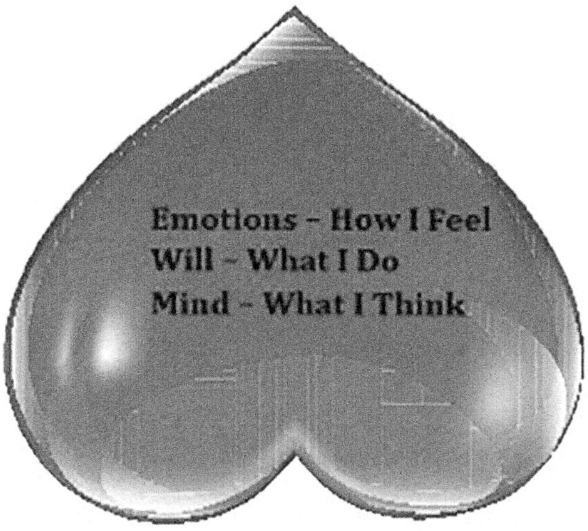

When the heart is flipped upside-down, (and it can), I know something is wrong! I know I have been listening to the wrong voice. I need the Savior to rescue my heart and place it right side up. When my heart is right side up, I can think biblically. In other words, the Spirit is in control.

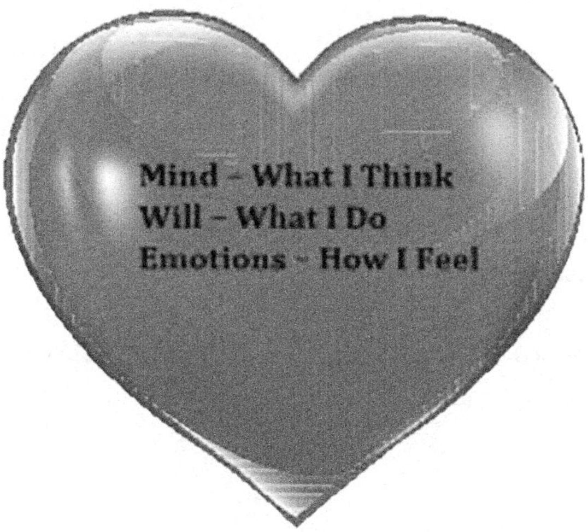

2. John MacArthur, Jr. *The MacArthur New Testament Commentary: Galatians* (Chicago, IL: Moody Press, 1987), 64.

Do you see it?

Note: In the past, I have wasted my time and energy striving to rescue my own heart when I realize it has flipped upside-down. I have learned, after sheer exhaustion, that it is much easier to cry out for the Savior to deliver me. Thankfully, He always hears my cry for help and rescues me.

5. Now, as we look back at Galatians 3:1, to whom might Paul be referring by using this particular word, "bewitched," and more specifically the verb's tense, mood, and voice? What do you see?

Paul is writing to believers. Therefore, a believer can be bewitched. Did you notice the word "bewitched" is an aorist indicative active verb? You will recall, the aorist tense indicates a point in time. The indicative mood is a statement of fact, while the active voice signifies the subject is performing the action.

You may be thinking, *Why would this be allowed?*

6. Look at how Jesus warns His disciples in John 10:10. Answer the following questions using this verse:

    a. What does Jesus call the enemy in this verse? ___________________________________

    b. What verb is used in connection with the thief? _________________________________

Note: The verb "comes" is present indicative middle. The present tense represents a continuous action. The indicative mood is a statement of fact; and the middle voice means that the subject (the thief) is both initiating and participating in the action (coming).

    c. What is the Enemy's purpose in coming?

        1) _________________________________

        2) _________________________________

        3) _________________________________

7. Now read Ephesians 6:12. How might this verse shed light on what Paul is saying in Galatians 3:1?

Think about it. Paul is not addressing the false brethren because they are just pawns in the hands of the Enemy who hates the message of the cross.

8. Look at Colossians 2:13–15. Record what God did through Jesus Christ. Also, note what happened to the Enemy when Jesus was nailed to the cross?

9. Also, look at Hebrews 2:14–15. Record what the death of Jesus Christ accomplished in regard to the Enemy. Also, note the Enemy's agenda for the believer.

10. Now, look back at Galatians 2:4. How does the Enemy's agenda in Galatians correspond with his agenda in Hebrews 2:15? What do you see?

And finally, looking back at Galatians 3:1, in the English transliteration, the words "publicly portrayed," actually come from one Greek word, *prographo*, which means "to announce openly and plainly, to set forth as in a public-written notice."[3]

11. If you look at Galatians 3:1, what is Paul saying to the Galatians? ___________________

12. Now let's look at Paul's central question. What does Paul say in Galatians 3:2?

Isn't Paul just asking, "How does a person receive the Spirit of God?" If you think about it, this is <u>the</u> question. The answer, hinging on this question, will determine one's eternal destiny. Therefore, the answer to this question ***must*** be right. It is a matter of life and death.

13. Notice Paul gives only two options as answers. What does Paul contrast?

a. By ____

or

b. By ____

It may surprise you to discover, as it did me, that the words "works" and "hearing," are not verbs, as they are both nouns! Likewise, the words, "Law" and "faith, are both nouns. Therefore, whether one works or hears, this refers to a state of being.

3. Ibid. 1217.

The word "receive" is the main verb. It is in the aorist tense meaning at a point in time. Keep in mind, by asking, ". . . Did you receive the Spirit?" Paul is referring to the initial entrance of God's Spirit at justification.

Another way to state the same question Paul is asking the believers in Galatia is to *say*, "Were you saved by works or by faith?"

14. First, let's look at the phrase, "by the works of the Law." If you look at the phrase, what immediately comes to mind? In other words, who is the initiator of the works?

If man can be the initiator of salvation, which nullifies the grace of God, then why did Jesus come and die?

Isn't that what Paul just said in Galatians 2:21?

So, what person, other than Jesus Christ, do you know, past or present, who kept the entire Law perfectly and entirely? In other words, do you know anyone, other than Jesus Christ, who lived a perfect and sinless life in regard to God's Law?

15. So then, how is a person saved?

a. In order to answer this question biblically, look at Ephesians 2:8-9. What do you see?

Do you see that human tendency and propensity is to boast? Religion breeds boasters. Look back at what Paul said about himself in Galatians 1:14, when he identified his former way of life in Judaism. Record the phrases Paul uses to describe his life in Judaism.

Now, look again at Ephesians 2:8–9.

Note: The order matters! You will recall, grace has everything to do with God and nothing to do with man, except for man's sin and need. Therefore, grace always precedes faith. God is always the Initiator! Faith, on the other hand, is man's response to God's grace. Both are gifts from God.

b. From where does faith come? Look at Romans 10:17 in order to answer this question. What do you see?

c. So, since faith comes from hearing God's Word, how is it that man can hear? Who is the initiator or gives man the ability to hear the truth? Look at Revelation 2:7, 11, 17, 29; 3:6, 13, and 22. (**Note:** These references are taken from the letters written to the seven churches in Asia Minor in the book of Revelation.) What do you see?

From the closing lesson in *Cease Striving Book 1*, you will recall our working definition of faith reveals:

Saving faith has three components: (The Spirit + The Word)

↓ ↓

Firm conviction to God's Word

Personal surrender to God's Word

Obedience to the Word of God[4]

Always keep in mind: The order is critical. God is always the Initiator! In other words, humanity's ability to surrender the will and obey God comes from God. They are His gifts of grace and faith.

Isn't it true then that the works of the Law blind you to the grace of God because the flesh becomes the initiator—the source, rather than the Spirit of God?

16. Now let's examine Galatians 3:3. Notice Paul begins with his next series of questions (which looks just like his first question). What does he ask?

a) ____ ?

b) ____

____ ?

17. Notice that Paul's second series of questions (v. 3) actually answers his first question (v. 2). As you follow his flow of thought in verse 3, what did Paul assume was the answer to his question in verse 2? In other words, had they received the Spirit by the works of the Law or by hearing with faith? Do you see the answer in verse 3?

____

____

18. Once again, what does the "fool" have to do with his questions regarding salvation? Refer back in the lesson to Psalm 14:1. What is Paul saying?

____

____

Now let's look closely at the phrases, "having begun by the Spirit," and "being perfected by the flesh."

Note: The verb "having begun" (*enarchomai*) is aorist participle middle. Aorist tense implies at a point in time; middle voice indicates that the subject both initiates and participates in the action.

However, the verb, "being perfected" (*epiteleo*) is present indicative middle. The present tense represents a continuous action; the indicative mood indicates a statement of fact, and the middle voice means that the subject both initiates and participates in the action. Also note that the word "perfected" (*epiteleo*) means to finish or complete.[5]

4. W. E. Vine, *Vine's Expository Dictionary of Old and New Testament Words* (Vol 2: E-Li) (Grand Rapids: Fleming H. Revell, 1981), 71.
5. Spiros Zodhiates, *The Complete Word Study Dictionary New Testament* (Chattanooga, TN: AMG Publishers, 1993), 642.

19. As you look at the verb tenses, what do you see in regard to salvation (justification and sanctification)?

By stating, "*Having begun by the Spirit*," Paul is reminding the Galatians that the Spirit of God had been the Initiator of their salvation. They had forgotten that it had been the grace of God—God's Spirit taking the Word of God, to open their eyes to their need for a Savior. They needed to be reminded that they had responded in faith. Therefore, they needed to look once again at justification.

However, by asking, "are you now being perfected by your flesh," indicates that they had also failed to understand the process of sanctification. Somehow, they had believed the lie that they now needed to strive through the works of the Law to be made complete. In other words, their sanctification was all up to them.

I don't know about you, but I can relate. I too believed this lie, which resulted in striving and exhaustion! Ignorance of God's Word coupled with my residual flesh was a recipe for disaster. I spent years of my walk as a believer trying to do for God what only He could do—complete what He had started. Thankfully, the Book of Galatians was written for people like me!

20. Look at the following cross-references to gain insight into Galatians 3:3. Record what you see.

a. Philippians 1:6

If you look closely, you will see all three tenses of salvation in Philippians 1:6.

b. Philippians 2:13

c. Hebrews 12:2a

d. John 17:17

21. As you look at Galatians 3:3, along with the cross-references in the previous question, where are you in these passages? In other words, what is your flesh contributing to your salvation (justification, sanctification, and, eventually, glorification)?

In a nutshell, isn't Paul just saying, "The same way in which you received the Spirit is the way you live by the Spirit—by grace through faith (God-Initiated)? Isn't our part (work) to surrender our will and obey His Spirit as He leads in His Word?

22. Now let's look at how He accomplishes His will in our life. Read Galatians 3:4. What does He use in our life?

Note: The word, *suffer* (*pascho*), means to be affected by something from without.[6]

Personally speaking, the most helpful definition comes from the late missionary and author, Elisabeth Elliot, who succinctly defines the word, *suffering*, as, "Having what you don't want, or wanting what you don't have."[7]

Do you see the main and repeated subject? ______________________

Remember, at the root, it's all about us!

I have discovered, the long and hard way, that suffering occurs when the Lord uses someone (people) or something (circumstances) from outside (without) to press in on me. Prior to this revelation and in my ignorance, I made the issue flesh and blood. The solution for me was to get out of the pressing circumstance or get away from that person! I had no idea that the purpose of the squeezing was to show me what He sees and wants to put to death—*in me*, if only I will let Him.

In other words, there are areas in my heart that need to be cleansed and set free—areas that do not look like Him. These are places in my heart where I have not fully surrendered my will in obedience to Him. Oftentimes, at least for me, these are not willful areas but ignorant areas. Sadly, there are also willful areas. These are places that can own me (have power over me), and the Lord will have none of that! For He, alone, is the Master of my heart. He alone is God!

Therefore, the Lord, in His kindness (although it never *feels* kind) allows people and circumstances in our life so that He can save us from ourselves—from within. Romans 2:4 tells us that it is the kindness of God that leads to repentance.

That being stated, let's look closely at Paul's question, "Did you suffer so many things in vain—if indeed it was in vain?"

Now, let's consider the word *"vain"* (*eike*), which literally means "without purpose, inconsiderately, groundlessly, without cause, to no purpose."[8]

23. Given the information above, what is Paul communicating in Galatians 3:4?

Note: Suffering is the tool God uses to perfect His people. His ultimate purpose and plan are to conform us into the image of His Son (Rom. 8:29). Therefore, our suffering (whether with people and/or circumstances) is never in vain. In fact, from His perspective, it is necessary.

---

6. *Ibid.*, 1127.
7. Elisabeth Elliot, *A Path Through Suffering* (Grand Rapids, MI: Revell, 1990), 56.
8. Spiros Zodhiates, *The Complete Word Study Dictionary New Testament* (Chattanooga, TN: AMG Publishers), 511.

Look again at Hebrews 12:2b, which states, "...who for the joy set before Him endured the cross..."

Notice, in God's economy, the cross always precedes the joy. The same will be true for His followers (see Mark 8:34).

24. And finally, as we look at Galatians 3:5, notice that Paul shifts the focus from the Galatians to God and more specifically, the Father and the Spirit. What does Paul specifically tell us about God the Father (5a)?

"Does **<u>He</u>** (emphasis added) then, who ______________________________

and

____

Note: Both verbs, "provides" and "works," are translated from present active participles. Remember, the present tense signifies continuous action; while the active voice, means that the subject is performing the action.

Also, the word, "miracles" may be difficult to understand in this verse. The Greek transliteration is *dunamis*, which literally means, "achieving power; intrinsic (inherent) power.[9] *Dunamis* is where we get our English word, dynamite.

With all of this in mind, what is Paul saying about the Father in verse 5?

25. Now let's look at Galatians 3:5 in its entirety. Fill in the blanks:

"Does **<u>He</u>** then, who ______________________________

and

____

↓

do it

↙ ↘

by ______________________________ or by ______________________________?

What do you say? How did God the Father provide the Spirit? (Notice, you can only answer from one of two options). Having walked through the lesson, how you would answer.

9. *Ibid.*, 485.

WHAT ABOUT YOU?

Is there a circumstance or a person (people) at this moment squeezing you?

Are you shocked, discouraged or even appalled by what is coming out of you?

If so, write it down here. There is something very illuminating when the Lord gives us the courage to take the thoughts out of our head and write them down on paper so that we can see them objectively.

Have you been making the situation a flesh and blood issue?

If so, confess this to the Lord because He already knows!

Ask the Lord what He is trying to show you about *your* heart. Typically, whatever has been coming out of you is what He is trying to show you.

For example, if anger has been your response, confess this to the Lord. More than likely, you are most angry with Him. However, knowing that it is not right to be mad at God makes it hard to see and even more difficult to confess.

When this happens to me, I have learned to cry out for the Lord Jesus to save me (Ps. 34:6). In the past, I unknowingly tried to fix it myself. I have spent years striving to save myself, by what I considered good things; for example, more prayer, more Bible studies, more time fasting—MORE.

Don't get me wrong. I am not disregarding prayer, Bible study, fasting (etc.). I am not saying you are not to participate in these things. I am saying that you cannot do these things in order to get something or manipulate God. It is impossible for man to put God in his debt. It's the mindset that thinks, "Well Lord, I've done _______ and _________, and now, You owe me ___________ and __________."

Whether willful or innocent, it's the mindset that places God in our debt, as if He owes us something for the things we have done. In other words, these things will not be the means of our salvation; rather, the Lord Jesus will be salvation; whether it is from the penalty, power, or presence of sin).

Thankfully, the Lord in His kindness has granted me repentance by revealing to me the simplicity of the gospel. You see there is only one Savior—Jesus. His work to save is a completed work involving all three aspects, namely: justification, sanctification, and glorification.

Grace is teaching me that when I cease striving to be God (save myself from the *power* of sin), then and only then, will I know that He is God. In other words, I am learning to come to Him in the state that I am in, whether it is weakness or hurt or anger or disappointment or discouragement—due to my sin, the sin of another, or just because I live in a fallen world that is dying, I am learning to cease striving to make myself better.

When I realize that something has power over me, I am learning to cry out and pray,

"Lord Jesus, You have used this (circumstance or person) to squeeze me. You have shown me that _______________ is in my heart. Lord Jesus, You are right, and I am wrong because ____________ has power over me. Thank you for showing me what is in my heart. Please forgive me and save me from the *power* that ________ has had over me. I am in need of a Savior. Lord Jesus, You are my Savior."

As for you, whatever circumstance or person(s) He has brought to mind, He has done so because He wants you to see what He sees so that He can save you from its power.

Will you let Him save you from whomever or whatever has power over you right now?

LESSON 2

SALVATION: WORKS OF THE LAW OR FAITH IN CHRIST JESUS

GALATIANS 3:6–14

As we continue in our study, you can see the ongoing contrast in the Book of Galatians is clearly between the works of the Law and faith in Jesus Christ. In other words, man would instead strive for something only God can provide. Indeed, there is something inherent within humanity's fallen flesh that desires to be like God because deep down, people love themselves and want the glory that is due to God alone. And since the Fall (whether heavenly or earthly), God's creation (whether angelic or human) has been in an all-out futile attempt to rob God of His glory. Sheer insanity!

In this lesson, Paul, under the inspiration of God's Spirit, will masterfully address the issue by using someone that every Jew (including the Judaizers) know and revere—Abraham. You will recall from a previous lesson, Abraham's salvation occurred before circumcision and over four hundred years before the Law was given to Moses, making Abraham the perfect example for faith. In other words, man was saved by grace through faith before any work could be credited to man's account.

Keep in mind as you go, Paul's message was directed to the believers who were being disturbed by the Judaizer's distorted message. Notice he does not address or argue with the Judaizers, but rather focuses on those in the church by reminding them of the truth from God's holy and inspired Word.

Observe, as the Spirit of God will use the Word of God to correct the Judaizer's false doctrine. Keep in mind Paul is merely the human instrument God chose to accomplish His purpose.

1. Let's begin by reminding ourselves of Paul's main question to the Galatians; in fact, it was the only thing he wanted to find out from them (Gal. 3:2). He asked, "Did you receive the Spirit by:

   ____

   or

   ____?"

2. And again, in verse 5, he asks them the same question. Except this time, the question is from God's perspective, stating, "Does He then, who provides you with the Spirit and works miracles among you, do it by:

   ____

   or

   ____?"

Now observe as the Spirit of God using the Word of God prompts Paul to respond to lead the Galatians to the correct answer. It's amazing!

3. Let's begin by reading Galatians 3:6-14. Count the number of times the passage uses all caps.

Note: The use of all caps in this passage is an indicator that Paul is referring back to the Old Testament.

a. How many times does Paul refer the Galatians back to the Old Testament to answer his question?

____

We would do well to learn from Paul here. When false teaching slips into the church (and it will), notice that Paul does not confront the false teachers. He doesn't argue with them or engage with them at all.

Instead, in referencing the Old Testament six times in this section, Paul demonstrates his ultimate dependence upon the power of God's Spirit using God's Word to teach, reprove, correct, and train in righteousness (2 Tim. 3:16). We would do well to follow his example.

b. If you look at 2 Timothy 3:17, you will discover why. What do you see?

Note: The word "adequate" means, "complete, sufficient, completely qualified. More closely synonymous with the word, *whole* (*holokleros*), as used in 1 Thessalonians 5:23, one in which all the parts are complete or whole and what they are supposed to be so that they might serve their destined purpose."[10] The antonym is "crippled, maimed, lacking."[11]

Likewise, the verb "equipped" (*exartizo*) means "to fit completely."[12] Interestingly, the verb is a perfect passive participle. The perfect tense indicates that the equipping is a completed action from the past that has present and future results. The passive voice suggests that the subject is being acted upon by an outside source, which in this case, would be a reference to God.

Therefore, the Spirit of God is doing the equipping. We, on the other hand, are following as He leads by surrendering and obeying His Word.

Furthermore, I found Dr. Zodhiates' explanation very helpful as he connects verses 16-17 together, stating, "*Exartizo* means to equip, outfit, furnish. The participle is causal, and the sentence therefore reads, '. . . that the man of God may be competent because he has been equipped [outfitted, furnished].' God's Word is that which gives one the necessary skills and tools to be capable in performing every good work."[13]

c. Think about it. What would be the opposite of 2 Timothy 3:17?

Are you beginning to see that every time you and I refuse to surrender our will in obedience to the Spirit's prompting of God's Word, we are rendered useless?

---

10. Spiros Zodhiates, *The Complete Word Study Dictionary New Testament* (Chattanooga, TN: AMG Publishers, 1993), 259.
11. *Ibid.*
12. *Ibid.*, 601.
13. Ibid.

As you meditate on these truths, can you see exactly what the enemy wants to accomplish within the churches of Galatia? Knowing he has no ownership or power over those who belong to the Lord, the only tactic he has left is to try to render the believer useless. No one is immune. Lord, save us all!

Now let's get started with the people and places in Scripture the Spirit prompted Paul to consider. The same voice in the Old Testament is speaking in the New Testament.

4. Read Galatians 3:6. Look familiar? If you recall, we discussed in detail Genesis 15:6 in the lesson entitled, "The Issue: Circumcision."

   a. In the way of review, what does Paul remind the Galatians about Abraham?

   Abraham ____________________ __________________,

   and

   ↓

   it was ____.

Note: The verb, "believe" (*pisteuo*), and the noun, "faith" (*pistis*) have the same meaning. They are just different parts of speech; therefore, they can be used interchangeably.

Saving faith has three components: (The Spirit + The Word)

↓ ↓

Firm conviction to God's Word

Personal surrender to God's Word

Obedience to the Word of God[14]

Always keep in mind: The order is critical. God is always the Initiator!

The word "reckoned" (*logizoma*) is an accounting term that means to impute or put to one's account. The word "reckoned" is where the doctrine of imputation originates. Also, the passive voice is specifically used here. [You will recall that the passive voice is used when the subject is not the one performing the action but rather is acted upon from an outside source. In this case, God.]

   b. Using the information provided, as you look again at the verbs "believe" and "reckoned," in Galatians 3:6, what do you see?

14. W. E. Vine, *Vine's Expository Dictionary of Old and New Testament Words* (Vol 2: E-Li), (Grand Rapids, MI: Fleming H. Revell, 1981), 71.

Commenting on this portion of the lesson, one precious young lady in my leadership class shared the following observations, stating,

The Lord God gave Abraham the conviction, and Abraham surrendered and obeyed the Word. Then, God imputed His righteousness to Abraham. I don't start or finish the work! The Lord is on either side of my obedience. He prompts and He finishes. He goes before and He follows. He surrounds me in all His work. I am not left alone to do God's bidding, as the Enemy would have me believe. The Lord Jesus follows and lays a blanket of righteousness—His Righteousness over me.[15]

Watching the peace that was clearly visible on her beautiful face and seeing the tears well up in her eyes as she spoke immediately brought two Scriptures to mind.

First, Philippians 1:6, in which Paul states, "For I am confident of this very thing, that He who *began* a good work in you *will perfect* (complete) it until the day of Christ Jesus" (emphasis added). Do you see that He is the one who began the good work of salvation, and that He is the one who will complete His work on your behalf? These, my friend, are words of grace!

Secondly, Psalm 139, which states, "Thou hast enclosed me behind and before, and laid Thy hand upon me. Such knowledge is too wonderful for me. It is too high, I cannot attain to it" (Ps. 139:5-6). Beautiful response to a beautiful Savior, don't you think?

5. Now, let's look at Paul's admonition to the Galatians in verse 7, following the example of Abraham in verse 6. What does he caution?

Note: In essence, isn't Paul stating that those who are indeed sons of Abraham are spiritual sons through faith, and not merely because of their nationality?

6. Now look at Galatians 3:8 and answer the following questions:

   a. What did the Scripture foresee about God?

   b. How would God justify the Gentiles by faith?

   c. How was the gospel preached to Abraham beforehand?

   d. Look now in the margin of your Bible in the cross-reference section to discover from where Paul is quoting?

15. Karen Nixon shared in Leadership class with her permission.

e. What did the LORD God mean when He promised, "All the nations shall be blessed in you?" In other words, how is it possible to bless all nations through this one man, Abraham? [**Hint:** Who came from his line?]

7. Galatians 3:9 begins stating, "So then," which is a conclusive statement that connects verse 9 with verse 8. So, what is Paul's conclusion in verse 9? Note what Paul calls Abraham in this verse.

Note: The word "bless" (*eulogeo*) is worth further examination. According to Dr. Zodhiates, the subject and recipient can alter the interpretation. For example, when the word is used concerning humanity, it means to speak well of someone with praise and thanksgiving; to invoke God's blessing upon, which is God's action or intervention to accomplish His will in their life.[16]

Moreover, when used regarding God toward man, it means to distinguish with favor (grace) to act in man's life and accomplish His purposes instead of allowing men to have their way. When the subject is God, His speaking is action, for God's speech is energy-released. When God is said to bless us; He acts for our good as He sees our need and not necessarily our desire. Therefore, He blesses by intervening.[17]

Dr. Zodhiates in his invaluable dictionary mentions Acts 3:26 as an example, where it states that God sent His Son to bless us, to intervene in our lives with what He planned to do for us. Likewise, in Ephesians 1:3, He blesses us with all spiritual blessing, means the one who intervened and acted so that our spirits might be made conformable to His Spirit. Therefore, the *eulogeo* of God is His action or intervention in men's lives to bring them into the desired relationship with Himself.[18]

Furthermore, the word blessed is a present indicative passive verb. Present tense suggests continuous action. The indicative mood is a statement of fact. The passive voice indicates that the subject is being acted upon.

Now, with all of the information provided, what is Paul saying in Galatians 3:8-9?

8. As you read Galatians 3:10, what do you see about those who are depending on the works of the Law?

Note: As you might have already deduced, the word "curse" (*katara*) is the exact opposite of *bless* (*eulogeo*). The word "curse" has to do with the rejection of Christ (God's provision and greatest blessing). According to Dr. Zodhiates, it involves both the sentence of divine judgment and the ruin therein inflicted.[19]

---

16. Spiros Zodhiates, *The Complete Word Study Dictionary New Testament* (Chattanooga, TN: AMG Publishers), 677.
17. *Ibid.*
18. *Ibid.*, 678.
19. *Ibid.*, 841.

9. Why, according to verse 10, are they under a curse?

Are you watching how God's Spirit uses God's Word with each point Paul makes? Here, Paul is quoting from Deuteronomy 27:26; Psalm 119:21, and Jeremiah 11:3.

10. What was Paul's logical conclusion in verse 11? In other words, what, according to Paul, was evident?

a.

Again, as we have seen previously, the word *justified* is in the passive voice, meaning that the subject is being acted upon.

b. Why (v. 11)? For ___

Galatians 3:11b is quoted in Habakkuk 2:4, Romans 1:17, and Hebrews 10:38. In essence, it is one of the key verses in both the Old and New Testaments.

c. When you read, "THE RIGHTEOUS MAN SHALL LIVE BY FAITH" (v. 11b), do you see also, "For by ***grace*** are you saved through ***faith***" (emphasis added)? Although not stated, where is grace in Galatians 3:11b?

11. Read Galatians 3:12. Remember, when you see a reference to, "the Law," think, the "works of the Law." With that in mind, what do you see in verse 12a?

a.

b. Now look at the Old Testament passage quoted next from Leviticus 18:5 and Romans 10:5.

Commenting on Galatians 3:12, MacArthur states, "God's written law itself marks the danger of trying to live up to its standard, which is **perfection**. If you are relying on works of the law as your means of salvation, **then you have to live by them perfectly**" (emphasis added).[20] Contemplate the deception and the pressure of thinking you can perform the works of the Law perfectly. Blessed grace of God, only our Lord Jesus perfectly and completely obeyed the Law of God!

12. Now, after looking at the Scriptures, to whom does the Spirit point next in Galatians 3:13? ___

13. What do you learn specifically about Jesus Christ in verse 13?

a.

b.

20. John MacArthur, Jr. *The MacArthur New Testament Commentary: Galatians* (Chicago: Moody Press, 1987), 77.

The word "redeemed" (*exagorazo*) means, "to buy out from."[21] *Exagorazo* was the word commonly used to purchase a slave from the slave market.

Moreover, the phrase "having become a curse for us" comes from the verb, *ginomai*, which means "to begin to be, to come into existence."[22] Here it is used in aorist participle middle, meaning at a point in time, the subject (Christ) both initiated and participated in becoming a curse for us.

Herein is the doctrine of substitution. Jesus died in our place.

c. Now to discover at what specific point in time our perfect, sinless Savior became a curse for us read the following cross-references and record what you see.

1) Matthew 27:45-46 -

2) 2 Corinthians 5:21

Why did He become sin for us? ____

3) 1 Peter 2:24

Why did He bear our sins in His body on the cross?

d. Now, look at 1 Peter 1:18-19. What do you learn about the cost of your redemption?

Note: You and I were purchased from the slave market of sin. The purchase price was priceless, innocent, and precious blood.

You and I were very costly!

Can you imagine then what it means to the Father when a person rejects the gift of His Son?

---

21. Spiros Zodhiates, *The Complete Word Study Dictionary New Testament* (Chattanooga, TN: AMG Publishers, 1993), 597.
22. *Ibid.,* 367.

14. Quoting again from the Old Testament (Deut. 21:23), what does Paul remind the Galatians (and us) about the curse in Galatians 3:13b?

Consider, again, the words of MacArthur, who states, "In ancient Judaism, a criminal who was executed, usually by stoning, was then tied to a post, a type of tree, where his body would hang until sunset as **a visible representation of rejection by God**. It was not that a person became cursed by being hanged on a tree but that he was hanged on a tree because he was cursed" (emphasis added).[23]

You see, Jesus' death served as further confirmation to the unbelieving Jew that He could not have been the Messiah, for God would not curse or reject His Messiah. Moreover, they saw no need for a Savior to die in their place, because they were counting on their own "righteous" works for salvation.

15. As we conclude this lesson in Galatians 3:14, how is it possible that the blessing of Abraham might come to the Gentiles; and how might we receive the promise of the Spirit through faith? (**Hint:** Look for three key words.)

-------------- -------------------- -------------------------

16. As you look over Galatians 3:6-14, what does it mean to be **<u>in Christ Jesus</u>**? Be very specific, looking in each verse. Record what you see.

17. What, then, does it mean when a person is **<u>not</u>** in Christ Jesus? Again, be very specific looking in each verse. Record what you see.

23. John MacArthur, Jr., *The MacArthur New Testament Commentary: Galatians* (Chicago: Moody Press, 1987), 78.

Terrifying thought, isn't it?

18. One final question. When false teaching creeps in and *bewitches* you, your family, and/or church, what have you seen threaded throughout Galatians 3:6-14 that should serve as a biblical example to follow?

Will you be ready?

Look at the following illustration of Galatians 3:1-14 using the stick figure.

Galatians 3

A *Bewitched* Person

A fool has said in his heart, "No God for me!"

In other words, I'll be god! I've got this!

A *Bewitched* Believer

A fool has said in his heart, "No God for me!"

In other words, "Justified by grace through faith," but living (sanctification) by works!

↙ This mindset results in rendering: ↘

A Bewitcher Person

Dead in Transgressions and Sin

Heavy

Weary-laden

Commands are burdensome

A Bewitched Believer

Useless

Now, let's narrow our focus in on the believer who is bewitched. Look at the following visual for help:

The *Bewitched* Heart of a Believer

An incorrect theology (thinking) leads to wrong living and entangling emotions!

A believer can be bewitched (trapped) into *thinking* you have been saved (justified by grace through faith), and yet, now, you are being saved (sanctified) by works of the Law.

<u>Galatians 3:2</u>

Question: This is the only thing I want to find out from you: Did you receive the Spirit?

By works of the Law?

OR

By hearing with faith?

<u>Galatians 3:3</u>

Question: Are you so foolish? The answer is YES; we can be! Do you know that? Keep in mind we still have residual flesh!

Question: Having begun by the Spirit (justification), are you now being perfected (sanctification) by the flesh?

Example of Galatians 3:6-14: Abraham's salvation—before circumcision, before the Law!

Genesis 15:6—Abraham believed God (Word), and it was reckoned to him as righteousness!

Both the Old and New Testament

THE RIGHTEOUS MAN SHALL LIVE BY FAITH (Hab. 2:4; Rom. 1:17; Gal. 3:11; Heb. 10:38.)

↓ ↓ ↓

BY GRACE Through Faith! Sanctification Personal surrender to God's Word

Obedience to God's Word

Do you see that the life of a believer is *being saved* **by grace through faith**?

A life that says:

"Yes" to God's Spirit

and

"No" to our flesh!

"No" to the world!

"No" to the Enemy!

So, whether it is justification (have been saved), sanctification (being saved), or glorification (will be saved);

All of our salvation is by grace through faith!

Notes

Lesson 3

Salvation: The Law or The Promise

GALATIANS 3:15–25

In the past two lessons (Galatians 3:1-14), we have examined how Paul addresses the topic of salvation by contrasting the works of the Law versus faith in Christ. We discovered that the works of the Law amount to nothing more than striving in the flesh in an attempt to please God. In fact, according to Scripture, anything added to the finished work of Christ is a futile attempt to nullify the grace of God and a declaration (whether by words or works of the flesh) that Christ's death on the cross was needless (Gal. 2:21). Think about it, if the works of the Law can save mankind, then why would Jesus have had to come and die? The obvious conclusion then is that the works of the Law cannot save man, and Christ's death alone justifies men before God.

Now, in this lesson, (vv. 15-25), Paul will continue to solidify his defense of grace alone through faith alone as he further expounds on the contrast between the Law and the promise. You will discover, as did the Galatians, that salvation comes by way of the promise and not by the Law. You will also uncover the purpose of the Law as we proceed through Paul's argument that salvation from God is by faith alone in His promised seed, Jesus Christ.

1. Let's begin by reading Galatians 3:15-25.

2. Now, after reading these verses, what is repeatedly being contrasted?

the ______________________ and the ______________________

Do you see that Paul is contrasting the Law and the Promise? As you may have discovered while reading Galatians 3:15-25, Paul's defense can be very difficult to follow. Let's face it, Paul was a genius, and he argues, at times, like a very gifted lawyer.

Therefore, I have enlisted the assistance of a very bright attorney, Megen Prewitt, to help us unravel Paul's flow of thought. For example, after studying these verses and voicing the complexity of Paul's argument to Megen, she explained Paul's method of reasoning by stating,

> *Whenever I'm going to write a paper and submit it to the Court to ask the Court to rule for my client, the written part with my arguments and supporting case law/statutes is called a brief.*
>
> *To support an argument, I most often use either a statute or case law. A case law would be opinions written by higher courts, like the Arkansas Supreme Court or the United States Supreme Court. In each opinion, the judges write out (in a very similar way as Paul did in his epistles), how in specific detail, they arrived at their decision in the case. The opinion logically walks through each issue in the case. Each point that they make becomes the rule of law (that other courts and attorneys can rely on), and that is called a holding.*[24]

As you consider what Megen shared, do you see that Paul argues for the Promise, and the opposing counsel, in this case, the Judaizers, support the works of the Law? With each side presenting their case, God's Word, and more

24. Attorney, Megen Prewitt, shared with full permission.

specifically, the salvation of Abraham concerning the Law (Gen. 15:6) is the standard. The Judge and supreme ruling court is God Himself, and because He is the source of Law, every opinion must align with His Word.

So, follow along, as Megen has so graciously set each case in a visual to illustrate the two opposing arguments: The Promise (in the left-hand column) and The Law (in the right-hand column). Now, re-read Galatians 3:15-25 through the lens of an attorney. Pay close attention to the two distinct sides and the conclusion at the end of each point. This will prove very helpful as we proceed in the lesson.

Galatians 3:15-25

3:15 [Man's Covenant]

Brethren, I speak in terms of human relations:

even though it is only a man's covenant, yet when it has been ratified,

no one sets it aside or adds conditions to it.

3:16 [Promise]

Now the promises were spoken
to Abraham and
to his seed.

He does not say, 'And to seeds,'
as referring to many,
but rather
to one,
'And to your seed,'
that is, Christ.

3:17 [Law]

What I am saying is this:

the Law
which came 430 years later
does not invalidate a covenant
previously ratified by God
so as
to nullify the promise.

↘ ↙

3:18 [**Conclusion**]

The Promise Has Priority

For if the inheritance is based on law,

↓

it is no longer based on a promise;

but God ↓

has granted it to Abraham by means of a promise.

3:19-20 [Law]

Why the Law then?
↓
It was added because of transgressions,
having been ordained
↓
through angels
by the agency of a mediator,
until the seed would come
↓
to whom the promise
had been made.
Now a mediator is not for one party only;
whereas God is only one.

3:21 [**Conclusion**]

Is the Law then contrary to the promises of God?

May it never be!

For if a law had been given, which was able to impart life, then righteousness would indeed have been based on law.

3:22 [Promise]

But the Scripture has shut up
everyone
under sin,
so that
the promise
↓
by faith in Jesus Christ
might be given
to those who believe.

3:23 [Law]

But before faith came,
↓
we were kept in custody
under the law,
being shut up
to the faith
↓
which was later to be revealed.

↘ ↙

3:24-25 [**Conclusion**]

Therefore

the Law has become our tutor to lead us to Christ,

so that

we may be justified by faith.

But

now that faith has come, we are no longer under a tutor.

3. Now, looking at what Megen so beautifully put together, answer the following questions:

a. How does Paul refer to the Galatians in verse 15? ____________________

Now, that's a far cry from, "You foolish Galatians" isn't it?

b. In what terms is Paul addressing the brethren (v. 15)? __________________

Do you see that Paul begins this portion of the argument with an example that they would have each understood in terms of human relations—the making of a will or covenant agreement?

Note: You may recall from a previous lesson that the term *covenant* is the Hebrew transliteration of the word *berith* and the Greek transliteration of the word, *diatheke*. However, when used in classical Greek, it always involves a disposition a person makes of his property in the prospect of death. Its use in Galatians 3:15 was intended for classical interpretation regarding the will of one's property upon death.[25]

c. So what do you learn about a man's covenant (will) once it has been ratified according to verse 15?

1) ____

2) ____

Now, let's continue looking at the flow of Paul's argument in verse 16 as Paul shifts from human covenants to His divine promise. Do you see that Paul is arguing from the lesser to the greater? In other words, Paul begins his argument stating that if a human covenant is binding, and cannot be altered (v. 15), how much more binding and unalterable would a promise made by God be (v. 16)? Brilliant strategy!

4. Now, record to whom God's *promises* were made (v. 16)? ____________________

and

____

Note: This is the first time the word "promises" (*epaggelia*) is used in Galatians. Here the word is used as "a legal term meaning a summons or promise to do or give something with the intention that the thing promised is a *gift graciously* given and it is not a pledge secured by negotiation" (emphasis mine).[26]

5. Did you notice that Paul differentiates between the singular use of the word "seed" (*sperma*) and the plural use of the word "seeds"? Why does Paul place such special emphasis on its singular use? In other words, who does the *seed* represent?

Although Paul references the promise of the *seed* regarding Abraham (Genesis 12-22), the first mention of the promised *seed* is actually in Genesis 3:15. Theologians refer to this passage as the Protevangelium or the first mention of the promise of the gospel (good news). Let's pause and look at the first reference to the promised seed.

6. Let's start in Genesis 3:15 to discover what the LORD God said about His seed. [Notice the context is immediately after the Fall of Man in the Garden.]

a. Begin at verse 14 to discover to whom the LORD God is speaking? ____________________________

25. Spiros Zodhiates, *The Complete Word Study Dictionary New Testament* (Chattanooga, TN: AMG Publishers, 1993), 424.
26. *Ibid.,* 609.

b. What will the LORD God put between the the serpent and the woman in verse 15

c. Notice again what the LORD God says, "I will put enmity between _______ and the _______ between your ___________ and her ______________."

d. What will the *seed* of the woman do to the serpent?

e. What will the serpent do to the woman's *seed*?

There are several things you need to see in this verse. First, the woman does not have seeds (*sperma*). Reproductively, a woman has eggs (*ova*). Therefore, this is a prophecy concerning the virgin birth. The *seed* would be none other than Jesus Christ.

Secondly, the *seed* of the woman would bruise (crush) the head of the serpent. Head wounds are fatal; therefore, Jesus would have the final victory! Still, the serpent would bruise (crush) the *seed* of the woman's heel. Did you know that crucifixion was commonly known as *the death of the heel*?

Death, by crucifixion, was the death of asphyxiation. It was a slow, agonizing death, which involved extreme torture. Until death occurred, the victim would press his heel into the cross to push up to allow air into his lungs while he hung on the cross. There was never a doubt when someone died on a cross because his heels were a bloody mess due to hours of pushing up for air. Typically, the Roman guard would have to break the legs of the victim to expedite death.

[By the way, Jesus' legs were never broken (Jn. 19:32-33). Moreover, He dismissed His spirit when His work was complete fulfilling the Old Testament prophecy that no bone of His would be broken (Jn. 19:30; Ps. 34:20).]

You see the provision for the *seed*, which resulted in our salvation, was established long before Abraham, even long before the Garden; in fact, the plan was from eternity past (Rev. 13:8).

Now, let's return to Galatians.

7. What does Paul say, then, about *the promise* of the seed regarding *the Law* in Galatians 3:17? Try to use your own words rather than just copying the verse.

Note: The word "ratified" means "to establish or to confirm before, previously."[27] Furthermore, the word is a perfect participle passive verb. You will recall, the perfect tense indicates a completed action in the past with the present and future results. The passive voice shows that the subject, (Abraham), received the action of the covenant made by God Himself.

---

27. Spiros Zodhiates, *The Complete Word Study Dictionary New Testament* (Chattanooga, TN: AMG Publishers, 1993), 1222.

And if you think back to the lesson on Abraham's life, you will recall that the covenant God made with Abraham occurred while Abraham slept (Gen. 15:12). In fact, on the day the covenant was made, God Himself passed between the pieces of flesh. On that day, God inaugurated the covenant, which He had made with Himself from eternity past. On that day, God made a covenant with God, while Abraham (and all men slept—a euphemism for spiritual death) in terror and great darkness (Gen. 15:12).

Do you see that *the Law* or the works of the Law could not invalidate the covenant God had previously (some 430 years earlier) made with Abraham? God's promise to Abraham concerning the *seed* could not and would not be nullified. God's covenant was unconditional and not based upon what humanity could or could not do. Only the God-Man could accomplish what God had promised.

Therefore, Abraham's salvation, as recorded in Genesis 15:6, was *by grace through faith,* and it occurred *before* circumcision (Gen. 17), and long before the Law (Ex. 20). Abraham looked forward to *the promised seed*, Jesus Christ. We, on the other hand, look back at the same one and in the same way—by faith in His *promised seed*, Jesus Christ.

8. Now, read Galatians 3:18. Before you attempt to interpret the verse, look at the following information that will prove most beneficial.

Note: The word "granted" is from *charizomai*, which is a specialized word, denoting not merely a gift, but a gift, which is "given out of the spontaneous generosity of the Giver's heart, with no strings tied to it."[28]

It is unique in that *charizomai* has the same Greek root and meaning as the word, *grace* (*charis*). Therefore, it represents the "free act of the one who gives without any expectation of payment, which at once shows the difference between law and grace."[29]

Additionally, the word translated "granted" is in the perfect tense, which indicates a completed action in the past with present and future results. God is always the initiator of grace. People are merely the recipients.

9. Now, look at 1 Peter 1:3-4 to gain insight into this *inheritance* Paul references. What do you see?

Also noteworthy, according to Zodhiates, the word "inheritance" (*kleronomia*) is just another way of saying, "Divine salvation."[30]

10. Now, look at Galatians 3:18. Can you follow Paul's logic in this verse? With all of the information previously provided, what is Paul's conclusion (**Hint:** Look at Megen's conclusion).

Do you see that the Promise has priority over the Law?

11. Now, look at Galatians 3:18 in a slightly different way for clarity's sake.

28. Kenneth S. Wuest, *Word Studies in the Greek New Testament: Galatians, Vol. One* (Grand Rapids: William. B. Eerdmans Publishing Co., 1972), 102.

29. *Ibid.*

30. Spiros Zodhiates, *The Complete Word Study Dictionary New Testament* (Chattanooga, TN: AMG Publishers, 867).

a. Who grants the inheritance? ______________________

b. To whom is it granted? ______________________

c. By what means did He grant it to Abraham? ____________________________

Then, if this is true (and it is)...

d. Is it possible that the inheritance of salvation can be based upon the Law? _________

So, if the Law was never meant to be the means of salvation, why was it created in the first place?

12. Paul asks the same question in Galatians 3:19, and then answers his question. What do you see?

a. Why was the Law added? ____

Note: The word "transgression" (*parabasis*) is not the common word for "sin" (*hamartia*), which means to miss the mark. *Parabasis*, in its simplest definition, says, "to step beyond." It refers to the act of a person stepping beyond a fixed limit into forbidden territory.[31]

For clarity, Dr. Wuest explains,

> Before the law was given by Moses to Israel, the wrong doing of man was recognized as *hamartia, sin, a deviation from the course of right conduct. But when the law was given, sin was seen to be not merely the following of evil impulses, but the violation of explicit law. Thus, the exceeding sinfulness of sin was recognized by the human race, which otherwise might not have been evident. The law, therefore, was not given because of the existence of transgression, but to show hamartia (sin) in its true light, an overstepping of what is right into the realm of what is wrong. This revelation of the true nature of sin would cause man to fear God's wrath, which in turn would give strength to the weakness of man's moral sense and thus educate his conscience and make it more sensitive to sin.*[32]

So now, as you read what Dr. Wuest explains, why, then, was the Law given?

b. According to Galatians 3:19, through whom did the Lord God ordain the Law?

1) Through ______________________________

2) By the ____

and

3) For how long? ____

Note: The reference to the Law *having been ordained through angels* may be a new, confusing, and somewhat obscure thought. If you were to trace the cross-references in your Bible, you would find the following references listed: Deuteronomy 33:2, Acts 7:37-38, 53, and Hebrews 2:2. Each verse mentions that the angels were somehow involved when the Lord God gave Moses the Law.

Due to the obscurity of the topic, I will defer to Dr. MacArthur, as he explains Galatians 3:19, stating,

---

31. Kenneth S. Wuest, *Word Studies in the Greek New Testament: Galatians, Vol. One* (Grand Rapids: William. B. Eerdmans Publishing Co., 1972), 104.
32. *Ibid.*

The covenant of the Law was inferior to the covenant of promise because it was ordained (diatasso, a technical word for carrying out laws) through angels by the agency of a mediator. God gave the covenant of law through two sets of mediators, first through the angels and then by them, through Moses to the people.

God was the Author and Giver of the covenant of law, and He was present with Moses on Mt. Sinai when it was given (Ex 19:18-24). But in a way not fully explained, the law was given by God to Moses through angels (Acts 7:53; Heb 2:2).

When God gave the law, the setting was awesome and forbidding. God warned the people not to come near the fiery mountain, "Lest He break forth upon them" (Ex. 19:24).

But God gave the covenant to Abraham as Friend to friend (see Gen 12:1-3; 15:1-7; 18:1-33). The promise of salvation by faith was so precious to the heart of God that He gave it to Abraham in person. That is the way God desires to come to every person who will have His Son as Lord and Savior, the seed of Abraham who was to come to whom the promise had been made.

Moses was great, and the angels were great, but they were mediators. Paul warned the Galatians not to exalt Moses or angels over God Himself as the Judaizers were doing. [33]

13. Now, let's look at Galatians 3:20 to determine what Paul meant when he stated, "Now a mediator is not for one party only; whereas God is only one." Due to the difficulty in translation, I will defer, once again, to comments made by Dr. MacArthur, who states,

The Greek text of Galatians 3:20 is difficult to translate and interpret, but Paul seems to be pointing out that a mediator (literally one who stands between two parties) is needed only when more than one party is involved. God gave the covenant directly to Abraham without a mediator because He was the only one involved in making the covenant. Abraham was a witness to the covenant and a beneficiary, but he was not a party to it. Abraham had no part in establishing or keeping the covenant. That responsibility was God's alone.

The covenant of the law, however, not only involved mediators (angels and Moses) but mutual obligations on the two parties (God and Israel). The stipulation of that covenant was, "You shall walk in all the way which the Lord your God has commanded you, that you may live" (Deut 5:33). Man's part was to obey, and God's (part) was to give life, to save. The problem was that man could not keep his part, and therefore, God could not grant salvation.[34]

In summation, grace is unconditional. There is nothing man can do to either earn or deserve it. Where grace is concerned, God acts alone. However, the law is conditional, and although we may try, we cannot keep the Law of God without God.

14. Now, let's look at the second question Paul asks concerning the Law in verse 21.

a. What is his question?

b. What does he conclude? ____!

c. Now, what is the rationale for his answer? (Once again, you might refer back to Paul's conclusion [and Megen's] on page 25.)

33. John MacArthur Jr., *The MacArthur New Testament Commentary:Galatians*, (Chicago: Moody Press, 1987), pp. 87–88.
34. *Ibid.*

For clarification, consider again, the following from Dr. Wuest, who explains so beautifully, stating,

> The law and the promises are not in conflict because each has a distinct function. The law is a ministry of condemnation. The promises are a ministry of salvation. The law judges a person on the basis of obedience or disobedience. The promises judge man on the basis of faith. The law, whose ministry is one of condemnation, was not intended to express God's attitude towards man; God's attitude towards man is one of grace. The law is not the basis of God's judgment of man. **A sinner who rejects Christ, goes to the Lake of Fire for all eternity, not because he has broken God's laws, for his sin is paid for. He goes to a lost eternity because he rejects God's grace in the Lord Jesus** *(emphasis mine).*[35]

As I read the last part of his explanation, I thought, Lord, this is so true! To reject Christ is to reject God's grace!

15. Now, read Galatians 3:22. Look back at the diagram Megen provided on page 216-218 (it will change when you renumber the workbook) and answer the following questions:

    a. What had the Scriptures done to all people?

    b. Why, or for what purpose? ". . . so that

Do you see that God's purpose all along was faith in His Son?

16. Now, look at Galatians 3:23.

Before faith, in what was man *kept*? In ____

Note: According to Dr. Wuest, the word "kept" means "to keep in a ward under lock and key. The law was a jailer who held in custody those who were subjected to sin, in that they should not escape the consciousness of their sin and their liability to punishment."[36]

17. So, what is the first part of Paul's conclusion in verse 24?

    "The Law has become our ______________________. . ."

Note: The term "tutor" is an interesting term. When we think of the English term, we think of an instructor who comes alongside a teacher. However, the Greek word used here has more to do with a slave employed in Greek and Roman families to watch over a boy who is 6-16 years old. The slave was entrusted with the moral supervision of the young man.[37] In other words, rather than serve as a teacher or instructor, the job of the slave was to keep the boy out of trouble.

18. As you review the analogies of the jailor (v. 23), and the slave or tutor, whose job was to oversee the moral supervision of a child (v.24), what is the purpose of the law concerning each? In other words, what was the Law designed to lead to in each case and why (v.24)?

---

35. Kenneth S. Wuest, *Word Studies in the Greek New Testament: Galatians, Vol. One* (Grand Rapids, MI: William. B. Eerdmans Publishing Co., 1972), pp.106-107.
36. *Ibid.,* 109.
37. *Ibid.,* 110.

Do you see that the jailor and the slave were only outside sources to help regulate morality? What man needed most was an inside Source.

Note: Keep in mind that the word translated "justified" is in the passive voice, meaning that the subject is being acted upon. In other words, we are justified by grace alone from an outside Source. For no man can justify himself in the eyes of a holy God.

19. Now, look at Galatians 3:25. What do you learn in this verse about faith, and what might that have to do with our being justified (v. 24b)?

What is the basis of faith? Think about our working definition of faith from previous lessons. Isn't it based upon the promise from God (His Word) regarding His seed, Jesus Christ? Faith always and only finds its foundation in God's Word and God's Son.

One final thought. As I was considering the Law versus the Promise, I could not help but think back to the Israelites. I kept pondering the fact that for anyone to believe that the Law can save him or her is such a debilitating and depressing deception.

Have you ever considered that every other form of religion is under this same deception? People truly think so highly of themselves. Do you ever wonder why God had such grace and mercy on you? This thought causes my heart to become overwhelmed with gratitude and great joy. What about you?

Now one final assignment:

20. Let's take the time, before we end this lesson, to look back at the Israelites and their response to Moses in the giving of the Law.

Look at Exodus 19:3, which states, "And Moses went up to God, and the LORD called to him from the mountain, saying, 'Thus you shall say to the house of Jacob and tell the sons of Israel . . .'"

a. What is God's message to Israel in verses 4-6? Read these verses and record what God requires?

b. How do the people respond when Moses recalls all the words of the Lord to them (v.8)? Do you see Moses, the mediator?

c. And again, when the Word of the Lord is recounted to the people later in Exodus 24:3, how do the people respond?

d. Now, look at Exodus 24:4. What does Moses do?

e. Now, record what the book is called in verse 7?

f. What happens when Moses takes the book of the covenant and reads it in the hearing of the people? What do they say?

So, do you think they mean it? I do. In fact, I think they mean it with all of their heart.

So, what is the problem? ____

You see the entire Old Testament (covenant) is filled with God's people trying to follow the law and failing miserably. Only one would come to earth and keep the Law that God required. Only the promised *seed*, Jesus Christ, kept the law perfectly. And the fact that He now lives in us to do for us what we cannot do is nothing shy of amazing grace!

Why in the world would anyone want to go back up under the Law? That, my dear friend, is Paul's entire point in Galatians 3:15-25.

WHAT ABOUT YOU?

Have you based your salvation (justification, sanctification, and glorification) upon the Law or the promise, His seed, Jesus Christ?

What have you turned to for salvation from the *penalty* of sin?

Where do you go when sin has *power* over you? Whether it is your own willful choices, or the sin of another that has wounded, hurt, or deeply affected you, or whether it is from the sin resulting from this fallen world in which we live.

Think about it, the flesh, whether it is the dominating source as in the case of an unbeliever or the residual flesh that opposes the Holy Spirit in the life of a believer, wants to usurp God's Word. Since the fall of humanity, all flesh wants to be god! All flesh loves itself most! All flesh wants its own way! No flesh wants God (Rom. 3:10-18).

For the believer, the only way the flesh is put to death is by God's Spirit. He is the initiator of grace. Our only *correct* response is to surrender our wills and obey Him in faith. When He convicts our heart with the Word of God, He is inviting us to be filled with His Spirit as we surrender our wills to His will (Word) and obey Him. When that happens, there is more of the Spirit and less of the flesh.

Do you think that's what the author of Hebrews means when he encourages believers to, "Fix their eyes on Jesus, the author, and perfecter of faith, *who for the joy set before Him endured the cross, despising the shame...*" (Heb. 12:2; emphasis mine).

Think about it, in full surrender and obedience to the Father's plan to save, the Lord Jesus endured the cross and despised the shame, for the joy set before Him. Don't you think the joy set before Him included His Father's good pleasure and glory?

In His grace, He extends this invitation to those who are His. We too, are called to surrender to His will and obey Him. When we do, the Spirit of God puts the residual flesh to death resulting in more of the Spirit and less of the flesh. This process called sanctification results in a heart filled with love, joy, peace . . . (Gal. 5:22–23).

Isn't that what we as His followers desire? Do you realize that the desire just described comes from God's Spirit within you? According to Scripture, our flesh, when left to itself, will oppose and usurp God at all times.

Recently, I ran across an excellent and encouraging statement made by pastor and author, Paul David Tripp, who says, "God's call to obey is itself a grace. In this call, He is actively rescuing (saving) *you from you* (emphasis added).

Before this statement, I'm not sure I had ever seen the call to surrender and obey as a *grace* from God. But truly it is. Admittedly and sadly, I have seen it more as drudgery, punishment or something rather harsh that I have to endure.

Can you say like John the Baptist, "He must increase, but I must decrease" (John 3:30)? Isn't that what you truly want?

Are you, like the Israelites, depending on your ability to keep the Law? Or is your complete dependence for salvation (justification, sanctification, and glorification) based upon the promise of God, His seed, Jesus Christ?

LESSON 4

SALVATION: SLAVES OR SONS

GALATIANS 3:26—4:11

Over the past three lessons (Galatians 3:1-25), Paul has been explaining salvation by way of contrasts. So far, we have seen that salvation is: by faith, not works (vv. 1-14), through the promise and not the Law (vv. 15-25), and now in this lesson, we will discover that salvation in Christ makes us sons not slaves.

We will begin by looking specifically at Galatians 3:26-29, which beautifully serves as a hinge between contrasts. Let's get started.

1. Since this section serves as a hinge, we must look back to see the connection. Re-read Galatians 3:22-25 and answer the following questions:

    a. Notice that the Scripture has shut up <u>all men</u> under sin (v. 22). Why or for what purpose?

    b. Now, fill in the blanks from verses 23-25.

        But before __________________ came...

        ... being shut up to _____________ ______________, which was later to be revealed.

        Therefore, the law became our tutor to lead us to ______________________,

            that we may be justified by ________________________.

        But now that ___________________ has come...

    c. Do you see the key repeated word? What is clearly the subject? ______________

    d. And in whom is our faith to be placed (v. 24)? ____________________________

Let's pause here and take a closer look at faith and its Source.

2. Begin by reading Philippians 2:5-8 and answer the following questions:

    a. What did Christ Jesus (2:5b) do to Himself in verses 7-8?

        1) He ____________________________ Himself.

How did He empty Himself? By ____.

2) He _________________________ Himself.

How did He humble Himself? By ____

____.

Now, let's think of our definition of faith, which involves the surrender of our will and obedience to God's Word. When you read Philippians 2:5-8, and consider the Garden of Gethsemane, where Jesus, as a Man, surrendered His will to the will of His Father, do you see that Jesus Christ is the *Example* and *Source* of faith?

In other words, the *grace* of God the Father, Son, and Spirit saved mankind through the *faith* of Christ Jesus. Do you see that the Source of *grace* is God alone? Can you also see that the Source of *faith* is also God alone? And now that Christ's Spirit lives within the believer, we too are able to surrender our will and obey His Word because the Source is in us to accomplish *for* us and *through* us what man (Adam) chose not to do.

b. Now, let's re-read Galatians 3:23-25 in light of Philippians 2:5-8. It might read,

But before *faith* (Christ Jesus) came...

...being shut up to *the faith* (Christ Jesus), which was later to be revealed.

Therefore, the law became our tutor to lead us to *Christ* (faith),

that we may be justified by *faith* (Christ Jesus).

But now that *faith* (Christ Jesus) has come...

3. Now with that in mind, read Galatians 3:26-29 and answer the following questions:

a. How are we made *sons of God* according to verse 26? Through ______________.

Note: Truly, God is the Creator of all men, but not all men are *sons of God*. There is a qualifier to be called *sons of God*.

b. In whom is the basis of faith (v. 26)? _______ _____________ ________________

c. Now, looking at verse 27, what is true of those who are *sons of God*?

1) ____

2) ____

Now, let's look at each part of the verse individually before we try to understand it in its totality.

d. First, let's consider what it means to be *baptized into Christ*.

Note: The word, *baptized* (*baptizo*), means "to be put or to place into."[38] In this verse, it is used metaphorically in reference to the Holy Spirit.

Additionally, the word, *baptized,* is an aorist indicative passive verb. The aorist tense indicates a punctiliar action at a point in time. The indicative mood signifies a statement of fact, and the passive voice means that the subject was acted upon making him or her the recipient.

38. Kenneth S. Wuest, *Word Studies in the Greek New Testament: Galatians, Vol. One* (Grand Rapids: Wm. B. Eerdmans Publishing Co., 1972), 111.

1) Now with this information, what does it mean to be *baptized into Christ*?

Now, let's pause for a moment to contemplate what the verse does <u>not</u> mean.

2) Do you see how a casual reading of verse 27 could lead to an interpretive error regarding baptism? Explain.

e. Secondly, what does it mean to *clothe yourself with Christ*?

Note: The word, "clothed" (*enduo*), in its most basic sense, means "to put on." In this verse, it is used metaphorically of one who puts on or assumes a new character, for example, the new man.[39] Dr. Wuest, adding clarification, explains, *enduo* "refers to the act in which one enters into an actual relationship with someone else."[40]

Similarly, I found the antonym very helpful, which means to be naked.[41] Immediately, my mind went back to the Garden when sin entered.

1) Look back at Genesis 3:7. What did Adam and Eve *know* and then *do* immediately after they had eaten from the forbidden fruit?

What did they *know*? ____

What did they *do*? ____

Do you see that the first man's attempt to cover himself is still man's propensity today?

2) Now, look at Genesis 3:21. What was the LORD God's provision to cover man's nakedness?

3) Do you see the promise of the gospel in Genesis 3:21? Explain your answer.

f. With all that has been stated, can you explain Galatians 3:27?

4. Now as we continue to read Galatians 3:28, Paul gets very specific. To better understand what Paul is saying, fill in the blanks using the diagram on the next page:

39. Spiros Zodhiates, *The Complete Word Study New Testament Dictionary* (Chattanooga: AMG Pub.,1993), 587.

40. Wuest, *Word Studies*, 111.

41. Zodhiates, *The Complete Word Study New Testament Dictionary*, 587.

3:28 There is neither ______________________

nor

______________________,

there is neither ______________________

nor

____

there is neither ______________________

nor

______________________;

↓

for (because) you are ____________ ____________

↓

________ __________ ______________.

There's that repeated phrase again, "in Christ Jesus."

5. Now, look back over the couplets mentioned in verse 28. What does each represent?

Do you see physical state or natural realm assigned nations, stations in life, and gender by an all-knowing and all-loving sovereign God? Truly He has assigned our lot in this life (Ps. 16:5-6).

6. Now read Galatians 3:29. Notice the verse is a conditional statement, which contains an *if*, and a *then*, statement. Record what you see.

If ____

↓

Then ____

Do you see that although we are diverse in the natural realm, in the spiritual realm we are one in Christ?

7. Now, before we conclude, let's look at a couple of cross-references to gain insight into Galatians 3:26-29. Look at each cross-reference and any additional information that will help you better understand Galatians 3:26-29.

a. 1 Corinthians 12:13 -

b. Ephesians 4:4–6 -

8. And now, just as we did in a previous lesson, look over Galatians 3:26-29 and record what it means to be **in Christ Jesus**. Be very specific as you examine each verse.

9. Taking these same verses, what, then, does it mean when a person is **not** in Christ Jesus? Again, be very specific-looking in each verse. Record what you see.

Now, let's pick up with Paul's analogy of the *heir* as we continue into Galatians 4. Read Galatians 4:1-2. Notice in these verses, Paul began, once again, with a contemporary life illustration. [You may recall Paul did the same thing in Galatians 3:15 concerning the ratification of a legal will upon death. Now, in Galatians 4 he expounds on the stipulations of the will concerning the heir.] Oftentimes, Paul used everyday analogies to drive his point home to the recipient. Let's unpack his correlation.

10. Follow the diagram to discover facts about the heir in verses 1 and 2?

4:1 Now I say

as long as the heir is a ________________,

he does not differ at all

↓

from a ____________________________

although he is ____________________ of ____________________________,

4:2 but he is under ____________________________

and

____

until the _________________ ______________

↓

by the ____________________________.

Note: The word "child" (*nepios*), is literally "one who cannot speak; one not yet of age."[42] Dr. Wuest adds, "an immature person both intellectually and morally."[43]

In addition, the word, "slave" is translated from the Greek word, *doulos*, meaning, "one who is in permanent relation of servitude to another, his will being altogether consumed in the will of the other."[44] Be careful, however, not to confuse a voluntary *doulos* in Jesus Christ with the *doulos* who is under the Law.

Also, the terms, "guardians," and managers, will be helpful words to understand. The first word "guardian" (*epitropos*) applies to the one who governs over a child. Whereas, the "managers" (*oikonomos*) is a term used to describe one who supervises over the property of a child.

11. Now with this in mind, answer the following questions using verses 1–2.

    a. What is the legal position between the child and the slave? ________________

    b. How long is the child under the supervision of the guardians and managers?

____

12. Now let's see how Paul compares the physical illustration used with the spiritual realm. Read Galatians 4:3–4a. To help answer the question, note that the word, "bondage" (*douloo*), means to be subjugated or subdued.[45] Do you see the word "slave" (*doulos*)? In addition, it is a perfect participle passive verb. You may recall that the perfect tense represents a completed action in the past with present and future results. The passive voice signifies that the subject has been acted upon.

Likewise, the words, *elemental things* (*stoicheion*), is a reference specifically to the ceremonial ordinances established under the Mosaic Law for the Jew; but for the Gentile of this time period, it refers to pagan ceremonial and ritualistic observances.[46] In either case, the *elemental things* involved the idea of striving to achieve divine acceptance through human effort.

a. An excellent cross-reference at this juncture is Colossians 2:8. Look at this verse and record the company that the "elementary things" keep. What are *elementary things* associated with in Paul's mind?

Paul warns, "See to it that no one takes you captive (kidnaps you) through:

1) ____

and

2) ____

according to the

3) ____,

according to the

4)____

rather than

42. Ibid., 1009.

43. Kenneth S. Wuest, *Word Studies in the Greek New Testament: Galatians*, Vol. One (Grand Rapids: Wm. B. Eerdmans Publishing Co., 1972), 113.

44. Spiros Zodhiates, *The Complete Word Study New Testament Dictionary* (Chattanooga: AMG Publishers, 1993), 483.

45. *Ibid.*, 484.

46. Wuest, *Word Studies*, 114.

according to ______________________________.

b. As you survey the items listed among the "elementary things," who do you see?

____

c. Notice who these "things" oppose? ___________________________

In his commentary on Galatians, Dr. John MacArthur gives an excellent example of "elementary things" in the life of the late John Wesley. He states,

> *John Wesley was an honor graduate of Oxford University, an ordained clergyman in the Church of England and orthodox in theology. He was active in practical good works, regularly visiting the inmates of prisons and workhouses in London and helping distribute food and clothing to slum children and orphans. He studied the Bible diligently and attended numerous Sunday services as well as various other services during the week. He generously gave offerings to the church and alms to the poor. He prayed and fasted and lived an exemplary moral life. He even spent several years as a missionary to American Indians in what was then the British colony of Georgia. Yet upon returning to England he confessed in his journal, "I who went to America to convert others was never myself converted to God." Later reflecting on his pre-conversion condition, he said, "I had then the faith of a servant, though not that of a son."*
>
> *Wesley tirelessly did everything he could to live a life acceptable to God, yet he knew something vital was missing. It was not until he went "very unwillingly to a society in Aldersgate Street" one evening that he discovered and claimed true Christian life. "I felt my heart strangely warmed," he wrote, "I felt I did trust in Christ, Christ alone, for salvation; and an assurance was given me that He had taken away my sins, even mine, and saved me from the law of sin and death." Things were no longer* **elemental** *for Wesley. He had entered "the heavenlies."*[47]

While at the Aldersgate Society, Wesley heard Martin Luther's preface to the Epistle to the Romans. Clearly, the Spirit of God using the Word of God spoke to Wesley's heart and drew him to Jesus Christ. Do you see the grace of God? Do you see it was *by grace* that Wesley was saved as he responded *in faith*?

d. Now as you look at Wesley's life, how does his conversion explain Galatians 4:3-4a perfectly? Be sure and include a list of the "elementary things" in Wesley's life pre-conversion. What do you see?

Do you see the deception of thinking He needs you, when in truth, you desperately need Him?

WHAT ABOUT YOU?

Does Wesley's testimony resonate in your heart? Are you striving to earn justification? Or are you more like the Galatians, who having been justified by Christ now find yourself striving to be sanctified (Gal. 3:3)?

---

47. John MacArthur Jr., *The MacArthur New Testament Commentary: Galatians*, (Chicago: Moody Press, 1987), pp.106-107.

What does your life's testimony really look like?

Has something, other than Christ, taken you captive? If so, ask the Savior to save you from the **power** that it has taken hold of in your life. Whether it is the penalty of sin (justification) or the power of sin (sanctification), the Savior is waiting to deliver.

Will you let Him?

Now, some might read the *things* Wesley was doing pre-conversion and think, "What's wrong with *these things*?" And the answer would be everything and nothing! Everything, if you depend on *these things* to save you. Nothing, if Christ in you has led you to follow Him in *these things*. Do you see that *these things* do not lead a person to Christ but will follow a true believer? In other words, *these things* will not be the source of salvation for the believer; rather, they are the fruit of someone who has been saved. There is only one Source—Jesus Christ!

Look once again at Galatians 4:3. Do you see that man is in bondage and great need? Now, look at the first words in Galatians 4:4, "But, when the fullness of time came, God..." Beautiful words are they not? **But . . . God**. They are rescuing words. Words of grace! Do you see it?

13. Now, let's examine the rich theology and amazing grace in Galatians 4:4–6. Answer the following questions using these verses.

    a. What do you learn about God the Father in verses 4 and 6?

        1) God ________________________________ (v. 4)

        2) God ________________________________ (v. 6)

    b. When did God send His Son (v. 4)? ________________________

Notice that God "sent forth" His Son. First, the Greek word "sent forth" (*exapostello*), literally means, "to send out of the place where one is."[48] Do you also see the word, apostle?

    c. What does *sent forth* imply?

____

____

    d. Now, what do you learn next about His Son in verse 4?

        1) Born of a ________________

        2) Born under the ____________

Note: The word, "born," is translated from the Greek verb, *ginomai*, which means to begin to be, to begin to exist into any state. It is an aorist tense (at a point in time), participle middle (meaning the subject both initiates and participates in the action).[49]

You see God sent His Son from eternity past. Although fully God, Christ became flesh at a point in time (in fact, when the fulness of time had come). He did not cease to be God, for that is impossible; rather, He became human—in fact, the God-Man. Therefore, Galatians 4:4 speaks to the Incarnation of Christ.

    e. This information begs the question, "Why?" Why did God become a man? You will find the answer to this question in Galatians 4:5–6. What do you see?

48. *Zodhiates, Word Study Dictionary*, 600.

49. Ibid., 367.

1) In order that He might _____________ those who were under the Law,

2) That we might receive _____________________ as ________________.

Note: You will recall from a previous lesson, the Greek word translated "redeem," means to buy or purchase out of the slave market of sin. The antonym of redeemer, interestingly, is slave or *doulos*.

Also note the word, "adoption" (*huiothesia*), which is a beautiful term, meaning, "to place as a son; to receive into relationship. It is used figuratively in the New Testament to those whom God through Christ adopts as His sons and thus makes heirs of His covenanted salvation."[50]

14. The term "adoption" (*huiothesia*) is a technical term used in Scripture only by Paul. It is used a total of five times in Scripture, including here in Galatians 4:5. Look at the other four times it is used to gain further insight into the meaning of this beautiful picture of grace. Record any additional insights to add to Galatians 4:5. What do you see?

a. Romans 8:15:

b. Romans 8:23:

c. Romans 9:4:

d. Ephesians 1:5:

15. Now, let's look a little closer at Galatians 4:6.

a. What occurs *because we are sons?* _____________________________________

b. What, specifically, is the Spirit called in this verse? ___________________

c. Where does He dwell in reference to man? ____________________________

Amazing thought, isn't it? Amazing grace!

d. What is the Spirit of His Son doing in our hearts? ______________________

_________________________________ (And you thought you were the one doing this?)

Do you see it takes God to communicate with God?

50. Ibid., 1404.

Note: The term, *Abba*, is transliterated from the Aramaic, meaning, "Father, My Father. It is always used of God the Father."[51]

John MacArthur, commenting on this term, states, "*Abba* is a term of endearment used by young children of their fathers and could be translated "daddy" or "papa."[52] The term is personal. It speaks of relationship. It communicates love, dependence, and need.

16. Now, a closing statement by Paul can be found in Galatians 4:7. What is Paul's conclusion?

Therefore, you are no longer a ____________________, but a ________________________;

and

if a ____________________,

↓

then an ____________________ through God.

Do you see that Galatians 4:4–7 explains the roles of the Godhead in our salvation? The Father, who executed the plan to save mankind, sent His Son into the world to accomplish the plan of salvation. The Son, having completely submitted in perfect obedience to the Father's plan, accomplished the work of redemption through His death. With the work complete, then the Father could send the Spirit of His Son to apply that finished work to our hearts.

The Father **arranged** (His plan) the work of salvation.

The Son **accomplished** the work of salvation.

The Spirit **applies** the work of salvation.

So where are you and me?

Are we not merely the recipients of His work? Are you a grateful son (daughter)?

17. In this last section of the lesson, we will look at Galatians 4:8–11, where Paul will turn back to the believers in Galatia and ask them a rhetorical question. Using verses 8–11, answer the following questions.

   a. Paul reminds the believers of a time when they did not know God (v. 8). What was their former state according to verse 8?

Note: The word, *nature* (*phusis*), literally means "natural birth or that which belongs to a person or thing by virtue of its origin."[53]

   b. What does Paul remind the Galatians regarding the nature of those things in which they were formerly enslaved (v. 8)?

51. Ibid., 58.
52. MacArthur, *The MacArthur New Testament Commentary Galatians*, 109.
53. Kenneth S. Wuest, *Word Studies in the Greek New Testament: Galatians, Vol. One* (Grand Rapids: Wm. B. Eerdmans Publishing Co., 1972), 118.

In essence, Paul does not deny the existence of the things by which they were enslaved, but he does deny their deity.

c. As you read Galatians 4:9, do you distinguish a difference between knowing God and being known by God? Explain your answer. (An excellent cross-reference here would be Matthew 7:21-23. Look specifically at verse 23.)

Note: The word translated "known" in this verse (*ginosko*) describes an experiential and relational knowledge. It is in the passive voice, meaning that the subject has received the action and therefore has been acted upon.

d. What rhetorical question does Paul ask the Galatians in verse 9?

e. There it is again. Paul brings up the elemental things we looked at earlier in the lesson. What two new facts do you learn from Paul about the elemental things in verse 9?

1) ____

and Isn't this the enemy's goal?

2) ____

Note: The word "weak" (*asthenes*) means without power.[54] In other words, the things you are turning back to have no power to rescue you.

What/whose power are the *elemental things* missing? __________________________

Why would anyone ever want to return to that state? That is the question that has bewildered and astonished Paul.

f. Now, look at verse 10, as Paul names the elemental things to which they wanted to return. What do you see?

1) ____________________________

and

2) ____________________________

and

3) ____________________________

and

4) ____________________________

54. Spiros Zodhiates, *The Complete Word Study New Testament Dictionary* (Chattanooga: AMG Pub.,1993), 274.

g. To help understand, look at Colossians 2:16–17, where you will see some of the same things listed.

What does Paul call all these things in verse 17? ______________________________

Who are these things a mere shadow of? In other words, Who is the substance of the shadow?

____

Note: Paul, in both Galatians and Colossians, is expressing the same thought. These *things* represented the ceremonial law, which was established in Leviticus. They were useful and effective as guardians and managers until Christ came. However, now that Christ has come, He is the substance or the fulfillment of the ceremonial law. All these things pointed to Him. He is the fulfillment of them all.

Think, for example, about the purpose of the Sabbath Day, which was established by God as a day of rest from work on the seventh day of the week. Christians often treat Sunday as a Sabbath Day. Jesus Christ is why we have a Sabbath Day. We rest in His completed work on the cross. Christ's resurrection on the first day of the week is why we meet and worship on the Lord's Day (Sunday). The resurrection is a picture of the Father accepting His Son's work, which was evidenced when Christ was raised from the dead. Had the Father not accepted Christ's work, He would have remained in the grave as all men who had previously gone before Him. His life was sinless. His blood was perfect. No other sacrifice would be necessary.

As the author of Hebrews records, "But when Christ appeared *as* a high priest of the good things to come, *He entered* through the greater and more perfect tabernacle, not made with hands, that is to say, not of this creation; and not through the blood of goats and calves, but **through His own blood, He entered the holy place once for all *time*, having obtained eternal redemption**" (emphasis mine; Hebrews 9:11–12).

h. Now, look at Galatians 4:11. What do you sense in Paul's words?

Martin Luther, as quoted by Dr. Wuest, says of this verse, "These words of Paul breathe tears."[55] Can you imagine the time, energy, and even danger Paul encountered to bring the gospel to the Galatians, only to hear that they wanted to turn back?

WHAT ABOUT YOU?

This lesson is personal.

As you ponder the contrast in this lesson, would you describe your religious life today as a life of slavery or a life of son-ship? (A life of son-ship speaks to the sweet relationship of a Father with his child, and vice versa.) Is it a dull and burdensome servitude, or would you explain it as joyous, restful, and light?

If you can truthfully answer dull and burdensome servitude, I invite you to look at Matthew 11:28–30. The Savior is bidding you to, "Come." Whether you need to be justified from sin's *penalty* or sanctified from sin's *power*, this verse is for you.

Are you willing to make the exchange?

55. Kenneth S. Wuest, *Word Studies in the Greek New Testament: Galatians, Vol. One* (Grand Rapids: Wm. B. Eerdmans Publishing Co., 1972), 123.

Now, in keeping with our stick figures, let's summarize Galatians 3:1—4:11.

You will recall that Paul contrasts three things in these verses, namely:

- the works of the Law versus faith in Christ (Gal. 3:1–14)
- the Law versus the promise (Gal. 3:15–25)
- slaves versus sons (Gal. 3:26—4:11)

In each lesson, we see Jesus Christ emerge as the fulfillment of each. For example,

- Jesus Christ is both the source and the example of faith!
- Jesus Christ is the promise of God (The Seed)!
- And, Jesus Christ is the Son of God!

Do you see the good news of the gospel of Jesus Christ?

Therefore, considering this Good News, let's look at the difference Jesus Christ makes in the life of a believer as contrasted with the unbeliever. To do so, we will refer to our stick figures for a visual.

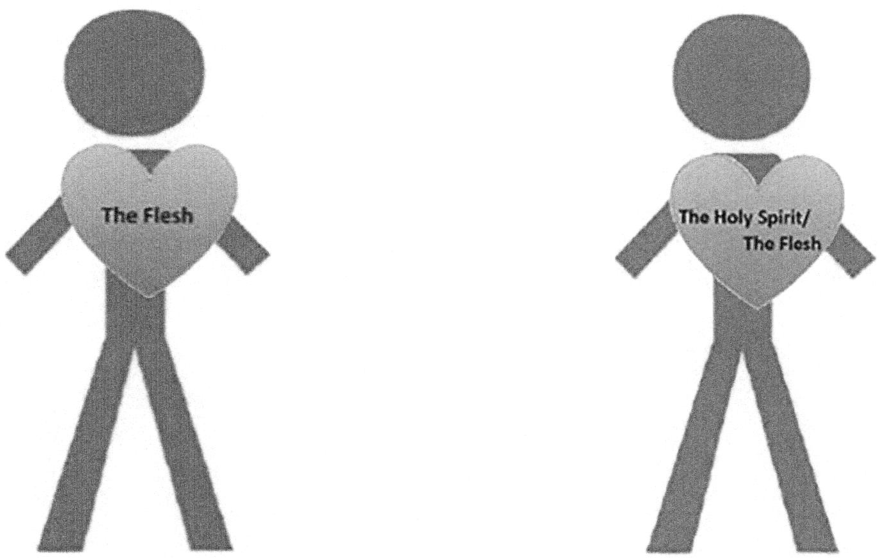

The Unbeliever Versus The Believer

Striving: to do the works of the Law
under the Law
as slaves to sin

Resting: in the faith of Jesus Christ
in the promise (Seed)
in the Son of God

As you look at the visual, who makes the difference in the believer?

Do you see that the answer is clearly Jesus Christ through His indwelling Spirit?

Now, considering the contrasts Paul uses in Galatians 3:1-4:11, let's re-visit the questions Paul asked the Galatian believers at the beginning of Chapter 3.

1) Who has bewitched you (3:1)?

2) Did you receive the Spirit by works of the Law, or by hearing with faith (3:2)?

3) Are you so foolish? Having begun by the Spirit, are you now being perfected by the flesh (3:3)?

4) Does He then, who provides you with the Spirit and works miracles among you, do it by the works of the Law or by hearing with faith (3:5)?

Do you see the foolishness of the false teachers in the face of the wisdom of God, His Son?

Do you see that it is Christ in you who is the One saving you completely? When I say completely, I mean from the penalty of sin (justification), and from the power of sin (sanctification), and someday, from the very presence of sin (glorification). He is the Difference Maker!

Do you also see that as believers, our residual flesh is drawn to the works of the Law and enslavement to sin? Our need for Christ to continue to save us did not cease when He entered our hearts. He is still saving us from the deception that our flesh can accomplish His Word.

Lesson 5

A Spiritual Parent's Lament

GALATIANS 4:12–20

At this juncture in the letter, and following Paul's reprimand to the foolish Galatians, Paul expresses a very personal and heartfelt plea to them as their brother, pastor, and even their spiritual father (mother).[56] If you are a parent, you can sense the anguish in Paul's words as he travails on their behalf. You too may know a great fear and immense suffering as you have watched a child that has been influenced and led astray by the wrong crowd. Many a parent has suffered great turmoil as their son or daughter has willfully chosen to leave their loving care and instruction only to follow the enemy of their soul. Whether they were aware the enemy was behind it or not, the destruction left behind has taken its toll.

Similarly, on a spiritual level, eventually, every pastor or Bible teacher who has been entrusted with the care of their children has felt the intensity of Paul's struggle as well. Let's face it; the Enemy does not fight fair. He sets his target on those who are physically and spiritually weak and immature. He takes advantage of vulnerable situations. He strikes when our defenses are down or at times when "the rug has been jerked out from underneath" during the shock of tragedy.

As we continue through our study of Galatians, we understand Paul knew the battle is not with flesh and blood (Eph. 6:12). Sadly, the Galatians did not. They had no idea that behind false teachers, the Enemy is at work in great opposition to God's Word and His work. Because of the Enemy's deception, Paul had become their enemy. The same thing can happen today. Frequently, when we do not like the message from God's Word, we point our guns at the messenger. This is exactly what was happening to the churches in Galatia.

My prayer, as you continue in this lesson, is twofold in purpose. First, I pray that Paul's words will serve as a warning to believers within the church. The devil is a real and present enemy, and we are all at risk. He uses false teachers to target God's people. He attempts to lure the believer away from God's people and God's Word. His tactic is to isolate and separate, to kill, steal, and destroy (Jn. 10:10).

And secondly, I pray that Paul's words would serve to both instruct and encourage the pastor, teacher, or discipler who may, from time to time, find themselves experiencing the heartache of watching a spiritual child turn, not only from the truth but also from you. My prayer is that you would not take it personally and make it a flesh and blood issue and that the Lord would give you great clarity of mind as you continue to teach the truth, no matter the pain or outcome. His Word will prevail. It will accomplish what God has purposed despite the opposition.

With these things in mind, let's proceed. Begin by reading Galatians 4:12–20. Can you see Paul the brother, the pastor, and the spiritual mother (*in labor*) in these verses? Now let's examine the three sections a little closer.

---

56. Note: In this lesson, I have used the words "father" and "mother" interchangeably in regard to spiritual maturity and in matters of discipleship. Again, I am indebted to the insights from Eric Alexander regarding the outline from Galatians 4:12–20. For more information see Galatians 4:12–20 [online]; accessed February 8, 2019; available at http://tapesfromscotland.org/Audio3/3852.mp3Internet.

Paul, the Brother

1. What is Paul doing in Galatians 4:12? ____

Note: The Greek word translated "beg," when used in the New Testament, means, "to make one's need known, to beseech, to ask by praying specifically."[57] Here in Galatians 4:12, the verb is present tense, meaning that Paul is continuously praying on their behalf.

2. What specifically is Paul praying for the Galatians in verse 12? ____________________

____

At first impression, it appears as if Paul may be prideful by advising, "*Become as I*," but be careful here. Could Paul be saying, "I too was once like you—in bondage to the law? Become as I am now, not bound to the law but to the promise, which is in Christ Jesus."

Moreover, Paul had been willing to leave his countrymen to become like one of them, a Gentile. Why would Paul ever want to return to his former Jewish customs and live under the law? That is precisely the point Paul is making to the Galatians.

WHAT ABOUT YOU?

Have you ever felt the weight of what Paul is verbalizing in verse 12? Have you ever witnessed a brother or sister in Christ run headlong into a trap where you too were once ensnared? Did you beg them to listen as you warned them of the danger ahead? Have you ever found yourself pleading with the Lord on another's behalf? Isn't this what Paul is doing?

If you can identify with Paul in verse 12, you know the intensity of the words he is saying. He speaks from a heart of great love for his brothers and sisters in the Lord. He sees the vulnerable situation that they are in and knows that apart from the grace of a loving Savior, they are in great danger of falling.

Paul, the Pastor

3. Now, look at Galatians 4:13–18 as we see Paul move from his position as their brother in Christ to pastoral mentor and counselor. Answer the following questions using verses 13–18:

a. Who preached the gospel to the Galatians for the first time? _______________

b. What do we learn from Paul about his physical condition while preaching in Galatia?

____

Note: The Greek word translated here as "illness" (*astheneia*) is actually better translated, *weakness*.[58]

Therefore, by using the term, "illness" (*astheneia*), Paul is just describing a symptom, and we are left to speculate the disease (*nosois*) from which he suffered. In other words, all that we can say for certain is that Paul's disease (*nosois*) had left him very weak (*astheneias*).

Bible scholars are divided when it comes to Paul's specific disease. Some speculate that Paul suffered from malaria, which left him in a very weakened condition. Prior to his visit to the southern region of Galatia (Acts 13:14-14:28), Paul had visited the swampy lowlands of Pamphylia, where mosquitos might have been an issue.

---

57. Spiros Zodhiates, *The Complete Word Study New Testament Dictionary* (Chattanooga: AMG Pub.,1993), 405.
58. Ibid., 271.

Others believe Paul suffered from some sort of eye condition and based their assumption by using the text. They would use passages such as Galatians 4:15, which states, "For I bear you witness that if possible, you have plucked out your eyes and given them to me," and later, at the close of the letter, "See with what large letters I am writing to you with my own hand" (Gal. 6:11), as internal evidence to support their theory that Paul had some sort of ophthalmic issue.

Although there is internal evidence within the text, which seems to support both theories, no one can say exactly what Paul's physical issue was for sure. One thing we do know, while going out on his first missionary journey, Paul had become very ill and had to stop in the region of Galatia to recover. While in Galatia, "his sickbed became his pulpit," and many received Jesus Christ (Acts 14:1). [59]

c. Whatever the illness (weakness), Paul tells us a few things regarding the Galatians and his illness in verse 14. What do you see?

1) It was a ________________________ to you...

2) It was a ______________________________ condition (as opposed to spiritual)...

3) The Galatians did not ________________________________

or

________________________________ Paul (because of it).

Note: The Greek word translated "despise" (*exoutheneo*), means, "to treat with scorn and contempt."[60] Likewise, the word "loathe" is from *ekptuo*, which means "to spit out, to reject."[61]

4) Rather, they had ____________________________ Paul

↓

as ____,

as ____.

Note: As you can tell from Paul's recollection, the Galatians had been very warm and receptive to him.

d. What question then does Paul ask the Galatians in verses 15?

e. Based on all the information you have been given, what point is Paul trying to make with the Galatians from verses 14–15?

59. Kenneth S. Wuest, *Word Studies in the Greek New Testament: Galatians, Vol. One* (Grand Rapids: Wm. B. Eerdmans Publishing Co., 1972), 125.
60. Ibid., 606.
61. Spiros Zodhiates, *The Complete Word Study New Testament Dictionary* (Chattanooga: AMG Publishers, 1993), 553.

f. Now, look at Paul's conclusive question in verse 16. What does Paul ask the Galatians?

Great question, isn't it? Do you see that Galatians 4:16 really gets to the heart of the matter? Now, let me ask Galatians 4:16 in a different manner.

g. As you read Galatians 4:16, how had Paul become their enemy?

Have you ever become someone's enemy by telling them the truth? As I thought about the answer to this question, my mind went immediately back to the Old Testament story of a prophet named, Micaiah. Now turn to 1 Kings 22 to see why.

4. Let's begin by reading the entire chapter of 1 Kings 22.

Note: It is essential to place 1 Kings 22 in context; therefore, we must first understand that the events in this chapter take place during Israel's divided kingdom.

The nation of *Israel* (Northern Kingdom) consisted of ten tribes, while *Judah* (Southern Kingdom) consisted of two tribes (Judah and Benjamin). Each of these kingdoms had its own king. The king of Israel at this time was Ahab, while the king of Judah was Jehoshaphat.

In general, the kings of Israel (Northern Kingdom) were evil. In fact, there was not even one good king in Israel who sought after God. Moreover, every time you read about Ahab, you will discover he had a problem with the Word of God (1 Kings 16–22).

Now, at the time of 1 Kings 22, Ramoth-gilead was under Syrian domination. (You may recall from Scripture, Ramoth-gilead was one of the chief cities of Gad, which had been set apart by God as an allotment to the Levites and an appointed city of refuge [Deut. 4:43; Josh. 20:8]. Therefore, the city was one of utmost importance.)[62]

We learn immediately in verse one, Israel has had three years of peace with Aram (Syria), but all of that is about to change because Ahab wants Ramoth-gilead back. We are told that Jehoshaphat, the king of Judah, has come down to the king of Israel (1 Kings 22:2). Maybe he has come down to visit his son, Jehoram, who had married king Ahab's daughter, Athaliah, in an effort to form an alliance with Israel. Sadly, Athaliah was said to have been "almost as wicked as her mother Jezebel."[63]

Let's pick up on the story from here. Answer the following questions using 1 Kings 22.

a. What does Ahab ask Jehoshaphat during his visit (v. 4)?

62. Merrill F. Unger, *Unger's Bible Dictionary*, (Chicago: Moody Press, 1971), 911.

63. Merrill C. Tenney, *Zondervan's Pictorial Bible Dictionary* (Grand Rapids, MI: Zondervan Publishers, 1967), 407.

b. How does Jehoshaphat answer (v. 4)?

Note: Is he really like Ahab? Jehoshaphat was considered a good king in Judah's history, who sought the LORD GOD. He had destroyed the high places and the Asherim from Judah (2 Chron. 17:6). But do the people and horses really belong to him?

Be aware that at any moment, pride can creep in and take over. Every God-fearing person is vulnerable and will not be totally delivered from the sin of pride until glorification. Had Jehoshaphat forgotten that every good and perfect gift is from above, from the Father (James 1:17)?

Furthermore, be careful with whom you form an alliance. They may not be seeking the same One you seek. They may have a form of godliness but deny its power (2 Tim 3:5).

c. What else does Jehoshaphat add in verse 5?

d. What does Ahab do in verse 6?

1) How many prophets does Ahab consult? ______________________

2) How do Ahab's prophets respond to his request (v. 6)?

e. What does Jehoshaphat say to Ahab in response to his prophet's report (v. 7)?

Did you notice Jehoshaphat's distinction in verse 7? He requests a prophet of the LORD. He knows that Ahab's prophets are on his payroll. He knows that they would never go against Ahab. In essence, Jehoshaphat wants to hear the truth.

f. Notice how Ahab answers Jehoshaphat in verse 8? What does he say?

Knowing that Jehoshaphat will not go into battle without inquiring of the LORD, Ahab sends men to summon Micaiah (v. 9).

g. Now, describe the scene in verse 10 while they wait on Micaiah.

h. Did you notice in verse 11, that one of Ahab's 400 prophets, named Zedekiah, distinguishes himself in front of the royal scene? Record below what he does and says.

Note: Did you happen to pick up on the phrase, "***made*** horns of iron ***for himself***..."? Anytime you see this phrase in Scripture; you can bet there will be trouble!

i. Notice again, what all the prophets of Ahab prophesy in verse 12.

j. Meanwhile, the messenger who is sent to summon Micaiah forewarns the prophet of the LORD in verse 13. What information does he provide ahead of time for Micaiah?

k. How does Micaiah respond in verse 14?

l. Now, when Micaiah comes to Ahab and is asked about going to war, how does Micaiah respond initially in verse 15?

m. What does Ahab know immediately regarding Micaiah's initial response (v. 16)?

Doesn't Ahab's response tell you that deep down he knew the truth?

n. Now, record what Micaiah tells Ahab he saw regarding Israel and Israel's shepherd (Ahab himself) in verse 17a.

Israel - ____

Israel's shepherd (king Ahab) - ______________________________

o. Now, record what the LORD says in verse 17b regarding each:

Israel's shepherd (master) - _______________________________

Israel - ____

Basically, the prophecy concerning Israel states that when Ahab is gone there will be peace, right? Ahab knows precisely what the prophecy implies. Look at his response.

p. How does Ahab respond to the word of the LORD in verse 18?

q. Now look at verses 19–22 and in particular, the scene that Micaiah witnesses.

Did you notice that "***all*** of the host of heaven" (emphasis added) was standing by the LORD on His right and on His left (v. 19)? The *host of heaven* is a reference to the angelic beings. The mention of ***all*** includes both the obedient and disobedient demonic realm that followed Lucifer in his rebellion against God. ***All*** answer to God.

Just as we see in the Book of Job, *the sons of God* (angelic hosts) must all present themselves before the LORD, and Satan also comes among them (Job 1:6). Nowhere is the sovereignty of God more visible than when we see in Scripture how all the good and evil created beings must present themselves and answer to a holy God. He is over ***all*** His creation. Therefore, He can use the evil/bad to accomplish His purpose and to fulfill His plan without usurping the will of the created being (whether angelic or human).

r. Now compare this heavenly scene with the earthly scene described earlier in verses 10–12. What do you see? Be specific.

Do you see two realms? Do you see the LORD sitting on His throne? Do you know that His throne is called the *throne of grace* in Hebrews 4:16? Do you see the grace of God in the prophecy recorded in 2 Kings 22, forewarning king Ahab what is about to happen? If that's not God's grace, I am not sure what is. Ahab is told ahead of time exactly what the LORD is going to do. There is no deception. In fact, what exactly does the LORD tell Ahab about his prophets in verse 23?

Do you see that Ahab is given the truth ahead of time?

s. Why do you think the LORD forewarns Ahab? What is He giving Ahab the opportunity to do?

Once again, and this time, for the last time, Ahab will choose to reject God's Word. Do you see that to reject God's Word brings disaster and death?

t. Now, as you continue to read verses 24–27, record how Micaiah is treated for telling Ahab the truth.

u. Now, as the story concludes, briefly describe what happens to Ahab in verses 29–36? Be sure and record the deception of Ahab in verse 30 and the result of the "random" arrow that kills him in verse 34. What do you see?

Do you see that although the arrow, humanly speaking, may have been random, God's Word hit the mark? Be assured His Word will never miss the mark!

v. Now, look at verse 32 regarding Jehoshaphat. For further insight, see 2 Chronicles 18:31 for more information. What do you see about king Jehoshaphat and the mercy and grace of our loving God?

w. Now, look back at 1 Kings 22:36–37 and compare these verses with what Micaiah prophesies in verse 17. What do you see?

x. Now read 1 Kings 22:38 and compare it with 1 Kings 21:19. What do you see?

Some final thoughts regarding 1 Kings 22 and Galatians 4:16:

First, the Word of God cannot be shaped to fit what people like, desire, or see. The person who speaks for the LORD cannot change God's message. In fact, this message cannot be changed or altered by anyone at any time. It cannot be controlled or manipulated. It will say things to you and me that we do not particularly like. We are not asked to like it, nor are we asked to understand it. We are invited to submit our will and obey it even when it proves very costly.

Secondly, if you have been called by God to teach His Word, always speak the truth of God in love. That type of love is not defined in how you say something (although that is very important) but that you are willing to speak the truth. Even when you know it may cost you significantly. Our first love is to be the Lord our God, which will always result in our love for others.

You will be accountable to speak the truth; however, you will not be responsible for the choice of the listener nor the outcome. Let's face it; the truth of God is not a popular message these days. Therefore, more than likely, in all honesty, you may not be very popular nor have a well-liked ministry.

Oftentimes, we believe the lie that we need to protect the other person from the truth. We convince ourselves that it is about not wanting to hurt the other person. When that happens, we enter into deception because we talk ourselves into protecting the lie. It's as if we think the lie or deception is not going to hurt them or us. In other words, we sometimes think it is better for someone to believe a lie than know the truth. When in fact, if we would just be honest with God and ourselves, at this point we have just placed ourselves as God because our real desire is to protect and please ourselves.

Always keep in mind that you have One to please and in pleasing Him, you will more than likely not be pleasing others. When you think about it, it all boils down to the root issues in the Garden: "Who is God?" and "Who do you love most?"

If we truly understand that He alone is God and love the Lord our God most, we will say only what He says. However, when we think that we are God because we really love ourselves more, then we will be inclined to tell people what they want to hear so that they will like us.

WHAT ABOUT YOU?

Have you become someone's enemy because you told them the truth from God's Word?

Are you willing to face the fallout even if you are the only one, like Micaiah?

If summoned to the authorities, would you be willing to speak the truth in love?

Did you notice that Micaiah was not confrontational? He did not barrel in on his own authority and wield the Word of God without first being summoned. Nor did he back down when the opinion of the majority pressed him.

When someone asks for your counsel, do you give her the Word of God or your own opinion? Are you willing to tell people, when asked, what God's Word says about their situation, or are you more concerned with what they will ultimately think about you?

Don't you think in these perilous times, the Lord is looking expectantly for someone to speak the truth? Often, in my head, I hear when asked to speak to an issue, "Will anyone say what God is saying?"

What will you say? Will you be a useful tool for the Master in these dark times, or will you choose to be rendered useless by the Enemy?

5. And now, we need to focus our attention on false teachers. Paul gives us some critical information about them in Galatians 4:17. What do you see?

    a. They ____________________ _________________ you, not __________________________.

    b. They wish to _______________ ______________ ________________ ...

    c. ...in order that you may _____________________ _______________________.

Do you see what they are really after?

Note: The word "seek" (*zeloo*), means "to be filled with zeal or to make a show of zeal, to profess affection in order to gain someone as a follower."[64] Additionally, the word "seek" can be used in a good or bad sense, depending on who or what is being sought.

By these things, can you see the true motive of their heart?

6. Now let's pause to consider some ways false teachers may eagerly *seek* you out but not commendably? What might that look like?

    a. Look at Psalm 5.

Note: The context of Psalm 5 is the person who takes pleasure in wickedness (v. 4); who speaks falsehood (v. 6); who is a person of bloodshed and deceit (v. 6).

Now, look at verse 9. How does he operate? What does he use as his bait?

    b. Now, look at Romans 16:17–18 and answer the following questions:

        1) Who is Paul addressing in verse 17? _____________________________________

        2) Whom is Paul warning against?

            a) ____

            and

            b) ____

            contrary to ____.

        3) What is his counsel (v. 17)?

            a) ____

            b) ____

        4) To whom are these men slaves (v. 18)? __________________________________

            a) Who is the one behind their enslavement? __________________________

        5) What do they use? ____

64. Spiros Zodhiates, *The Complete Word Study New Testament Dictionary* (Chattanooga: AMG Pub.,1993), 699.

6) Whom do they deceive? ____

Beware when someone begins to come after you with smooth and flattering speech. Be on guard for those who would rather have you follow their counsel than the Word of God. Did you notice that their target was the Word of God? Doesn't this sound just like Galatians 4:17?

Now, let's examine the words "shut out" (*ekkleio*), which means, "to alienate or cause separation."[65] According to Wuest, the context suggests that the Judaizers were attempting to shut the Galatians out, either from the benefits of the gospel of grace or from fellowship with Paul.[66] Don't you see where it could be both?

7. Now, as you look at Galatians 4:17, what is the motive behind false teachers who seek you out to shut you up? Why are they doing this? What are they really after?

8. Now, as you consider what false teachers are doing and why they are doing it, who else in Scripture can be described the same way?

________________________________ (Scary thought, isn't it?)

9. And finally, before we leave Galatians 4:17, we need to examine 2 Corinthians 11:13–15. Answer the following questions:

    a. What does Paul call the false apostles (13)? ______________________________

    b. What are they doing in verse 13? ____

    ____

Note: The word "disguising" (*metaschematizo*), literally speaks of an outward change in form only without any change inwardly.[67] Look closely at the Greek word. Do you see the word, *scheme*? Isn't that what Paul warned in Ephesians 6:11?

Also note that *metaschematizo* is the exact opposite of the word, "transform" (*metamorphoo*), which is used when the change is inwardly and results in an outward transformation.

Furthermore, the verb "disguising" is a present-passive participle. You will recall from previous lessons, the present tense represents an ongoing continuous action, and the passive voice indicates that the subject is being acted upon.

    c. So, who is the outside source acting upon false prophets/teachers? What does verse 14 say?

Notice the word "disguises" (*metaschematizo*) again is used regarding Satan. In other words, Satan may be able to change his outward appearance; but inwardly, he is filled with darkness, and any simulation of light is false.

---

65. Kenneth S. Wuest, *Word Studies in the Greek New Testament: Galatians, Vol. One*, (Grand Rapids: Wm. B. Eerdmans Publishing Co., 1972), 128.
66. *Ibid.*
67. Spiros Zodhiates, *The Complete Word Study New Testament Dictionary* (Chattanooga: AMG Pub.,1993), 972.

d. Notice what the false teachers are, in connection to Satan (v. 15)?

e. What do his servants disguise (*metaschematizo*) themselves as in verse 15?

Note: Anytime you see the phrase, "disguise **themselves**," you know there is a problem with the truth.

f. What will be their end (v. 15)? ____

10. Now, what is the correlation between Galatians 4:17 and 2 Corinthians 11:13-15?

11. And now, we would be remiss if we did not consider what our Lord Jesus taught regarding false prophets. Look at Matthew 7:15–20, and this time, rather than asking questions from the text, allow your built-in teacher, the Holy Spirit, to show you the truth (John 14:26). Record the insights He shows you.

12. Returning to the Book of Galatians, let's see what Paul does affirm. Look at Galatians 4:18. What does Paul regard as *good*?

Note: The word "commendable" (*kalos*) in this verse means "to be right and good in character."[68] Today, we overuse and misuse the word "good." However, notably, in Scripture, the word "good" is used as a description of God. So, the next time you see the word "good" used in Scripture, think *God-good.*

13. So, what is Paul recommending (v. 18)? What/Who would Paul consider commendable?

____

In short, Paul is warning the Galatians of those who eagerly seek them out but not in a commendable way. He tells them (and us) instead to eagerly seek those who will point them to the Lord Jesus and His Word rather than to themselves. For Paul, the only commendable way is Christ.

Now, let's move from Paul's pastoral role to his final self-description, the Galatian's spiritual mother. Note the term "mother" has been chosen due to the description of "being in labor" (v. 19).

PAUL, THE SPIRITUAL FATHER

14. What does Paul call the Galatians in verse 19? ____________________________________

68. *Ibid.,* 814.

Note: The term "my children" (*teknion*), is a relational term of endearment used figuratively of a teacher to his pupils.[69] In 1 John 2:12, this same term (*teknion*) is used to describe those "whose sins were forgiven for His name's sake." In 1 John 2:13-14, John qualifies those who are his *teknion*, based upon their spiritual level of maturity. John's *teknion* was divided into three specific groups, namely: "fathers," "young men," and "little children," from a different Greek word (*padia*), meaning spiritual baby or immature one.

15. What specifically does Paul say about the *teknion* in verses 19-20?

a. I am in _____________ until ____

but

b. I could wish ____

for

c. I am ________________________________ about you.

First, the term, *labor* (*odino*), is used figuratively to describe the intense labor at the birth of a child.[70]

Second, the term "formed" (*morphoo*) was used earlier in the lesson regarding 2 Corinthians 11:13–15 as the opposite of Satan's disguise. *Morphoo* refers to the act of giving outward expression of one's inner nature.[71]

Equally important, *morphoo* is an aorist subjunctive passive verb. The aorist tense indicates an action, which occurred in a moment in time (as opposed to present, continuous action). The subjunctive mood is the mood of probability used to express an action, which may or should happen but may not be true at present. The passive voice means that the subject has been acted upon and therefore receives the action.

16. Now, with all the information provided above, what is Paul saying to the Galatians in verse 19?

Note: Paul's love for the Galatians is compared to the love that a mother has for her child. No matter the intensity of the pain in labor, the love for the child far outweighs any physical discomfort the mother may have experienced. As their spiritual father, Paul likens the pain he is suffering on their behalf with the pain a mother experiences during childbirth. He is hopeful that no matter the intensity, it will be well worth it in the end.

Paul's purpose in labor is that Christ would be formed inwardly in them, which always results in an outward transformation. Paul could not do this for them. They could not do this for themselves. The Spirit of Christ living within them had to be the source. At an appointed time, as the Spirit of God revealed His Word to their hearts,

69. *Ibid.,* 1370.

70. *Ibid.,* 1498.

71. Kenneth S. Wuest, *Word Studies in the Greek New Testament: Galatians, Vol. One* (Grand Rapids: Wm. B. Eerdmans Publishing Co., 1972), 129.

they, in turn, could choose to surrender their will and obey His Word. Their surrender and obedience would result in maturity and growth. In other words, Christ would be manifested in their lives. When this transformation occurs in people, there is less of the residual flesh and more of the Spirit.

However, the subjunctive mood indicates that if they chose not to surrender and obey at the appointed time when the Spirit of God revealed His Word, they would remain spiritually immature. Their lack of maturity would result in uselessness to the Master. Most assuredly His goal for all His children is spiritual growth and maturity so that a dark and lost world may see Jesus Christ through them.

17. And now, let's complete the lesson by looking at verse 20. What is Paul's desire and why?

18. Why does Paul want to be with them (v. 20)? For I am ____________________________ about you."

Note: The term "perplexed" (*aporeo*), is used figuratively here meaning "to doubt, hesitate not knowing how to proceed, determine, speak or act."[72]

As you look at Galatians 4:20, can't you hear Paul's tone? His spiritual children are in a dangerous situation. False teachers have come in and have caused enmity between him and the (spiritual) children he loves. His tone, at first, may have seemed harsh and abrupt. But that is not his heart toward them. Can't you hear Paul saying, "I wish I could be present with you because, rather than having you read my words you could listen to the intensity and inflection in the tone of my voice"? Sometimes, words communicated via letters, emails, or text messages can seem cold and unfeeling. Sometimes, it is just better to go face-to-face or at least make that phone call if possible. In any case, it's evident that Paul longed to see them.

And lastly, doesn't every parent, whether physical or spiritual, feel perplexed at one point or another. Think about it, if Paul, the apostle, is perplexed about what to do with his spiritual children, how much more should we be perplexed? And how encouraging it is to read that even Paul, at times, became perplexed!

Thankfully, like Paul, we do not have to remain perplexed. We have a Savior who lives within by His Spirit who uses His Word to speak to our hearts.

In closing, read 2 Corinthians 4:7–10. What do you see?

Note: The "treasure" in our earthen vessels is a reference to Christ in you, the hope of glory (Col. 1:27). Notice what God uses to form Christ in you. Notice also the purpose in verse 10.

Isn't that what Paul is saying in Galatians 4:19–20?

Now, in keeping with the stick figures, look at the next two pages for a visual of Galatians 4:16–20.

72. Spiros Zodhiates, *The Complete Word Study New Testament Dictionary* (Chattanooga: AMG Publishers, 1993), 235.

Galatians 4:16-20

The Heart of a False Teacher

Galatians 4:16-17

Eagerly seeks you out: Smooth and Flattering Speech

Psalm 5:9

Psalm 55:21

Romans 16:18

They wish to shut you out: From Jesus Christ

↓ From God's Word

(alienate and separate) From True Teachers of Grace

They "labor" to point you to themselves

Heart's Motive: You may seek them!

The focus is on the flesh!

The Heart of a True Teacher

Galatians 4:18-20

Is eagerly sought after: To point others to Christ

To point others to God's Word

They wish: To be present with you now (v. 20)

They "labor" that Christ be formed in you (v. 19)

↓

(surrendered and obedient will)

Heart's Motive: You may seek Jesus Christ!

The focus is on God's Grace!

Galatians 4:16-17

Cross-References

The Heart of a False Teacher

Romans 16:17-18

Cause dissensions

Hinder the teaching of God's Word

Slaves to their own appetites

Use smooth and flattering speech

Deceive the hearts of the unsuspecting

↓

(without guile/duplicity)

Matthew 7:15-20

Jesus warns: BEWARE false prophets!

They come to you!

Outwardly: Dress as sheep

Inwardly: Ravenous wolves

Known by their fruit!

↓

Deeds of the Flesh (Gal 5:19-21)

2 Corinthians 11:13-15

Called deceitful workers

Disguise themselves as: Apostles of Christ

↓ Servants of +R

Satan himself is disguised as an angel of light

The "Potential" Heart of a True Teacher

Remember, the potential is still there for one's residual flesh to rear its ugly head.

Therefore, everything that is *habitually* true about the false teacher can also be said of the true teacher who is quenching or grieving the Spirit of God. In other words, the residual flesh looks just like the flesh of an unbeliever.

Lesson 6

More Groundwork

GALATIANS 4:21—5:1 (PART ONE)

You will recall in a previous lesson; we paused to lay some necessary groundwork by looking at the life of Abraham in Genesis. We spent time looking at Genesis 15 and 17 where Paul argues that Abraham was saved (Gen. 15:6) *before* circumcision was inaugurated (Gen. 17:10-11).

And now, we find ourselves needing to look back again at the life of Abraham and even more specifically, at Sarah and Hagar, to understand the next section in Galatians 4:21—5:1. So before we dive into this next portion in Galatians, we will need to go back to the beginning where the foundation was laid.

You will notice by reading Galatians 4:21—5:1 that Paul picks up in his summary of the Book of Genesis as if the audience of Gentile believers could follow along without much explanation. Do you think that's because Paul had already taught the believers in Galatia from the Book of Genesis? I think so. Apparently, Paul had previously laid a firm foundation *because* his teaching would have come solely from the Old Testament *because* at this point in Church history, the New Testament had not been written.

There is a rich lesson all of us could learn from Paul's approach in Galatians. Anyone who says we do not need the Old Testament or that it is outdated, could not be further from the truth. In fact, we need the Old Testament to understand the New Testament. With that being stated, let's go back to the Book of Beginnings and do the necessary work of laying Galatians 4:21—5:1 on the firm foundation of Genesis 16, 20, and 21. Are you ready to get started?

Let's begin by putting Genesis 16 in context. To recap, remember the grace of God as He called Abram from the land of Ur, from his relatives and his father's house to Himself (Gen. 12:1–3). In short, God's promise to Abram included three things, namely:

- Land
- Descendants
- The Seed

Do not miss the grace of God in Abram's call, for Abram was not looking for God. In fact, Abram was dead in his transgressions and sin. He was a polytheist, meaning he worshiped and served many gods. But God, who is rich in mercy came looking for Abram (Eph. 2:4).

Notice everything God took him *from* (his land, his relatives, his father's house) was necessary to lead him *to* something and Someone far greater! Isn't that what happened to you and me when He called us to Himself?

As we fast forward to Genesis 15, we find Abram inquiring of the LORD regarding God's promised heir, since he is childless. He specifically asks the LORD about Eliezer, his servant (v. 2-3). Do you sense that innate within fallen humanity lies the propensity to try and help God out? However, the LORD's response is clear, "This man shall not be your heir; but one who will come forth from your own body, he shall be your heir" (v. 4).

And now, in Genesis 16, we find Sarai, who remains barren at this point, trying to help God out (as if God needed the help of any human being). Except this time, her solution includes the legal system of their day, called the code of Hammurabi. According to this ethical code, which was operative during ancient Babylonian history, it would have been perfectly legal to have a child by a servant in the home.

Note: Remember, although something may be legal, there is a higher code than people's code—God's Word.

1. Let's pick up on the story from this point and answer the following questions from Genesis 16. **Note:** We will start in Genesis 16, but we will need to go to other places in Genesis to help fill in the story.

    a. Notice in verse 1, who is Sarai's maid? ______________________________

    b. From where has Hagar come? ______________________________

Note: Remember, symbolically in Scripture, Egypt is always a picture of the world.

2. Now, to understand Genesis 16, we must go back and read Genesis 12:10–20.

    a. First, why are Abram and Sarai in Egypt (v. 10)? ______________________________

Note: Figuratively, a famine represents a circumstance of testing orchestrated by God. It is a circumstance of squeezing, so to speak. It presents a time in our life when we go looking for help to survive. Did you notice that Abram went "down to Egypt," rather than "up" to God? Geographically, he would have had to travel down, but do not miss the spiritual undertones implied in this verse.

Famines, orchestrated by God, are a time of testing God's Word in our life. The result of this testing can be good or bad. They are good, when they result in our turning to God and His Word for direction and help. They can be bad when we turn to our flesh or the world for help. Let's continue to see the Word God is testing in Abram's life.

Look specifically at verse 12 and compare it with what God had promised earlier in verse 3.

    b. Do you see Abram's lack of faith in what the LORD had promised earlier?

    What do you see?

    c. Notice as you read, Abram came up with a plan to save his own life. What does he do in verse 13?

    d. In whom is Abram depending on for his life (v. 13)? ______________________________

    Isn't he really depending on himself and his alternate plan as well?

    e. Technically speaking, from Abram's perspective, this is not a "complete" lie, for Sarai was his half-sister. Read Genesis 20:12 to see how Abram justifies his lie, but this time, to Abimelech. What do you see?

Note: You may be thinking, *If Sarai is his half-sister, what makes this a lie?* Let's answer this question by asking another question, specifically: Is Sarai functioning in a relationship with Abram as his sister or his wife?

Isn't Abram's "half-truth" just his way of protecting himself? Isn't that what you and I are doing when we lie?

Moreover, since God had clearly promised the "seed" through Abram's line, wouldn't it matter if Sarai became the wife of another man? Can you see the Enemy's attempt to use fear and unbelief in an effort to thwart God's plan? Beware; this is still his method of operation today.

f. Now, let's look back and specifically focus on Genesis 12:16. Do you see where Hagar is first mentioned (even if not by name)?

How did Abram acquire her? What do you see?

g. Now, look at verse 17. Who intervened on Abram and Sarai's behalf?

______________________________ Were they asking for help? ____________________

Wouldn't this qualify as another picture of God's grace?

h. Notice in Genesis 12:20, when Pharaoh throws Abram and Sarai out of Egypt for lying, who and what is escorted out with them?

i. Now, look at Isaiah 31:1-3. What do you see and how do these verses describe what happened in Genesis 12:10-20?

WHAT ABOUT YOU?

Think about the famine in your life right now. Maybe you are in the famine of loneliness, fear, or discouragement. Perhaps you are facing a physical or spiritual drought that is causing your mind to be in great turmoil and doubt.

Where do you run in the time of need or trouble?

Are you running to the world for help? Woe to those who do. At first, it seems as if Abram got by with his lie, but in Genesis 16 we will see how it all catches up with him.

Are you trusting in your own alternate plan to save yourself (whether from the penalty or the power of sin)?

Are you in the habit of telling little "white" lies to protect yourself?

Has the LORD God given you a word from His Word, and now, in the delay of it all, are you sensing the need to help God?

Have fear and unbelief caused you to doubt a clear word from the Lord?

Would you be willing to confess these things to Him? Would you be willing to ask Him to grant you repentance and get you back on track for His plan in your life?

3. Now, let's look back in Genesis 16 and pick up on Abram, Sarai, and Hagar. Using Genesis 16, answer the following questions.

    a. Notice in verse 2 who Sarai blames for her barren state? What does she say to Abram?

    b. What is her alternative plan (v. 2)?

Perfectly legal solution, right? What's wrong with her plan?

Note: If you look at Genesis 16:2 from a spiritual standpoint, we may need to rethink what is happening in the church today. For example, only God can produce a spiritual child, right? In other words, we cannot manufacture or reproduce a child of God. However, if you look at some of the "strategies" in the church today, is that not what you see?

Like Sarai, our desire is for spiritual children. Have we in some way, devised our own plans and ways to get them? Sobering thought. With that in mind, I cannot help but wonder just how many Ishmaels are in the "church" today. How many are products of our flesh trying to help God out, and how many are legitimately born of God by His Spirit?

    c. What do we find Abram doing in verse 2?

Note: There is nothing wrong with Abram listening (which means to hear with obedience) to his wife, *unless*, what she is saying does not align with God's Word. And in this case, legal or not, what she is concocting does not!

Do you see where Sarai is now attempting to "help God out of His dilemma"? Is our God ever in need of our help? Is He ever in a dilemma? Can you also discern the absurdity of this way of thinking and how contrary it is to God's Word and way of thinking?

    d. Now, look at verse 4. Following her conception, what is Hagar's estimation now of her mistress, Sarai?

Note: The word, "despised" means to make light of. Isn't that the way the world estimates the life of a believer? We must expect the world to turn on us when we run to it for help rather than the LORD.

e. Notice Sarai's response as her own plan is accomplished in verse 5. Do you see how she blames everyone but herself? Record your thoughts.

f. Now skip down in the story to verse 15.

What does Abram call the name of his son, whom Hagar bore? ____________________________

Note: Do you see how Ishmael is a product of the flesh?

g. How old is Abram when Ishmael is born (v. 16)? ______________________________

Note: Keep in mind that Sarai is ten years younger than Abram, which would have made her seventy-six years old at the time of Ishmael's birth.

4. Now, as you read Genesis 17:1, note Abram's age in verse 1? ______________________

With this information, and looking back at Genesis 16:16, how much time has elapsed in Abram's life? ___________

You will recall from a previous lesson; we looked specifically at Genesis 17 concerning the LORD God's encounter with Abram as He revealed His name, God Almighty (*El Shaddai*). You will also remember that when God progressively reveals His name to man it always coincides with man's need at the time of revelation. In this case, God Almighty was about to perform His Word in Abram's life at a time that was physically and reproductively impossible for both he and Sarai.

We also examined Genesis 17 in light of the establishment of circumcision, which was a sign of the covenant God was making with Abraham (Gen. 17:10-11).

As a way of review, what does circumcision of the flesh outwardly have to do with what is about to happen in the life of Abraham as God fulfills His promise through Isaac? Do you have any thoughts about the timing of his circumcision?

Think about it. Circumcision is a removal of the flesh involving a reproductive organ. God is about to act. Isaac, the promised son, will come in His time. Remember, His Son will come through this line. Therefore, there must be a removal of flesh.

The flesh impedes the fruit of God's Spirit; therefore, the flesh has to go! Under the direction of God's Spirit using God's Word, Abraham must do it.

You see Isaac's birth was not like Ishmael's birth. Ishmael's birth came naturally. But Isaac's birth would be supernatural. Although Sarah was reproductively dead, God Almighty intervened. There is no other explanation.

Keep these things in mind as we proceed.

5. Now, skip over a couple of chapters to Genesis 21. Answer the following questions from this chapter.

a. What does the LORD do for Sarah in verse 1?

b. What do you learn about the timing of conception in verse 2?

c. What does Abraham call the name of his son, whom Sarah bore to him (3)? ______________________________

d. What does Abraham do to Isaac on his eighth day of life and why?

e. How old is Abraham when Isaac is born (v. 5)? ______________________________

f. What is Sarah's response in verse 6?

Do you see the fruit of God's Spirit here? I see great joy!

Now, look at verse 8. We are told that Isaac grew and was weaned. On the day he was weaned, Abraham celebrated with a great feast.

g. What does Sarah see Ishmael doing at the feast (v. 9)? ______________________________

Note: One of the cross-references to Genesis 21:9 is Galatians 4:29. Interestingly, the term used to describe Ishmael's action in Galatians 4:29 is "persecuted," which is translated from the Greek verb, *dioko*, meaning, "to pursue; repeated acts of enmity."[73] Further informative is that the imperfect verb tense is used, which signifies a continuous or linear action in the past. In other words, the flesh will always mock or persecute the Spirit with repeated acts of enmity. Moreover, the antonym of *dioko* is to "guard, watch, to keep carefully; to deliver."[74]

As you connect Genesis 21:9 and Galatians 4:29, do you see that there is much more going on in this verse than just from the physical realm? In fact, there is a very real spiritual lesson for you to see here. You will recall that Ishmael is a product of the flesh. Isaac, on the other hand, represents the Spirit. With this in mind, what can you expect the flesh to *always* do in response to the Spirit of God?

Isn't that true in your life as well? Do you sense, at times in your life, when your residual flesh mocks or makes light of the Spirit of God? Do you see the flesh's inherent and unrelenting hostility toward the things of God? What, then, are we to do?

---

73. Spiros Zodhiates, *The Complete Word Study New Testament Dictionary* (Chattanooga: AMG Publishers, 1993), 474.
74. *Ibid.*

h. What was Sarah's response in verse 10?

i. How does Abraham feel (v.11) about Sarah's request in verse 10?

Obedience to God's Word can initially cause our hearts great distress, but in the end, it is meant to ultimately save us!

j. Now, look as God weighs in on the matter. What does God tell Abraham (vv. 12–13)?

Did you notice that this time, Sarah and God are saying the same thing? This time, Abraham is told to listen (with the intention of obeying) what Sarah had proclaimed (v. 10).

k. How does Abraham respond to the LORD God (v. 14)?

l. What do you learn about Abraham's obedience to the LORD when given a difficult assignment?

m. What do you learn about how to deal with the flesh as you look at what Sarah said (v. 10) and the LORD confirmed (v. 12)? Be specific.

6. Did you happen to notice who was responsible for driving out the flesh? Do you see that in Genesis 21:10-12, Abraham is in the process of being saved by grace through faith? Explain your answer.

Thoughts to Consider:

As I think about Abraham's decision to go to Egypt for help, despite God's promise (Word), I cannot help but think about the church today. When you barter with the enemy (Pharaoh), you get his "help," which will always result in enslavement (Hagar). His "help" will always involve our flesh and the world. These are two things I see that have crept into the church today.

By running to Egypt (the world) instead of the Lord and His Word, we have polluted the *pure* milk of the Word (1 Pet 2:2; emphasis added). The Greek word translated here as "pure" means undiluted, unmixed. Sadly, in the church, we are mixing various forms of psychology such as behavior modification and medication to "help" us *cope* with our flesh. Where sin is involved, we have a cure—a Savior! We have bought into the lie that the Word of God is not enough. In our effort to help others (and God), we are counseling people with something other than God's Word. It's exactly what the false teachers in Paul's day was offering—Christ plus something else. We have gotten away from the truth that the issue is always the heart, and Christ is the *only* answer!

As I have stated in other workbooks, I am not against medical help. I am, however, against medical solutions for spiritual issues. The Lord, in His great mercy, may send you for medical assistance. He has given physicians the knowledge to keep our physical body healthy. I praise God for that kind of support. But again, when the issue is spiritual, we need a different type of help. Thankfully, our Great Physician specializes in hearts!

Furthermore, Abraham's life is symbolic of the Christian life. Within each believer, there is an Ishmael (the residual flesh) and an Isaac (God's Spirit). The Ishmael within will always mock Isaac; therefore, he must be cast out. Tragically, we would rather try to rehab our flesh than put it to death. Wouldn't you prefer a list of ten things to do if the other option required putting your flesh to death? I know my flesh would.

What is in your life that needs to go? What is the Spirit of God through the Word of God pointing at in your life?

7. Now, having laid the groundwork, it is time to read Galatians 4:21—5:1. Take the time in this lesson to diagram the passages. You will notice that there will be two distinct contrasts: two women; two sons, and two covenants, each proceeding from two very different places. What do you see?

I am attaching my diagram on the following pages just in case you need a visual.

Galatians 4:21-5:1

[You]

4:21 Tell me,

you who want to be under law,

do you not listen

to the law?

4:22 For it is written

that Abraham had two sons,

one by the bondwoman and **one by the free woman**.

4:23 But the son

by the bondwoman

was born according

to the flesh,

and

the son

by the free woman

through

the promise.

4:24 This is allegorically speaking:

for these women are two covenants,

one proceeding

from Mount Sinai

bearing children

who are to be slaves,

she is Hagar.

4:25 Now this Hagar

is Mount Sinai

in Arabia,

and

corresponds to the present Jerusalem,

for she is in slavery

with her children.

4:26 But the Jerusalem above
is free;
she is our mother.

4:27 For it is written,

"REJOICE,
BARREN WOMAN
WHO DOES NOT BEAR;
BREAK FORTH
AND
SHOUT,
YOU
WHO ARE NOT IN LABOR;
FOR MORE ARE THE CHILDREN
OF THE DESOLATE
THAN OF THE ONE
WHO HAS THE HUSBAND."

4:28 And you
brethren,
like Isaac,
are children of promise.

4:29 But
as at that time
he him
who was born according who was born according
to the flesh to the Spirit,
persecuted
so it is now also.

4:30

But what does the Scripture say?

"CAST OUT

THE BONDWOMAN

AND

HER SON,

FOR THE SON OF THE BONDWOMAN

SHALL NOT BE AN HEIR WITH THE SON OF THE FREE WOMAN."

4:31 So then, brethren,

we are not children

of a bondwoman, but of a free woman.

5:1 It was for freedom

that Christ set us free;

therefore keep standing firm

and

do not be subject

again

to a yoke of slavery.

Notes

LESSON 7

TWO PATHS: HUMAN EFFORT VERSUS GOD'S GRACE

GALATIANS 4:21—5:1 (PART TWO)

ONE PROPER RESPONSE

In this lesson, we will see a heartbroken and perplexed Paul (Gal. 4:12–20) turn to God's Word for God's perspective. Although Paul is troubled in spirit, he knows the solution resides in God's Word. For every question Paul asks, he knows the answer is in God's unchanging Word. Is that true for you? When heartbroken and perplexed, where do you turn? To whom do you run?

As we proceed, having laid the groundwork in Genesis, let's continue in Galatians as Paul completes his teaching concerning the theology of grace. Let's begin.

1. Notice this section of the study begins with another rhetorical question from Paul. What does Paul ask the Galatians in verse 21?

2. How does Paul answer his question in verse 22? What are his first four words?

    -------- --------- -------- --------------- ...

Do you see where he turns for the answer? Do you see where he points? To whom and what do you look?

3. What do we learn about Abraham in verse 22?

Now, read Galatians 4:21-31.

4. A quick observation in verses 22–31 will reveal one father (Abraham) but two mothers. Herein lies the contrast throughout the remainder of this lesson. Let's distinguish precisely what Paul is contrasting.

    a. First, how are the two mothers identified in verse 22?

        1)

        2)

    b. What do you learn about the son of each woman in verse 23?

        1)

        2)

As you recall the birth of each son, what is Paul contrasting? In other words, how were each born? Think back to the miraculous birth of Isaac. Remember the formula:

Dead + Dead = Dead **BUT** Dead + God Almighty = Life (Isaac)

1) What does Paul want the Galatians to see by contrasting these two births?

2) Now, consider what Jesus told Nicodemus in John 3:3, 6. How do these verses relate to Paul's analogy in Galatians 4:22–23? What do you see?

c. What do these two women represent allegorically (v. 24)? ______________ ________________________

In verse 24, Paul uses the words, "allegorically speaking," which may seem confusing. Maybe a better way to understand what Paul means would be to think in terms of "representatively speaking." Keep in mind the word "covenant" can be used interchangeably with the words "will and testament." Here, the word "covenant" describes a mutual relationship between two parties. It signifies the "setting up of that relationship, which is accomplished by the free act or choice of one person."[75]

You will recall that the covenant God established with Abraham occurred without any human cooperation (Gen. 15). For it was God's choice (will) to make a covenant with Himself while Abraham slept (which represents his spiritual state of death). The covenant God entered with Abraham was of His own gracious choice and was meant to secure a religious inheritance for His chosen people.[76]

d. What do you learn about the covenant in verse 24? List the facts.

1. From where did it proceed? ________________________________

2, What is said regarding the children this covenant bears?

3. Of whom is this covenant representative? ____________________

Note: Keep in mind that Hagar is an Egyptian slave. She represents bondage as opposed to freedom. Also, Egypt, in Scripture, describes the world and Pharaoh, who was the ruler of Egypt, is representative of the enemy. Do you see our three enemies (Eph. 2:1–3)?

Furthermore, you will recall the covenant made on Mount Sinai signifies the Law, which represents a conditional covenant wherein a divine promise is based on man's obedience.

a) What have we learned in a previous lesson regarding man's obedience to God's Law?

75. Spiros Zodhiates, *The Complete Word Study New Testament Dictionary* (Chattanooga: AMG Publishers, 1993), 425.
76. *Ibid.*

In essence, by analogy, Paul is comparing Hagar and her bondage with Sarah and her free state. Symbolically, each represents two covenants. Hagar and Ishmael represent the covenant of law and works, while Sarah and Isaac signify the covenant, which corresponds by grace through faith.

e. Now, what do you learn about Hagar in verse 25?

1) Hagar is (or represents) ________________________

↓

in ________________

and

corresponds to the present ________________

for

she is in __________________________ with her ____________________.

Note: The mention of "Arabia" is a reference to Israel's forty years of wandering following its disobedience to God's Word. The word itself means, *arid* and *sterile*.[77] MacArthur's insights are worth noting here as well. He states, "The descendants of Hagar through Ishmael eventually moved into the desert areas to the east and south of the Promised Land. They came to be known broadly as Arabs and their territory as Arabia, and it is significant that Mount Sinai is in what is still known today as the Arabian Peninsula."[78]

a) As you consider verse 25, what is Paul inferring about the present state or condition of Jerusalem?

b) How do you think the Judaizers felt to hear Paul's evaluation of their condition?

Do you see why they hated Paul and his message? They prided themselves on being Jews. After all, they were Abraham's children. Their identity rested in their lineage as Abraham's offspring. Paul was not only challenging their true identity; he was exposing it, which is why they hated him and his message of freedom in Christ.

c) Like Paul, Jesus encountered this same deceptive spirit with its subsequent hatred, which resided within the Pharisees. Look carefully at a similar encounter Jesus had with the Pharisees. Read John 8:33–45.

1) Of what do the Pharisees continue to remind Jesus (vv. 33, 39)?

2) How does Jesus respond to them? Look specifically at verse 37.

3) How do the Pharisees respond to the truth in verses 37, 40, and 45?

---

77. *Ibid.* 248.

78. John MacArthur, Jr., *The MacArthur New Testament Commentary: Galatians* (Chicago: Moody Press, 1987), 125.

4) Why did they respond in this manner according to verse 37?

5) Now, compare John 8:37, 40, and 45 with Galatians 4:16. What do you see?

6) Ultimately, Jesus exposed their true identity in verse 44. What did He say?

Do you see that the opposing spirit Paul is addressing is the same Enemy Jesus identified in John 8:33–45? By the way, that same Enemy is still opposing God's Word and anyone who is faithfully sharing it with others today.

Now, let's go back to Galatians.

f. What do you learn about the Jerusalem from above in verse 26?

1)

2) She (Sarah) represents ______________________________

a) As you contrast verse 25 with verse 26, what do you see?

Note: The earthly Jerusalem represents the legalism from which Paul had been rescued by God's grace. He knew the trap of human effort and self-righteousness. Therefore, here he contrasts the earthly Jerusalem with the heavenly Jerusalem, which had come from above and represented freedom.

In essence, what Paul is contrasting is human effort versus God's grace, the arid and barren versus the fruitful, the natural versus the supernatural, being in Judaism versus being in Christ. Paul knew both. One he describes as enslavement while the other represents freedom. There was no going back for Paul. Herein is his plea to the Galatians.

5. Now, look where Paul turns their attention. What are the first four words in verse 27?

________ _________ ________ _______________ ...

6. Record the Old Testament verse Paul quoted in verse 27.

Note: Paul quoted from Isaiah 54:1, which contextually, is a reference to Israel while they were in captivity in Babylon. To help us better understand the purpose of quoting from Isaiah 54:1, consider the following insightful information from Old Testament theologian and professor, John Oswalt.

First, Isaiah 54–55 should be read as a unit. Oswalt states, "Chapter 54 is a love song by God to Zion, His estranged bride, telling her all the things He is going to do in restoring her. Chapter 55 is the invitation proper, calling on the bride not to miss through unbelief what is hers.[79]

Moreover, Oswalt determines that in the first ten verses of Isaiah 54, God speaks to Israel in the image of a disgraced woman. For example, Israel is the barren one (vv. 1-3), the widow (vv. 4-5), and the divorced one (vv. 6-8).[80] Oswalt reminds the reader that in the ancient Near East the worst fate that could befall a woman was to have no children. He explains, "In Isaiah 54:1–3, God says that those who have experienced His grace will no longer be fruitless but will live lives of unexpected abundance, with more 'descendants' for which than they can account."[81]

According to Oswalt, a kind and loving God makes it clear in the climactic verses 9–10 that the issue is not captivity in Babylon but rather <u>alienation from His presence</u> (emphasis added).[82] In other words, Isaiah 54 is about reconciliation and restoration, and our gracious God is the Initiator of both. In reality, no human effort can free captive Israel. Did you notice the reason for God's discipline of Israel? It was not punishment for punishment's sake. It was necessary from God's perspective. Truly with the Lord God, it is always about being alienated and separated from His creation; this is what grieves His heart.

By way of further help in understanding the meaning of the words from Isaiah 54:1, MacArthur, explains stating,

> *Those words were originally written to cheer the Jewish exiles in Babylon but are here applied to Sarah, the barren woman whose barrenness seemingly stood as an impenetrable barrier to the fulfillment of God's promise to her husband, Abraham. As freedom and greater fruitfulness came again to the nation in Babylonian captivity, so it would come to the people in captivity to the law and its death penalty.*
>
> *As Zion was a mother of children by grace after captivity, so believers will multiply in grace in the heavenly Jerusalem, which was also figuratively barren for a long time. 'The general assembly and church of the first-born (Heb 12:23) was not occupied until Jesus was crucified and resurrected, taking captivity captive and removing the spiritual barrenness that no human effort under the Old Covenant could remove. Heaven, the Jerusalem above, will continue to be populated with the born-again saints of God until every predestined believer has entered.*
>
> *In one sweep Paul sets forth the common factor of divine power in behalf of Sarah, the captive Jews, and the church. The common element of all three is divine power granting freedom and fruitfulness. Everything in this trilogy is the result of regenerating grace, not human effort.*[83]

7. Now, as you think about what was happening in Galatia, why would Paul refer to Isaiah 54:1 here? What is our gracious God revealing to the Galatians?

Do you see that although in captivity, God in His grace, was offering Israel (His bride) restoration and reconciliation to Himself? Paul wants the Galatians to know that grace will meet man in his inability, weakness, and most vulnerable state. Why would the free Galatians ever choose to go back into captivity under the Law?

---

79. John N. Oswalt, *The NIV Application Commentary: Isaiah* (Grand Rapids, MI: Zondervan, 2003), 595.
80. *Ibid.*
81. *Ibid.*
82. *Ibid.*
83. MacArthur, *Commentary: Galatians*, 127.

8. With that being stated, of what does Paul remind his brothers in verse 28?

9. Like Isaac, the brethren in Galatia can now expect persecution. Notice in verse 29, from where the persecution for Isaac originated?

10. Think back to the last lesson and particularly, to Genesis 21:9. To what is Paul referring in verse 29?

11. The phrase at the end of verse 29, which states, "so it is now also," is another way of warning the Galatian believers. What is Paul warning?

12. Now, look once again as Paul redirects their attention in verse 30. What question does Paul ask?

But ____________ ____________ ________ ________________ ______________?

That needs to be the question we ask ourselves in any given situation at any time.

13. Notice that God's Spirit directs Paul's mind back to Genesis 21:10. (Note: This is how the Spirit still speaks to the heart of man today. He always uses His Word.)

How does Genesis 21:10 address the Galatian's situation? What is God's counsel to the Galatians (and us)?

14. Isn't Paul telling the Galatians that the flesh and the Spirit cannot co-exist because the flesh will always mock the Spirit? God's counsel to Abraham was to cast out Ishmael, which represents our flesh. What might that look like in the life of a believer?

As I contemplated the question above, the following thoughts came to mind:

First, only God's Spirit has the power and ability to cast out the flesh. He knows exactly what needs to go and how it needs to be put to death. Only God's Spirit knows the areas of our heart that are still in bondage to the flesh. He alone knows what has power over our heart, and He (our Savior) alone is well able to save us from this power.

The Spirit of grace (Zech. 12:10) uses the Word, which is a mirror into our soul (James 1:23), to show us the truth about our heart. When this happens, He is inviting us to be free. In other words, when God's Spirit uses the Word to expose our heart and bring conviction, we are experiencing God's grace!

The proper response to His grace is faith. Faith involves the personal surrender of our wills and obedience to the Word He has just revealed to our heart. As we respond in faith, there is less of our flesh and more of His Spirit. What I have just described is the process of spiritual growth. This is true discipleship. In a sense, when we surrender and obey His Word, we are turning from self to Christ, which is called repentance. Often when we think of repentance, we think only of our justification. But repentance (a turning from self to Christ) is a life-long process (sanctification) as well.

Think of salvation in this way; justification is when we first turned from self to Christ. Sanctification is a life-long turning from self to follow Christ; until finally, in glorification, we will never again need to turn from self to Christ because once we have seen Him face to face, there will be no question in our minds that He is God and we are not!

Pastor and author, Scott Patty, in his book entitled, Words of Grace, addresses the topic of repentance and some of its misconceptions by stating,

> *God grants the repentance that leads to life (Acts 11:18). The repentance that leads to life is for salvation. This is a controversial point of the gospel. Salvation requires repentance. Turning to Jesus in faith to follow Him is the only way a person is saved.*
>
> *The repentance that leads to life is the way of discipleship. This is a misunderstood point of the gospel. Discipleship requires ongoing repentance. Yes, we repent and believe to be saved, but our ongoing growth in Christlikeness requires that we continue to turn from our self-life to follow Him.*[84]

Never forget, whether we are talking about the salvation of man (justification, sanctification, or glorification), God alone is the one initiating and participating in this gracious rescue mission by granting repentance. Man cannot and will not repent on his own. Left to himself, man will always and only turn to himself for salvation.

Looking at our salvation through the lens of grace, pastor and author, Paul David Tripp, in his daily journal entitled, New Morning Mercies, explains, "God's call to obey is itself a grace. In this call, He is actively rescuing you from you (emphasis mine)."[85] I don't know about you, but this truth resonates in my soul and has become the daily cry of my heart.

The quote from Tripp caused my mind to think back in Scripture to His first call of grace to obey. Although grace finds its origin in eternity past, grace was first manifested on earth in the Garden. Adam had one command to obey, which was God's grace. In this call of grace to obey, God was rescuing man from choosing to eat from the Tree of the Knowledge of Good and Evil, which unbeknownst to man, was in effect, preferring the world, our flesh, and the enemy of our soul over and above Him (our greatest need).

Rather than gratefully accepting God's grace by faith, man chose his own way (or at least that is the lie he believed). For in truth, he chose the enemy's way instead of God's way. The choice to be "like God" propelled man into the greatest pit of darkness and deception and launched God into a search and rescue mission that is still actively in process today.

Do you see that the command to cast out the bondwoman is just another way of saying repent? Turn, by God's grace, from self (your plan, your will, your way) to Christ. In essence, God's grace is merely an invitation to be free whether it is freedom from sin's penalty, power, and someday, its very presence. Will you accept His gracious invitation?

---

84. Scott Patty, *Words of Grace*, (Nashville: B&H Pub., 2018), 99.
85. Paul David Tripp, *New Morning Mercies* (Wheaton: Crossway, 2014), January 27.

With these things in mind, let's look at our final verse of study in this lesson, Galatians 5:1, which serves as a hinge from theology (Chapters 1–4) to practical living (Chapters 5–6). In fact, all of Paul's letters can be divided into these two distinct parts: theology and practical application, or to put it another way, God's grace and our response in faith.

15. Answer the following questions from Galatians 5:1.

    a. Notice, Paul begins the transition with grace. What do we learn about Christ?

Now, in response to the grace of God through Christ, Paul will structure our response in both the positive and the negative.

    b. What will the positive response in faith look like in the life of a believer who has truly been set free?

Note: The verb used here is present imperative active. The present tense signifies continuous action. The imperative mood indicates a command, and the active voice means that the subject is performing the action.

With that stated, what is Paul saying to the Galatians?

Isn't Paul commanding the Galatians to keep standing firm in what Christ has accomplished in His finished work on the cross rather than rely on their own merit now that they are His? Commands, in Scripture, are always possible because the One commanding us resides within us to accomplish the command for us and through us.

In other words, the same Power that set them free from the penalty of sin is the same One who will keep them free from the power of sin. He is and will remain the firm foundation both now, and for eternity. We merely need to follow.

    c. Now that we have looked at the positive response, how does Paul state the same command in the negative?

We will pick back up on this verse in the next lesson, but for now, keep in mind that Paul is challenging the Galatians to avoid two extremes, namely: heathenism and religion. Christ had rescued them from the face of rebellion in which they were once trapped in their self-indulgent way of living. As Gentiles, they knew no other way. But God, rich in mercy (Eph. 2:4) . . .

Now, having experienced God's grace, they were facing the opposite extreme, which had disguised itself as an angel of light in the face of religion. From the face of rebellion (self-indulgence) to the face of religion (self-righteousness), both are an extreme error. Both point to self rather than Christ. The Galatians needed to repent. And God in His grace was inviting them back to Himself.

WHAT ABOUT YOU?

Do you find yourself under the power and control of a sin? Have you lost the joy you once knew so freely?

Is the residual flesh within you trying to usurp God's Spirit by placing you back up under the law of performance and striving? If so, this is a trap from the Enemy.

If you are reading these things, and the Spirit of God is convicting your heart under the weight of its truth, this is His invitation back to Himself. This is His grace. Will you properly respond in faith?

Notice that I qualified the response to faith with the word, proper. That's because sometimes our response to God's grace is unbelief. An improper response (unbelief) is a refusal to surrender our will and obey His Word. This occurs when I say. "No," to God's Spirit and, "Yes," to my flesh. A believer who chooses to respond incorrectly to God's grace can become hard, stagnant, and remain spiritually immature. In reality, the Enemy can render them useless.

Sadly today, discipleship is, all too often nothing more than a list of more things to do (especially when they appear religious). Our flesh is a sucker for self-help solutions. My flesh is a magnet for lists and will go to great lengths to avoid putting something I love (my god, my plans, my way, myself) to death.

The last thing we need is a list of more things to do. His Spirit calls us to put to death those areas of our flesh that compete and war against Him. Have you noticed we would prefer the list?

Consider the following excerpt from the book entitled, Devotedly: The Personal Letters and Love Story of Jim and Elisabeth Elliot, written by the Elliot's daughter Valerie Elliot Shepard. Shepard shares that while reading her father's journal, one entry caught her attention regarding grace.

First, the quote from her father, Jim Elliot's journal, reads,

> *I see clearly now that anything—whatever it be—if it is not on the principle of grace, it is not of God. Here shall be my plea in weakness; here shall be my boldness in prayer; here shall be my deliverance in temptation; at last, here shall be my translation. Not of grace? Then not of God." And here, O Lord Most High shall be Your glory and the honor of Your Son.*[86]

In her response to his entry, she candidly admits,

> *I was all too legalistic for at least twenty years of my adult life, believing if I could just be more disciplined, God would be more pleased with me, and I could climb the ladder of perfection, earning the reputation I desired. My own rules of godliness were my ideals. More than I loved Him, I loved my rules of what a devoted wife and Christian home should be. Therefore, to borrow from my father's words, I was not being "delivered in temptation," or being "bold in prayer," or understanding that His grace covered all my "pleas in weakness." Nor was I learning what my mother had told me throughout her life—how we shouldn't always be examining our own holiness but simply seeking to please Him, that it's up to Him to bring about change in us. As He helps us do His will, He conforms us into Christlikeness. It's all grace. It's not all about us.87*

Can you identify with the first twenty years of Valerie Elliot Shepard's adult life? I know I sure can. If, after doing this lesson, you sense the Lord is beckoning you out of the trap of sin's power, will you accept His gracious invitation?

---

86. Valerie Elliot Shepard, *Devotedly: The Personal Letters and Love Story of Jim and Elisabeth Elliot* (Nashville: B&H Publishers, 2019), 88.
87. *Ibid.*

In closing, consider the words of the late evangelist and author, Roy Hession, who states,

> *Where there is need, there is God. Where there is sorrow, misery, unhappiness, suffering, confusion, folly, oppression, there is the I AM, yearning to turn man's sorrow into bliss whenever man will let Him. It is not, therefore, the hungry seeking for bread, but the Bread seeking the hungry; not the sad seeking for joy, but rather Joy seeking the sad; not emptiness seeking fullness, but rather Fullness seeking emptiness. And it is not merely that He supplies our need, but He becomes Himself the fulfillment of our need...Grace, being what it is, is always drawn by need.*[88]

- Will you confess your need today?
- Will you bring to the Lord the sin that has power over you and let the Savior deliver you once again?
- Would you be willing to ask Him what that might look like in your life? In other words, is there an area of your heart in which you have been unwilling to surrender your will and obey?

With your permission here, I sense a personal word of counsel at this point:

Pause after each statement or question. Allow the Spirit to answer you from His Word. Sometimes, He will bring a word, a phrase, or even a memory. If He brings a memory, ask Him what He wants you to see. He will always answer with His Word. If He brings a word or a phrase (from His Word), find a concordance to discover His message to you.

At this point, I tell the women I counsel that He will not "rattle." By this, I mean He does not use many words, unlike the voice in my head that is rapidly firing without pause, which, I have learned is not from Him. I also know it is not from Him because it does not align with the Word. In fact, it is usually the exact opposite. The enemy's voice is condemning, hateful, accusing. It is usually accompanied by fear, anxiety, and great shame. The Lord's voice is gentle, hopeful, and convicting. He is always drawing me to Himself. The Enemy's voice tells me I am a failure and that I can never get it right and that I can never please God.

I liken the voice that is continual to a machine gun that doesn't come up for air. When God speaks to my heart, it is with a still small voice. The message is clear, concise, and I am not left wondering what He just revealed. His voice always aligns with His Word. I know He has put His finger on the issue of my heart and has given His Word to surrender and obey.

Will you surrender and obey Him?

I sense a word of caution is necessary here as well. When the Spirit of God uses the Word of God to speak directly to an issue in my heart, I know it is not a suggestion. It is a clear command to surrender and obey. I always caution the women I counsel to surrender and obey quickly. Do not delay and give man or the enemy an opportunity to persuade you otherwise.

The Savior is waiting. Will you join me in thanking our gracious God for His grace that is greater than all our sin (Rom. 5:20)?

To God be all glory as He continues to grant us repentance (from the world, our flesh, and the enemy) and lead us to Life (Jesus Christ)!

88. Roy Hession, *We Would See Jesus* (Fort Washington, PA; CLC Publishers, 1958), 41.

Lesson 8

Fallen from Grace

GALATIANS 5:1–12

As stated earlier, Chapter 5 in Galatians marks a turning point in the Book of Galatians. In fact, in every letter Paul wrote (all thirteen of them), there is one common *focus* throughout—Jesus Christ and Him crucified. There is one common *theme*, which is salvation "by grace through faith" alone (Eph 2:8). Likewise, Paul wrote each letter using the same method— theology first and foremost followed by practical application.

Grammatically speaking, Paul uses the indicative mood to present a proper theology. You will recall that the indicative mood indicates a statement of fact. In other words, the first portion of any letter written by Paul will begin with facts about God the Father, God the Son, and God the Holy Spirit.

However, in the practical application portion of any of Paul's letters, you will notice that he shifts to the imperative mood, which signifies a command to be surrendered and obeyed. In other words, because the grace of God is all that He is and has accomplished to save us (theology), then Christ, living in us by His Spirit, makes it possible for us to respond in faith (practical living) properly.

Finally, we must always keep in mind that the purpose of any revelation about the God the Father, Son, and Spirit is a gift from God for our benefit for the simple reason that who God is *always* correlates with what man desperately needs, which is God! Let's get started by looking at Paul's statement of fact (indicative mood) concerning Christ in verse one.

1. What does Paul remind the Galatians about Christ (v. 1)?

Note: Dr. Wuest, commenting on the freedom to which Paul refers, states, "The liberty spoken of here does not refer to the kind of life a person lives, neither does it have reference to his words and actions, but it has to do with the ***method*** by which he lives that life" (emphasis added).[89]

2. Now, watch as Paul shifts his attention from what Christ offers to the command we are instructed to obey (imperative mood). Like all other commands, there are always two options, and each diametrically opposed (Gal 5:1).

Either we will: 1) ____

OR

we will 2) ____

89. Kenneth S. Wuest, *Word Studies in the Greek New Testament: Galatians, Vol. One* (Grand Rapids: Wm. B. Eerdmans Publishing Co., 1972), 136.

3. Did you notice the word, "again"? What does that imply?

Again, citing from Wuest, he explains stating,

> *The Judaizers lived their lives by dependence upon self-effort in an attempt to obey the law. The Galatian Christians had been living theirs in dependence upon the indwelling Holy Spirit. Their hearts had been occupied with the Lord Jesus, the details of their lives being guided by the ethics that emerged from the teaching of the apostles, both doctrinal and practical. Now, in swinging over to law, they were losing that freedom of action and that flexibility of self-determination which one exercises in the doing of what is right, when one does right, not because the law forbids the wrong and commands the right, but because it is right, because it pleases the Lord Jesus, and because of love for Him.*[90]

4. Now, in summation and conjunction with Wuest's explanation, fill in the following blanks for clarity.

Basically, those who are coming back up under the law will need to rely on ________________________________; while those who come up under the finished work of Christ are relying upon the ________________ ________________ and are motivated by ____________________.

5. Before we leave verse one, let's look at some cross-references to help us gain insight into this command (imperative) to *keep standing firm*. Look at each reference and answer the following questions:

a. Romans 14:4 – Who can make us stand? ________________________________

b. 1 Corinthians 16:13 – In what are we to stand firm? ____________________________

c. Philippians 1:27 – How are we instructed to stand firm?

1) In ____

2) With ____

3) __________________ together for the __________________ of the __________________

Note: By the way, the only time we are instructed to *strive* is when the gospel is at stake.

d. Philippians 4:1 – In whom are we instructed to stand? __________________________

As you look at God's command in Galatians 5:1 and consider all the cross-references above, isn't Paul merely commanding us to stand firm in the *grace* of God?

Think of *grace* this way: Theologian and professor, J.I. Packer, defines *grace* as "God operating in love toward people."[91] Truly the *grace* of God that justified the Galatians (and us) is the same *grace* that will sanctify them (and us). When you think on the word, *grace*, remember it has everything to do with God. We are merely the recipients who either respond in faith by surrendering our will and obeying His Word; or in unbelief, which is evidenced by a refusal to surrender and obey.

Furthermore, as I think of the *freedom* that *grace* offers, I cannot help but hear in my head the words of one of my favorite pastors and Bible teachers, the late Wayne Barber, who would frequently say, "Freedom is not the

90. Ibid., 137.

91. J. I. Packer, *Knowing God* (Downers Grove, IL: IVP Publishers, 1993), 128.

freedom to do as you please. Freedom is the power to do as you should."[92] Thankfully, we know that the power source he is referencing is not us, but lives within us by His *grace*. Herein lies the message Paul was sending to the Galatians.

6. Now, let's look at Galatians 5:2-4 as Paul calls to the attention of the Galatians a hypothetical situation to consider. He begins verse two stating, "Behold," which, when you see this word used in Scripture, is a "call to attention to something or someone external to oneself."[93]

    a. What is the hypothetical scenario Paul lays out in verse 2?

    IF you ______________________________

    ____

In this verse, Paul uses the subjunctive mood, which indicates that the Galatians had not been circumcised but were on the verge of doing so.

    b. What does Paul testify to them (and every man) again in verse 3?

    ____

    ____

Did you catch the word, "obligation"? The word (translated from *opheiletes*) can be translated, "debtor" and signifies to owe. According to Zodhiates, *opheiletes* describes one who is morally bound to the performance of any and every duty of the Law.[94]

    c. What would this obligation to the whole Law mean in regard to Christ (v4)?

    ____

    d. What does it say about the one who is severed from Christ? What are they actively seeking (v4)?

    ____

Did you notice the harsh warning, *severed*? Can you imagine being severed from Christ? What might that mean?

Note: The word, "severed" (*katargeo*) means to be "idle, useless, ineffective, and unfruitful."[95] It is an aorist indicative passive verb. You will recall that the aorist tense indicates a punctiliar action in the past, and the indicative mood represents a statement of fact, while the passive voice means that the subject is acted upon.

In other words, by choosing to obligate oneself to keep the Law and seeking to be justified by the law (both phrases are in the active voice, meaning the subject is choosing the action), you will passively be severing from Christ. Moreover, the words, "obligation" and "severed" are linked with another result of choosing the Law over Christ.

    e. What is the final outcome of one who chooses the Law over Christ in verse 4?

    You have ______________________________ from ______________________.

---

92. Wayne Barber, *Living Grace* (Nashville, TN: B&H Publishers, 2005), 34. I highly recommend this book to anyone who wishes to understand the grace of God as it relates to our sanctification.
93. Spiros Zodhiates, *The Complete Word Study Dictionary New Testament* (Chattanooga: AMG Pub.,1993), 754.
94. *Ibid.,* 1079.
95. *Ibid.,* pp. 841–842.

Would it surprise you to know that the word "fallen," is the antonym of "stand firm?" With that being stated, what does it mean to *have fallen from grace*? [Hint: To answer this question look back over what it means to *stand firm* and think the opposite.] Record your findings.

Let's be careful as we look at this phrase, "fallen from grace." First and foremost, the Galatians were by no means in danger of losing their salvation, for that would be impossible since it does not align with the whole counsel of God's Word. At this point in the letter, the context of these verses is invaluable. Paul is talking to believers. Therefore, to have "fallen from grace" is not in reference to their justification or their standing with Christ. However, it is very much a warning to them concerning their sanctification.

In other words, to have fallen from grace is to lose sight of the grace of God necessary for daily living in this process of sanctification. In other words, someone or something has gained power over them in an area of their heart that does not align with the truth of God's Word. It is very much in keeping with the question Paul had asked the Galatians earlier in the letter. Record again the question he asks in Galatians 3:3?

Do you see that in Galatians 5:2–4 Paul paints a hypothetical picture of what it is like to be enslaved as a believer? In particular, he uses the trap of circumcision the Judaizers had used to entice or entangle the believers at Galatia. To go back up under the law to be sanctified would render the Galatians unfruitful, useless to the Master, and someday, standing before their Savior, very regretful.

7. What do I mean by regretfully standing before the Savior? To help us understand this statement, let's turn 1 Corinthians 3:10–15.

Note: First, we must put these verses in the context of what is called the Bema Judgment before which every believer will stand. In fact, Scripture speaks of two future judgments, specifically: one for the believer, which involves rewards (Rom. 14:10-12; 1 Cor. 3:10-4:4; and 2 Cor. 5:10), and one for the unbeliever, which involves being eternally separated from God's Presence and ultimately cast into the Lake of Fire (Rev. 20:11–15).

Now, let's examine 1 Corinthians 3:10–15 and answer the following questions. Did you notice that in these verses, Paul uses an architectural analogy in which to make his point?

a. What kind of foundation has Paul laid regarding the Corinthian church (vv. 10–11)?

b. To whom and what does Paul credit having laid the foundation (v. 10)?

c. Notice in verse 12, that there are others who will build upon the foundation. List the various materials that can be used according to Paul.

- ______________________________
- ______________________________
- ______________________________

- ______________________________
- _______________________________
- _______________________________

d. Do you see two categories or types of materials? Record your insights?

e. Now, look closely at verse 13. What are the materials above associated with in verse 13?

f. Why do you think Paul states, "each man"? What does this imply?

g. Notice in verse 13, there is a day designated to reveal the quality of material that was used to build upon the foundation of Christ. With what will the Lord use to test the material itself?

Note: No one knows for certain what the fire of testing will be. However, if I may, I would love to share a personal thought. If you look at Revelation 1:13–16, you will see a description of the glorified Christ Jesus. Look specifically at verse 14 and record the description of His eyes. What do you see?

Furthermore, look at Hebrews 12:29. How is God described in this verse?

Could the fire of testing occur when face-to-face we encounter the glorified Christ? One glance from Him and all things are "open and laid bare to the eyes with whom we have to do" (Heb. 4:13). Will His "eyes of fire" not reveal the truth about the material upon which we have been building? Will the materials upon which you have built upon Him be able to survive the eyes of His examination?

h. Now, look again at 1 Corinthians 3:13. What exactly will the fire test?

Notice Paul did not say, *quantity*. No amount of work will matter if the material used was insufficient.

i. What happens to the man that remains (v. 14)?

j. What happens to the man whose work is burned?

1) ______

but

2) ______

What does it mean to "suffer loss"? The Greek word used here means, "to receive detriment. A synonym means *to lose*."[96]

Note: Do you see that man's work and the material used are a reference to the same thing? Isn't it true that the gold, silver, and precious stones can survive the testing of fire, while the wood, hay, and straw serve as fuel for the fire?

k. So what might the Lord qualify as gold, silver, and precious stones? What is the difference in the materials used? Look at the following cross-references and divide the verses into two categories. In other words, what in these verses qualify as gold, silver, and precious stones, and what would the Lord qualify as wood, hay, and straw?

	Gold, Silver, and Precious Stones	Wood, Hay, and Straw
1 Samuel 15:22		
Psalm 40:6, 8		

	Gold, Silver, and Precious Stones	Wood, Hay, and Straw
Psalm 51:16–17		

96. *Ibid.*, 700.

Isaiah 1:10–20		
Matthew 23:23		

Do you see that the things in the wood, hay, and straw category could be labeled externally religious things? Religion (self-effort) calls us to burnt offerings and sacrifice, but God is looking for the heart that is surrendered to His will and obedient to His voice. Isn't it easier to do something for Christ rather than surrender our wills and obey?

Isn't the description of wood, hay, and straw just another description of materials that are idle, useless, ineffective, and unfruitful? Wouldn't the things done in the flesh qualify? Isn't that what Paul is communicating to the Galatians who are trying to be sanctified by self-effort and self-righteousness?

Just as circumcision was the snare of that day, can you think of traps today that mirror the external act of circumcision? These traps are areas of captivity to self-effort. They represent things that have the appearance of religion, but are motivated by self-effort, self-love, and ultimately self-glory. J. I. Packer describes the snares of religion as "the religion of aspiration and perspiration without either inspiration or transformation, the religion of low expectations, deep ruts, and grooves that become graves."[97] What about you? Are you in the grave of self-effort? What will the Lord see when He looks at you? Will there be anything left to lay at His worthy and precious feet?

Any thoughts?

8. Now, let's return to Galatians 5:5–6 and look at the exact opposite of verses 2–4.

   a. What are Paul and the Galatian believers doing in verse 5? ____________________

   b. Upon what are they waiting?

97. J. I. Packer, "An Introduction to Systematic Spirituality," in *The Collected Shorter Writings of J. I. Packer: Volume 2: Serving the People of God* (Carlisle: Paternoster Press, 1998), pp. 314–315.

c. How are they told to wait? Through the ______________________ by ______________

Did you notice that the waiting is through the Spirit versus the agency of human effort?

Note: Again, the context of these verses of Scripture is written from the position of the believer's sanctification as opposed to his justification, thereby making the righteousness a practical righteousness produced by the Holy Spirit as Paul and the Galatian believers surrendered their will and obeyed Him (exercised faith).

While studying Galatians 5:5–6, I found the following insights provided by Dr. Wuest most helpful. He offers three reasons to support that the text is about sanctifying rather than justifying righteousness. He explains,

> *First, it is righteousness that finds its source in the operation of the Holy Spirit. Justifying righteousness is a purely legal matter and has to do with a believer's standing before God. The Holy Spirit has nothing to do with that. The Father justifies a believing sinner on the basis of the work of the Son on the Cross.*
>
> *Second, the context is dealing with the Christian's experience, not his standing, with the method of living a Christian life, not the relation of that person to the laws of God.*
>
> *Third, love as a fruit of the Holy Spirit in the life of a Christian is spoken of in verse 6, which verse is bound up with verse 5. This shows again that the grace spoken of in verse 5 is sanctifying grace, of which the Galatian saints were depriving themselves by their act of depending upon self-effort in an attempt to obey the law.*[98]

As you look at verse 5–6, do you see that sanctification is by grace through faith? In fact, all of the tenses of salvation (justification, sanctification, and glorification) are by grace through faith proving that salvation is wholly an act of God.

Sadly, the Galatians had forgotten this foundational truth, and we are no less vulnerable today. When you combine the false teaching, which is rampant today, coupled with the propensity of our residual flesh, which is drawn to works, you have a recipe for disaster but for the *grace of God*. Thankfully, we have a Shepherd and Guardian to watch over our vulnerable hearts (1 Pet. 2:25). Oh, that we would let Him.

9. Now, in the lesson, Paul will reveal the *source* of their hindrance in verses 7–8. But first, as always, he will begin with a statement and then ask a question in verse 7.

a. What does Paul state about the Galatians in verse 7?

b. Now, what question does he want them to think about in verse 7?

c. What is this outside *hindrance* targeting? ______________________________________

Note: Is he targeting the Word or their obedience to the Word? And if the problem is obedience, the issue is love. Look at John 14:15, 21, 23-24.

98. Wuest, *Word Studies in the Greek New Testament*, 141.

You see the Enemy's target is God's Word because "faith comes by hearing and hearing by God's Word" (Rom. 10:17). However, what the Enemy fears most is your obedience to the Word. We can hear the Word of God but not be a doer of it. When we hear God's Word but refuse to surrender and obey it (faith), Scripture says we delude ourselves (James 1:22).

d. So why does the Enemy fear our obedience to God's Word? Look at James 4:7 and record the verse below in the order it is written (because the order in Scripture always matters).

1) ____________________

2) ____________________

3) ____________________

Note: The word "submit" is just another way of saying "surrender and obey" God. Do you see what happens when we submit to God? The Enemy is resisted! He has to flee and he knows it! And the last thing he wants is for you and me to know it.

Now look back in Galatians 5 and let's connect verse 7 with verse 8.

e. From where is the source of this persuasion **not** coming (v. 8)? ____________________

f. If not from God, then from where is the source coming? ____________________

Note: The word, "persuasion" (*peismone*), is interesting. The word used here means to "induce by words to believe."[99]

Do you see how the Enemy uses words to induce? If you are unaware that the Enemy still speaks today, you are most vulnerable for this type of persuasion, which is designed to hinder your obedience to truth. Did you happen to notice the difference in verse 8 between the words "persuasion" and "call"? Beware, one is an invitation, which leads to freedom, and the other is an enticement, which will lead to a trap.

10. Now, look at what Paul compares this *persuasion* to in verse 9. What do you see? ____________________

[**Note:** Leaven, in Scripture, is always a symbol for sin.]

Did you notice how much leaven it takes to leaven the whole lump of dough? Isn't it the little things we tend to excuse or let go that end up causing great danger?

11. Read Matthew 16:6–12. Notice in verse 6, Jesus gives His disciples a warning, and in verses 11–12, they understand the warning given and the symbolic meaning of leaven. What do you see?

____

____

Isn't this what Paul is doing in Galatians 5:8–9?

12. Now, watch in verse 10, as Paul encourages the Galatians. What does he tell them in verse 10?

____

Do you think Paul's confidence is in them? What do you see? ____________________

99. *Ibid.*, 143.

Note: The Greek word translated "adopt," is *phroneo*, which is more correctly translated along the lines of one's mind, will, and emotions. You will recognize these three things comprising the heart (soul).

13. Quickly, Paul turns his attention to the one who is causing the problem in verse 10.

How does Paul describe them? ____

The term, "disturbing" (*tarasso*), literally means to be agitated *in the mind*. Do you see how the Enemy will target the mind? Yes, the Enemy targets the Word of God, but in particular, what he fears most is your submission and obedience to the truth. It's the difference between head knowledge and heart knowledge.

When our minds have been targeted with a lie, our heart flips, and the emotion that is evoked most typically is fear. Only the Lord Jesus has the power to flip our heart back with the truth. As we surrender and obey the truth of God's Word, He flips our heart right side-up. He is the only one who can do this for us. Consider again, the following visual:

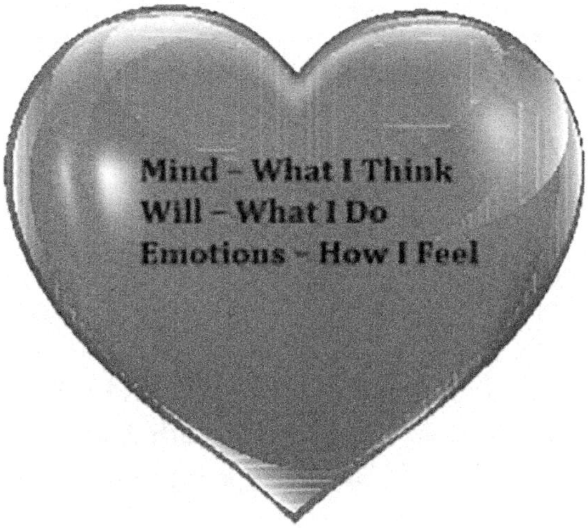

Figure 1 The Right -Side-Up Heart

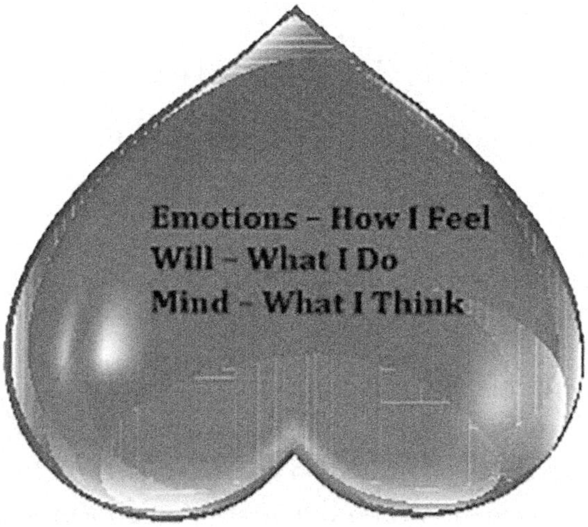

Figure 2 The Upside-Down Heart

Do you see that the heart controlled by the Spirit thinks biblically, which in turn, affects one's will and the emotions? However, the Enemy's target is the mind. If he can speak lies into the mind of man, eventually the will (what we do) and how we feel will be affected. In essence, our hearts (minds) have become *disturbed* and will flip upside-down. When this occurs, our minds are bombarded in the "what ifs," and the emotion of fear takes control. In other words, fear now has power in an area of our heart, and it is affecting what we do and what we think.

What the Enemy fears most is your obedience to the truth of God's Word. When you and I obey God's Word, we are exercising a willful love towards God. Therefore, the Enemy targets your mind with the emotion of fear. He is a bully. He presses and pushes himself on you in an attempt to control you. He uses manipulation to do so. The last thing he wants you to do is submit to God. When we submit to God, we resist the Enemy, and he has to flee (James 4:7). Note carefully the order.

Only the Lord Jesus has the power to flip our hearts right-side-up. He does this when we cry out for the Savior to save us. Then, as His Spirit uses the Word of God to reveal the truth and we surrender our wills and obey the truth (submit to God), our hearts flip back to right-side-up. We have resisted the Enemy, and he has to go!

The truth Paul gives the Galatians (from God's Word) when submitted to and obeyed will dispel the disturbance that has gained power over their minds. As they choose not to be circumcised (because it is not necessary), their surrender and obedience to the truth will cause their upside-down hearts to flip right-side-up, and the peace of God will reign in their hearts.

In other words, their obedience to the truth, which Jesus always equates with love (John 14:15; 21, 23–24), will cast out all fear because "perfect love casts out fear" (1 John 4:18). The word "perfect" literally means mature. As you and I mature in Him, we will not be weak and overcome by the Enemy because the Word of God abides within (1 John 2:12-14).

WHAT ABOUT YOU?

Has the enemy been disturbing your mind with the "what ifs" of life? Are the thoughts in your mind—affecting what you are doing (or not doing) and your emotional state? The best way to know if this is true in your life is to examine your emotional state. Is there some emotion in which you feel trapped? Is that emotion affecting what you are doing and thinking? Has that emotion taken control?

If the emotion in your heart right now is peace, then the Spirit of God is in control of your heart. You are thinking biblically, and in turn, have chosen to surrender your will and obey Him in all that you know at present.

However, if you are overcome with any emotion other than that which is from the Lord, (such as fear, anxiety, grief, anger, shame, doubt, etc.), then you can be sure your heart has flipped upside-down. Your emotions are now in control, and they are affecting what you do and what you think.

In other words, the spirit of fear is rendering you the opposite of 2 Timothy 1:7. Rather than His power, love (which is always equated with obedience), and a sound mind, you are reduced to being weak (and sometimes paralyzed with fear), hateful (disobedient), and thinking that you are going crazy! You, my friend, are in a trap.

I cannot tell you how many times I have found myself in this same snare. All it takes is a thought, a phone call, or a situation that has gone awry—basically, anytime I feel threatened, or someone in my family or that I love is vulnerable. The threats can be real or imagined. They can be physically or spiritually related. They are always masked by wrong thoughts against the character of God (usually His goodness is in question) or doubts against His Word.

Sometimes, confusion sets in our mind. We can know the truth in our head, but when we choose not to surrender our wills and obey it, we find ourselves upside-down and wondering why. This state is a description of deception. When what I think (even if it is the truth of God's Word) does not align with what I am doing, I am deceived and in a trap.

So, what do I do? This is when I run to the Savior and ask Him to rescue me from the power that "this emotion" has over me. Then I listen, as His Spirit so faithfully speaks a word of truth to my mind. When this happens, I ask the Lord to cause me to walk in faith, because He will be the cause if the response is faith. I typically ask Him what that truth would look like in my life. As He shows me, I surrender my will and obey His Word. Every time I surrender and obey His Word in this area of my heart, He leads me out of the trap. Do you see that when I submit to God, I resist the Enemy, and he has to flee (James 4:7)?

As I deny myself, take up my cross (the instrument of death He has chosen) and follow Him, He turns my heart right-side-up and the fruit of His Spirit reigns. Blessed Savior who continues to rescue my heart from the *power* of sin in this process called, sanctification.

14. As we return to Galatians 5:10b, what will happen to the one whom the Enemy is using to disturb the Galatians?

15. As we close this lesson in Galatians 5:11–12, what question does Paul ask in verse 11 to the brethren?

Note: Pharisee Saul, preached circumcision. Converted Paul preached Christ. So, his point in asking the brethren the question, "Why am I still persecuted?" is a legitimate concern for those who are His, because persecution is inevitable (see 2 Timothy 3:12).

16. What does Paul call the cross in verse 11? ____

Note: The Greek word "stumbling block" (*skandalon*), is where we get our English word translated "scandal" (scandalous). According to Dr. Zodhiates, *skandalon* is "the trigger of a trap on which the bait is placed, and which, when touched by the animal, springs and causes it to close, causing entrapment. In the New Testament, it is used figuratively in a moral sense. It is concerned mainly with the fact that it produces certain behavior, which can lead to ruin."[100]

Let's look at a couple of cross-references regarding the Person and the message of the cross as a stumbling block.

17. Read 1 Peter 2:7–8 and answer the following questions:

a. Record facts about the stumbling block.

b. According to verse 8, why do they stumble?

Now, let's go to 1 Corinthians 1:18–31 to discover how the word of the cross is a stumbling block.

18. Read 1 Corinthians 1:18–25. You will notice that the subject is *the word of the cross* (v. 18). Answer the following questions regarding *the word of the cross*.

a. What are the two groups of people contrasted in verse 18?

1. To those who are ____

2. To those who are _________________________ _________________________

b. Do you see what is causing the division? What exactly divided men in Paul's day and continues to divide men today?.

c. What is the description of *the word of the cross* to those who are perishing?

100. Spiros Zodhiates, *The Complete Word Study Dictionary New Testament* (Chattanooga, TN: AMG Publishers, 1993), 1292.

d. What is the description of *the word of the cross* to those who are being saved?

Notice in verse 19, Paul quotes from Isaiah 29:14. He then asks a series of rhetorical questions in verse 20.

e. If you had to summarize verses 19–20, what point is Paul trying to make?

f. Now, read verse 21. Will the world in its wisdom ever come to know God apart from God?

What does verse 21 tell you?

Isn't it true that apart from God man can never know God?

g. With what is God well-pleased to save those who believe?

With what message do you think He is well-pleased? In other words, what kind of preaching does the Father want to hear preached?

h. Now, look at verse 22 and answer the following questions:

1) What do the Jews want? ________________________________

2) What do the Greeks want? _____________________________________

i. What message did Paul give (v.23)?

j. What is the response to Paul's message of Christ crucified:

1) The Jews?

2) The Gentiles?

3) To those who are the called (both Jews and Greeks) in verse 24?

Christ crucified is the ______________________

and

____

k. What do we learn about God in comparison with man in verse 25?

1)

2)

l. Now skip all the way down to verse 30 and answer the following questions:

1) How are you and I *in Christ*?

2) What did Christ Jesus become to us?

a)

and

b)

and

c)

and

d)

m. Now, what is Paul's summation in verse 31?

n. As you look at verses 30–31 together, how does Paul come to his conclusion?

Don't you see that it has been God's plan of grace all along to save man? We are merely the recipients of His lavish grace. Hence, the reason we have no right to boast except in Christ alone.

Now, as you think about the Person and the message of the cross, which is a stumbling block to the Jews, do you see why the Judaizers hated and persecuted Paul? The hatred and persecution that existed in Pauls' day remains today.

19. And finally, Paul's word to those who were disturbing the Galatian believers seems harsh. What does he say in verse 12?

Dr. Wuest's insights are very beneficial here. He explains that in Paul's day, the heathen priests would castrate themselves as a sign of devotion, in particular, in the worship of Cybele (the Greek goddess of fertility and protection).[101]

Basically, Paul is sarcastically suggesting that if circumcision is necessary for salvation, why stop at circumcision? Why not castrate yourself and be really holy?

For the Galatians to turn to circumcision in order to be holy and acceptable to God, this would be the equivalence of returning to heathenism.

WHAT ABOUT TODAY?

The most popular messenger and message today promote human effort. Is not the tendency in many churches to substitute the message of the cross with self-effort? Are you hearing from the pulpit about the sufficiency of man, the promotion of man to just tidy up your act, pull yourself up by your bootstraps, do these five things—all, which involve you and your merit.

OR...

Is it to tell people they are in desperate need of a Savior, not only from the penalty of sin but its power? Is this the message in your church? Most assuredly the word of the cross is a message whereby we are saved by grace alone through faith alone? Is this your boast?

101. Wuest, *Word Studies in the Greek New Testament*, 146.

Notes

Lesson 9

Whom Do You Love?

GALATIANS 5:13–15

People, when left to themselves, through ignorance and arrogance, will lean toward two extremes: legalism and hedonism. Legalism is nothing more than self-effort attempting to secure and maintain self-righteousness. Legalism is disguised in the face of religion. On the opposite end of the spectrum, hedonism is an outright rebellion bound up in pleasure-seeking, which finds its root in self-gratification. Although seemingly contradictory, both legalism and hedonism find their origin in self.

Don't you sense the tug within? The Galatians sure did. They had been rescued from a life of self-indulgence, where every man did what was right in his own eyes. Yet now they were in danger of going to the opposite extreme of coming under the yoke of self-righteousness masquerading as the works of the Law. Do you see that, in either extreme, *self* is the focus?

Because this was true of the Galatians, it is an accurate assessment of all men. Remember, the flesh's desire to be *like god,* motivated by our love for self, entered at the Fall and remains an issue because our sin nature was not completely eradicated at justification. Although saved by grace through faith from sin's *penalty*, we continue to be in desperate *need* of a Savior to rescue us from the *power* of sin—as we live between the *already* (justification) and *not yet* (glorification). Praise God we have a Savior, Jesus Christ, who came and died to rescue us from the *penalty* (justification), *power* (sanctification), and *presence* (glorification) of sin. Hallelujah, what a Savior!

Keep in mind; the enemy is aware of the war within. He knows that we can be swayed to either extreme, which is why he sent the false teachers into the churches of Galatia. Be aware as you read Galatians; the Enemy still has his messengers today.

Therefore, we will begin this lesson (pages 1–3) in review by looking again at legalism, and then we will switch for the remainder of the lesson to the other extreme, as Paul addresses hedonism and its cure. Let's begin by re-visiting Galatians 2:4, as the Enemy's agenda is unveiled.

1. Answer the following questions using Galatians 2:4.

   a. *Who* had come into the churches in Galatia? ________________________________

   b. *How* had they entered in? ____

   c. *Why* had they "sneaked" in? ____

   d. *What* was their agenda? ____

The Enemy's plan could not be more visible, right? Are you aware the same thing is happening in the church today? Without God's Spirit faithfully illuminating God's Word to our heart, we too have the potential to vacillate between these two extremes.

2. Now, in review, let's go back to Galatians 5:1 to discover God's plan.

a. Whom did God the Father send to rescue us? ______________________________

b. Why had He come? ____

c. What was His agenda for us? ____

Do you see that God's plan all along was to set people free from the yoke and bondage of sin? It was for *freedom* that Christ came. He came to set captives free! The enemy's agenda, however, was and is to keep man in captivity.

Positionally, like the Galatians, you have been saved from sin's penalty, power, and presence. The work on the cross is a finished work. However, although saved from the penalty, power, and someday the presence of sin, we live in between the "already" and "not yet" of our salvation.

Experientially, sin can still have power over us and while on earth, and until glorification, we are still in the presence of sin. Our three enemies, the world, our flesh, and Satan remain a constant threat until we are glorified.

So, what hold can our flesh, the world, or the Enemy have on you now that Christ Jesus has set you free? His agenda is still captivity. He knows that your sin nature has not been completely eradicated, and therefore he targets your heart by using your flesh (inward) and the world (outward) as a lure to sin. As we learned in the previous lesson, the thing he fears most is your *obedience* to God's Word, which is far different from merely hearing the Word. Truly, there is a vast difference between being in the Word and the Word being in you. It's the difference between head-knowledge and heart-knowledge.

3. Look back at Galatians 5:7. Look specifically at what was being hindered?

4. One way the Enemy keeps you from the saving power of Christ is to keep you from God's Word. He knows Romans 10:17. Do you? Record the verse below.

It is true the Enemy targets the Word of God. If he can keep people from God's Word, he can keep them in captivity. But what he fears most is their *obedience* to God's Word.

5. Look at James 4:7 to see why. What do you see (in the order it is written)?

a) ____

b) ____

c) ____

Now, if you want to see something eye-opening, look at the antithesis of James 4:7. Record the exact opposite of this verse?

a) ____

b) ____

c) ____

Do you see that rather than submit to God, we are actually resisting Him? And when we resist Him we are submitting to the enemy? Do you also see that by making this choice, rather than flee the Enemy remains? Who in their right mind would choose to submit to the Enemy? Think about it, whether our enemy is our flesh, the world, or Satan (who is behind the other two), by choosing not to submit to God we are choosing our enemies. Sobering thought, isn't it?

6. Now, look at Ephesians 6:16 where Paul says the same thing James has said regarding faith (surrender and obedience) and the Enemy. What extinguishes the flaming missiles of the evil one?

As we have discovered, faith or submission to God involves the surrender of our will in obedience to His Word. When we submit to God, we resist the Enemy, and he has to flee. He knows this is true! Sadly, this truth eludes many within the church today. Do you see that a refusal to surrender your will and obey God's Word is like removing the shield God has provided, which now opens you up to the enemy's flaming missiles?

For example, I recently spoke in passing with a young man who was battling with pornography. I recall asking him as he shared his struggle what he was doing to combat the issue. He quickly stated, "I memorize Scripture." Great, I thought initially, but my next thought was, *Are you doing what the Scripture says?* The answer to this question is equally important.

Scripture memorization, although invaluable, is only half of the equation where sin is involved. We must also be doers of the Word if we are to commit it to our hearts. Surrender and obedience are evidence that *faith* is in action. Remember, it is by *grace* through *faith* we are being saved! God, in His grace, has revealed by His Spirit the Word to which we must surrender and obey. Grace is God's invitation. Faith is our response to His invitation. Either we will choose to submit (surrender and obey), or we choose unbelief (not to surrender and disobey). What are you choosing?

In Paul's day, the false teachers were adding the external act of circumcision to Christ. As I thought about this, I was reminded that many of the women I counsel today are opting to add some form of behavior modification or medication to cope with their sin, only to discover that these are *external solutions* to an *internal issue*—their own hearts. Jesus says, "For from within, out of the heart of men, proceed...", and then He lists thirteen things (although not exhaustive by any means) that proceed from a sinful heart (Mark 7:21–23). Remember, it is **not** Christ *plus* medication or Christ *plus* behavior modification when it comes to matters of the heart. The work that Jesus Christ did on the cross does not need to be supplemented by anything people can contribute or add. In fact, the only thing we bring into the equation is our sin.

If Jesus says it is an internal issue, why are we in the church wasting so much time on external solutions? External things may help you *cope* with your sin, but God sent Jesus Christ to die to offer a *cure*. He alone is the cure for sin. No wonder why He asks the man in John 5, "Do you wish to get well?" (John 5:6). Unbeknownst to most of us, we would instead opt to take a pill or perform from a list of ten things to do, when the alternative is to cry out in need for a Savior and then surrender our will and obey His. In our self-deception, we will do anything to keep from denying ourselves, taking up our cross, to follow Him. This, my friend, is what He continues to rescue us from—ourselves.

Please allow me to further explain.

As a nurse, I realize we have physical bodies. Our physical bodies (brain) can get sick. Thank the Lord for physicians and medication! However, there is a distinction between our physical and spiritual state of being, which is comprised of our spirit and soul/heart. That being stated, our souls/hearts includes our minds, wills, and emotions. Our conscience also resides within our souls. It serves as the moral regulators of our hearts.

We must be careful not to confuse our physical brains and our minds, which resides in our souls. In other words, the physical brain and one's spiritual mind are not the same.

For example, several years ago a woman came to me who was having panic attacks. Her concern was that they were occurring more frequently. In fact, she had just had one while driving in her car. Her greatest fear was that this would happen while her children were in the car and that she might have a wreck and injure them.

After we prayed together, she began to tell me about the anger in her heart towards another sister in Christ. In short, this woman was filled with unforgiveness, which was manifesting in slander. As she allowed the Lord to expose her heart, the Spirit of God used His Word to "reprove and correct" her heart (2 Tim 3:16–17). When she obeyed the Lord, her panic attacks ceased. In fact, it has been over eight years, and she has never had another one.

Similarly, another sister in Christ came for counsel after years of being on medication for her anxiety, depression, and insomnia. I did not even know this while counseling her. Her need for these medications was not the reason I was counseling her. Again, to make a long story short, this woman had been medicating the after-effects of an abortion. Her guilt in having hidden her sin was eating her alive from the inside out. However, when God's Spirit used God's Word to reprove and correct her heart, He set her free! Without my knowledge or counsel (which I would never do), she sensed the Lord leading her to stop taking her medications. That was many years ago.

So, what is my point in these examples? Neither of the women mentioned above was dealing with a genuine physical issue. The underlying (root) issue resided within their hearts (mind, will, and emotions). They both discovered that no pill or counsel could heal the sin in their hearts. They discovered that only grace alone through faith alone in Christ alone could heal their spiritual heart!

Anything added to Christ for salvation from sin's penalty, power, or presence is erroneous. In fact, the entire Book of Galatians, and in particular, the words of the apostle Paul, could best be summarized by the late New Testament scholar, William Hendriksen, who stated, "A Christ supplemented is a Christ supplanted."[102] In other words, when you add anything to Christ, you just changed the message of Christ. In essence, when you add anything to Christ, you are basically saying that Christ's death was not enough. It was insufficient. God forbid!

In our previous lesson we saw Paul warning the believers in Galatia about the danger of legalism, particularly, coming up under the law regarding circumcision (Gal. 5:1–12). In short, the Judaizer's message was Christ *plus* circumcision. Paul was writing to warn the Galatians that this message was not only dangerous, but it was also heretical.

And now we will see Paul address the other extreme, hedonism, which embraces the idea of using grace as a license to sin and do whatever you please. Allow me to remind you of the words of the late pastor and author, Wayne Barber, who stated, "Freedom is not the freedom to do as you please. Freedom is the power to do as you should."[103]

Similarly, consider the definition of freedom by pastor and author, Paul David Tripp, as he defines freedom so eloquently, stating,

102. William Hendriksen, *New Testament Commentary: Galatians*, accessed online at https://www.preceptaustin.org/index.php/galatians-3-commentary on March 6, 2019.
103. Wayne Barber, *Living Grace* (Nashville, TN: B&H Publishers, 2005), 34.

I have been liberated,
set free,
and given new life,
new hope,
new motivation,
and new peace
of heart and mind.
No, I have not been freed
from the authority of
another.
I have not been freed
to walk my own way,
to write my own rules,
or to do what I choose.
No, I have been given
the best of freedoms.
I have been freed,
not from God's rule,
but from my bondage
to me.
Following,
obeying,
serving,
submitting to God
is the thing I was created to do,
so it is the place where
true freedom is to be found.
Rebellion never gives life.
Self-rule never brings freedom.
So grace has worked to rescue
me from me,
so that I can know the true freedom
of serving Him.[104]

104. Paul David Tripp, *New Morning Mercies* (Wheaton, IL: Crossway, 2014), April 3 excerpt.

Beautiful explanation of freedom isn't it. As you continue to mediate on these words, let's get started.

7. Read Galatians 5:13 and answer the following questions:

a. What does Paul remind the Galatians in verse 13a?

"You were ___________________ to ____________________________ brethren...

Note: The Greek word translated "called" (*kaleo*), which means to be invited, is an aorist indicative passive verb. The aorist tense is an action in the past that is punctiliar, or at a moment in time. The indicative mood indicates a statement of fact, and the passive voice suggests that the subject was acted upon by an outside Source. Furthermore, the word "freedom" in this verse is a noun. It comes from the Greek word *eleutheria*, which means "a signal blessing of the economy of grace, which, in contrast with the Old Testament economy, is represented as including independence from religious regulations and legal restrictions."[105]

b. With these things in mind, what is Paul saying to the Galatians about their call to freedom?

c. Now, what does Paul warn the Galatians in verse 13b?

Note: For me, the most helpful definition of the word, "opportunity" (*aphorme*) comes from Dr. Wuest, who states, "*Aphorme* is a military term speaking of a base of operation." In other words, don't make your freedom from the law a base of operation from which to serve sin.[106] One might ask, "Then how do I not turn my freedom in Christ into an opportunity for the flesh?"

d. The answer is in Galatians 3:13c. What do you see? BUT

Note: There are four Greek words commonly used for our one English word, "love." What distinguishes the word used in Galatians, (*agapē/agapao*) is the Source. In 1 John 4:16, we are told that God is love (*agapao*). In other words, God does not merely contain love, nor does He just express love, but it is the very essence of His being. In essence, He is the source of *agapē/agapao*. Therefore, without God, people cannot love (*agapao*). It takes God within people, to love God and to love others. In addition, a person without God can only love one's self.

By definition, the Greek word for "love" (*agapao*), involves the direction of the will and finding one's joy in something or someone. It involves God doing what He knows is best for us and not necessarily what we desire.[107]

8. Notice Paul will reiterate what he has just stated by quoting, once again from the Old Testament, specifically Leviticus 19:18. What does he say in verse 14?

105. Spiros Zodhiates, *The Complete Word Study New Testament Dictionary* (Chattanooga, TN: AMG Publishers, 1993), 565.
106. Kenneth S. Wuest, *Word Studies in the Greek New Testament: Galatians*, Vol. One (Grand Rapids, MI: Wm. B. Eerdmans Publishing Co., 1972), 150.
107. Zodhiates, *The Complete Word Study Dictionary,* pp. 64, 66.

Notice, *who* we are told to love? ____

and

how we are told to love our neighbor? _______________________________

What, then, is Jesus saying about the love we have for ourselves?

Don't you sense the ever-present, ever-competing love you have for yourself? That awareness is your flesh. Similarly, do you sense a longing within to love the Lord God and others more? That consciousness comes from God's residing Spirit. Therein lies the competition for your heart.

Now, you may be wondering, "Just who is my neighbor?" Interestingly, the term "neighbor" (*plesion*) includes any member of the human family. The antonym is the word "enemy."[108]

9. Now, read Jesus' response in Matthew 22:34–39 to a Pharisee/lawyer who tested Him.

a. What did the lawyer ask Jesus?

b. What did Jesus say (v. 37)?

c. How does Jesus describe this command in verse 38? ___________________________

and

____

d. Now, look at verse 39. What does Jesus say next?

Note: The phrase, the second *is like it*, is the Greek word, *homoios*, which means, "one and the same, just like, equal, the same in kind or nature, in authority, dignity, and power."[109]

e. With the information above, what is the Lord saying about the importance of the command to love your neighbor as yourself?

108. *Ibid.,* 1178.
109. *Ibid.,* 1041.

Note: Do you see that the order of the two commands matter? In fact, a person cannot love (*agapao*) their neighbor as themselves if they do not first love (*agapao*) the Lord their God with all of their hearts. Moreover, man cannot love (*agapao*) God without the source of love (God Himself) residing within.

Christ Jesus living within us by the power of His Spirit is ***how*** we are able to love God. And loving the Lord our God with all of our hearts is ***how*** we can love our neighbors as ourselves. Apart from His love residing in us, we will only love ourselves. Once again, do you see that He is saving us from ourselves?

10. Now let's look at the opposite of loving (*agapao*) our neighbors as ourselves. How does Paul describe what that looks like in Galatians 5:15? Notice the words, "but if..."

Note: The word "if" in this verse is better translated "since," because it is used with the words, "bite and devour," of which both Greek verbs are in the indicative mood (statement of fact). When the word "if" (*ei*) is used with an indicative verb, there is no doubt the situation is occurring.[110] In other words, Paul is not writing about a potential problem in the church; he is confronting a real and present situation.

So, let's look at what the false teachers and their pseudo-message have stirred within the church. Read verse 15 and fill in the blanks:

5:15

But if you ________________________________

and ________________________________ one another,

____

take care

lest you be ________________________________ by one another.

Note: The word "but" is in direct contrast with loving your neighbor as yourself. Dr. Wuest, commenting on the words, *bite* and *devour,* explains that these were common descriptions used in the Classical Greek in connection with wild animals in a deadly struggle.[111] Both words are present indicative active verbs, meaning that the present tense signifies continuous or habitual action. As stated earlier, the indicative mood is a statement of fact, and the active voice indicates that the subject is performing the action.

Additionally, the word "consumed" refers to actions that lead to mutual injury.[112] Notably, it is translated from an aorist subjunctive passive verb. Remember, the aorist tense is a punctiliar action that occurs at a point in time (as opposed to present continuous action), and the subjunctive mood occurs when the action is thought of as possible or potential. Even more telling, the passive voice is used, which means that the subject is acted upon by an outside source.

Think about it. The *choice* to bite and devour another brother or sister in Christ will result in a mutual consumption, and neither of you has control over the outcome. In other words, both of you will suffer, and there is no winner. In fact, the Enemy is the outside source behind the consumption. A scary thought, isn't it?

---

110. *Ibid.,* 505.
111. Kenneth S. Wuest, *Word Studies in the Greek New Testament: Galatians, Vol. One* (Grand Rapids, MI: Wm. B. Eerdmans Publishing Co., 1972), 152.
112. *Ibid.*

11. What might be the underlying reason why we bite and devour one another?

Word of Caution: There is one sure way to know when the Enemy is at work in any given situation. Any time there is division, slander, lies, or destruction of someone's reputation within a family, whether it is your own personal family, or the family of God, you can be assured that the Enemy is behind the disruption, and he will not stop until he kills, steals, and destroys it (see John 10:10).

12. Now that you have a better understanding of Galatians 5:13–15, summarize what you see in these verses below.

Note: As you reviewed Galatians 5:13–15, did you see that love is the issue? Do you see that the antidote for biting and devouring others is to love others as yourself? But remember, you cannot love others as yourself until you first love the Lord your God with all your heart.

Do you recall when this root issue of love reared its ugly head? Think back to the Garden of Eden. The lure from the Enemy to be like god, coupled with the motivating love for self, became a recipe for disaster. Ever since the Fall, inherent within all flesh is man's desire to be like god, <u>because</u> we love ourselves most.

If you and I do not love God with all our hearts, it will manifest itself in a lack of love for our neighbors, which are basically any members of humanity. In other words, when the vertical love (between God and us) is either lacking or waning, the horizontal love (between us and others) will be significantly altered. Without the Source of love within, we basically love others for what they can do for us or give us. In other words, it is a self-serving type of love. In fact, this is how I typically know when I do not love God with *all* my heart. When this is true in my life, I cannot seem to get along with anyone else (horizontally). Something, someone has gained power over a part of my heart. In reality, I just love myself more than God in an area of my heart. Thankfully, the God of grace, in His kindness, is faithful to reveal this to my heart as it manifests itself in my treatment of others.

The Enemy wants me to blame the other person, or even worse, to blame God, when in fact, I am the guilty party. If I blame another person for my behavior, or worse, blame God, I will never be free. What I need to be freed from most is the love I have for myself. If you think back to Genesis 3:12, you will see Adam doing the same exact thing. First, He blames the woman for his sin, and ultimately, he blames the God who gave her to him. From Adam's estimation, everyone else is to blame for his sin but him. There is nothing new under the sun. The same is true of you and me today.

WHAT ABOUT YOU?

Who have you been biting and devouring?

Do you realize that while you are shooting your arrows at them, the Enemy is behind the entire situation shooting his flaming arrows at you?

We tend to make the issue flesh and blood through thoughts like, *If it's that person, it certainly isn't me! Could it be the spirit behind the person? Aren't these people just pawns that the Enemy is using?* This is how he lures you into their (aka his) trap. Remember, if he cannot have you (and he cannot), his goal is to render you useless. What better way than to lure you into the trap in which he has them?

I wonder what might happen if you asked the Lord Jesus to save you from the power this situation is having over you. I wonder if He might reveal to your heart with whom you are really dealing? I wonder if His Spirit might deliver you from the power that spirit has had over your heart?

What would that look like in your life? Ask Him. And then do what He says! I can assure you that His Spirit will recall His Word. When that occurs, you have just experienced God's grace. With every act of grace, God *invites* you to join Him rather than the Enemy of your soul. He is inviting you to respond in faith, which will involve your surrender and obedience to the Word He had just recalled to your memory when you prayed to be saved from the power of the sin that is trying to kill, steal, and destroy you. Will you respond in faith?

Remember, when you surrender and obey God's Word, you will resist the Enemy, and he will flee (James 4:7). Ensuing freedom will be the result.

Are you aware that the issues you are having with others is just a reflection of your relationship (love) for the Lord?

Who are you blaming for your sin? Do not be deceived into thinking that you can bite and devour others and then nestle up close to the Lord God in your quiet time? Whether you know it or not, how you treat others is a reflection of your relationship with the Lord.

ON A PERSONAL NOTE

The Lord reveals to my heart the issues I am having with Him by showing it to me through the problems I am having with others. These are inseparable. It's His kind way of showing me what He sees and wants to save me from. In other words, there is something in me that He wants to heal, restore, deliver, save, or rescue. However, at the time, it feels like anything but kind. In fact, it is at these times when He looks distant, hard, and uncaring. These are the kind of thoughts that enter my mind, which as you can clearly see, are against God's Word and His Character. Do you see the trap? Do you recognize the Enemy?

Ask the Lord to start with those with whom you have been biting and devouring. What's in them that has "poked" you? Every time I allow the Lord to search my heart in this way, He shows me that what I hate about them is in me and that it took this situation or this person to reveal this to me. Rather than blame them, or worse, God, I confess that what I hate about them is in me.

At this point, I cry out for Him to save me. I ask Him what that would look like in my life. Invariably, the Spirit of God will show me something in His Word that He wants me to surrender and obey. This is what it means to be saved by *grace* through *faith*. Except rather than being saved from the *penalty* of sin, I am being saved from the *power* that this sin has had over my life. This is the process of sanctification. This is His method He uses to conform me to the image of His dear Son.

By *grace* (when His Spirit takes His Word to reveal my heart) becomes His invitation for me to respond in *faith* (the surrender of my will to His will in obedience), or I can choose to respond in unbelief, which is a refusal to surrender my will to His will in disobedience. He will not usurp our will. In fact, our will becomes the material for sacrifice to a God who is more than worthy! Will you surrender?

We will look at this in greater depth in our next lesson. Suffice it to say that the answer will be expounded in Galatians 5:16 and following.

For now, will you spend some time with the One who has orchestrated that you be in this lesson at this particular time in your life? Do you think this is coincidental? It's actually a divine appointment. It's called grace!

What will you do with His invitation? How will you respond?

Notes

Lesson 10

THE FLESH Versus THE SPIRIT (Part One)

GALATIANS 5:16–21

Hopefully, in the last lesson, you allowed the Spirit of God to show you those areas of your heart that He wants to transform, areas where you want to be god because you love yourself more than you love Him and others. Maybe He put His finger, so to speak, in a place where you seem to be stuck or overcome.

Maybe you have found the Christian life frustrating because of the turmoil within. In this lesson, we will look specifically at the internal war that is taking place within the life of every believer. Hopefully, after this lesson, you will have a better understanding of the conflict within, and you will know how to cooperate with the indwelling Spirit as He wages war with your residual flesh.

If I had to label this section of Scripture, I would call it the "How to be Sanctified," portion of Scripture. Remember, Paul is writing to believers. He uses metaphorical words such as *running* (v. 7) and *walk* (v. 16), which are terms you would use to describe the process of sanctification.

In verses 16–24, Paul is contrasting the flesh of man with the Spirit of God. They could not be more conflicting. They are in extreme opposition. As you study Galatians 5:16–24, you will discover that *how you walk* is determined by *who you love most*. Let's begin with Paul's instruction.

1. Read Galatians 5:16–17 and answer the following questions:

a. What does Paul say to the Galatian believers in 16a?

"But I say, ________________________ by the ________________________________,"

Note: The term "walk" is used figuratively to describe how a person lives or one's lifestyle. The verb is present imperative active. The present tense specifies continuous action. The imperative mood signifies a command, and the active voice indicates that the subject is acting.

b. With the information provided, what might it look like to "walk by the Spirit"?

c. If the Galatians walk by the Spirit, what will be true of them (v. 16)?

"...and you _________ __________ carry out the _____________ of the ____________."

Note: To better understand this phrase, we must take a closer look at the words used. First, the Greek word translated "carry out" (*teleo*), in its simplest term means end or goal. However, in a complete definition, it means "to complete something, not merely to end it, but to bring it to perfection or its desired goal.[113]

Next, the word translated "desire" (*epithumia*) in verse 16 is a noun, which means an intensified desire. [**Note:** In Greek, anytime the prefix, *epi*, is used in front of a word, it signifies intensity.] *Epithumia* can be used in either a good or evil sense depending on the source. Furthermore, the word translated "flesh" (*sarx*) is used as a noun, which signifies a state of being as opposed to a verb, which would denote action and represents what someone is doing.

If you will recall from Part One of this study in Galatians, when the word, "flesh" is used (unless otherwise stated) you are to think of it in terms of man's desire to be god because his ultimate object of love is himself. The desire to be god because man loves himself is what entered at the Fall, and it is the state of every lost person on the face of the earth.

You will recall, however, that for the believer, although Christ resides within through the power of His Spirit, the flesh was not eradicated at conversion. Therefore, the residual flesh of humanity will remain an issue until glorification. When, prior to salvation, the flesh reigned and dominated; for the believer, Christ reigns. The flesh, for the believer, can only have power if we let it by saying "No" to God's Spirit, and "Yes" to our fleshly desires. Prior to salvation, we had no power within to say "No" to our flesh and "Yes" to God. In essence, for the unbeliever sin reigns. However, although sin in the life of a believer remains, it no longer reigns.

d. Now before we go further in the study, compare Galatians 5:16 with James 4:7. Do you see that Paul and James are giving the same instruction? Explain what you see.

Note: James instructs us *how* to resist the enemy, which causes him to have to flee *by* submitting to God. Likewise, Paul teaches us *how* to deal with the enemy called, our flesh. When you and I choose to walk by the Spirit, the flesh loses its power. In other words, the way to not carry out the desires of the flesh is to walk by the Spirit!

As I was considering what it means to "walk in the Spirit," I remembered the testimony of the late evangelist, Major Ian Thomas. I had had the privilege of hearing him speak at my former church about the time the Lord called me from what I now refer to as, *my* life, and into *His* ministry.

When I was six years old, I heard the gospel of grace and received Christ as my Lord and Savior, but found myself at the age of thirty-one, totally frustrated with trying to live the Christian life and continuously failing. I remember, just before Major Thomas came to our church thinking, "I cannot do this Christian life anymore." In my mind's eye, I had raised a white flag of surrender to the Lord and said, "I quit!" And I meant it with every fiber of my being! I was done!

What would happen next was nothing short of miraculous as, I believe the Lord saw the white flag I had raised in my head and said to my heart, "Good. Now I can do it for you!" From the moment Major Thomas stepped into the pulpit, and began to preach, until the week ended, was nothing short of a divine appointment. The Lord, in His grace, had sent Major Thomas into my life at that crucial moment to explain to me *how* to live the Christian life.

113. Spiros Zodhiates, *The Complete Word Study New Testament Dictionary* (Chattanooga,TN: AMG Pub.,1993), 1375.

As I look back at that week, I can only describe it as a time when I felt like I was drinking water from a fire hose. I could not write what he was sharing fast enough. My life would never be the same. At fifty-eight years old, I can look back and see this time as one of those major crossroad moments when grace came and rescued me from me.

In a book entitled, *They Found the Secret*, the author, the late president of Wheaton College, Dr. V. Raymond Edman shared Major Ian Thomas' testimony of when and how he learned to live the Christian life. In an effort not to miss anything crucial, I am recording Dr. Edman's exact words. Pay close attention to the quotes from Major Thomas, especially at the beginning of his Christian life. Notice the pronoun, *I*, as Major Thomas recounts his first seven years *in Christ*.

Dr. Edman writes,

> *Some Christians learn that the Lord can make life an adventure. Major W. Ian Thomas of England is one of them.*
>
> *The major is every inch a soldier. With his infantry battalion, he served in the British Expeditionary Forces in Belgium at the outset of World War II and took part in the evacuation at Dunkirk. Often in combat, in France, Italy, Greece, and elsewhere during that long war, he found the Lord Jesus to be his complete sufficiency. The major is likewise a soldier of the Cross, faithful to the Captain of our salvation.*
>
> *Reared in a 'respectable' middle-class English home, he was taken to church and taught its precepts. He learned little or nothing of the Bible, however, either at home or in the church attended by the family. At the age of twelve he was invited to a Bible study group of the Crusaders' Union by a lad of thirteen, who, during that year, had received Christ as his Savior. The Bible began to be meaningful to young Ian, and the following summer, at the age of thirteen he was converted to Christ at a Crusaders' Union camp. That decision was made when he was alone and simply by praying earnestly, 'Lord Jesus, please be my Savior!'*
>
> *At the age of fifteen, he felt convinced that he should devote all of his life to the service of the Lord Jesus. He told God that he would become a missionary. He began to preach, out in the open air at Hampstead Heath, at that early age. He was also actively engaged in Sunday-school work, as well as in the Crusaders' Bible class. Life began to be a round of ceaseless activity.*
>
> *In 1956 Major Thomas came to Wheaton College in Wheaton, Illinois for a week of meetings. In sharing with the students his experience of what Jesus Christ meant to Him, he gave the following account of those early years of ceaseless but ineffective activity.*
>
> *Speaking of his decision to become a missionary, he said: "I began to consider the best area in which I could become a missionary, and the best means I could employ to be the most effective—perfectly sincere and genuine questions." The first missionary influence upon young Ian's life came through a doctor serving in Nigeria, in the Housa Band. "First impressions are often the strongest," related Major Thomas, and so it became his ambition one day to go and join the Housa Band in Nigeria, West Africa. He thought the best thing for him to do was to become a doctor.*
>
> *At the university, Ian became a leader in the Inter-Varsity Fellowship group. If ever there was any evangelistic activity going on, this youthful zealot was "buzzing around the place, every holiday, every spare moment!" He started a slum club down in the East End of London. "Out of a sheer desire to win souls, to go out and get them, I was a windmill of activity, until, at the age of nineteen, every moment of my day was packed with doing things: preaching, talking, counseling."*

In the Major's own words, we continue his story. "The only thing that alarmed me was that nobody was converted! That gets a little discouraging after a bit, doesn't it? The more I did, the less happened, and it was not a question of insincerity. The prospects and environment were good; there was plenty of ammunition and plenty of target, but just nothing happened! I became deeply depressed because I really loved the Lord Jesus Christ with all my heart; I wanted to be made a blessing to my fellow men. But I discovered that forever doubling and redoubling my efforts in order to win souls, rushing here and dashing there, taking part in this campaign, taking part in that campaign, preaching in the morning, preaching in the evening, talking to the Bible class, witnessing to this one, counseling with another, did nothing, nothing, nothing to change the utter barrenness, the emptiness, the uselessness of my activity. I tried to make up with noise what I lacked in effectiveness and power.

"Thus by the age of nineteen, I had been reduced to a state of complete exhaustion spiritually, until I felt that there was no point in going on...

'Then, one night in November, that year, just at midnight, in my room at home, I got down on my knees before God, and I just wept in sheer despair. I said, 'Oh, God, I know that I am saved. I love Jesus Christ. I am perfectly convinced that I am converted. With all my heart I have wanted to serve Thee. I have tried to my uttermost, and I am a hopeless failure! So far as doing anything more, I am finished. I am not going to be a missionary. It is useless for me to continue like this. I hate this double life!' That night things happened.

"I can honestly say that I had never once heard from the lips of men the message that came to me then. I had never read it in print; but God, that night simply focused upon me the Bible message of Christ Who is our Life. This was the moment He had been waiting for; seven weary years He had watched me running round and round in the wilderness! He had been waiting for the time when at last I would fall down in hopeless despair. I heard His voice: 'To me to live is Christ...I am the way, the truth, and the life... If, when we were enemies, we were reconciled to God by the death of His Son, much more being reconciled, we shall be saved by His life... When Christ who is our life shall appear, then shall we appear with Him in glory.' Life! New Life! To me to live is Christ!'

"It just came from every area of God's Word, and very kindly and very lovingly the Lord seemed to make it plain to me that night, through my tears of bitterness: 'You see, for seven years, with utmost sincerity, you have been trying to live for Me, on My behalf, the life that I have been waiting for seven years to live through you. I have been there the whole time. All the things you have been pleading for, all the things for which you have been asking, have been yours since the day seven years ago, at your request and invitation, I came into your heart at that Crusader boys' camp; but you see, although you have given mental consent to the truth that I have been in your heart, and have accepted it as a theory, you have lived totally ignoring the fact. You have been busy trying to do for Me all that only I can do through you. Now supposing I am your life, and you begin to accept it as a fact, then I am your strength! You have been pleading and begging for that for seven years. I am your victory in every area of your life if you want it! I am the One to whom it is perfectly natural to go out and win souls, and I know precisely where to go to find them. Why don't you begin to reckon upon Me and say, "Thank you." ' "

That night, all in the space of an hour, Ian Thomas discovered the secret of the adventurous life.

He said: "With nothing to support the theory and without the testimony of any other known Christian to the facts, I simply said to the Lord Jesus Christ that night, 'Well, it is that or nothing! If this is true, then

I am going to thank Thee for it in sheer cold-blooded faith, with no evidence to support it, and nothing but a history of failure behind me! I am going to thank Thee that if Thou art my life, and this is true, then Thou art my victory, Thou art my strength, Thou art my power, Thou art my future! Thou art the One Who is going to go out now, clothed with me to do all that I so hopelessly have been trying to do in the past seven years! Then I went to sleep.

"I got up the next morning to an entirely different Christian life, but I want to emphasize this: I had not received one iota more than I had already had for seven years! I had had the Lord Jesus, equal to all my need and in whom I had been blessed with every spiritual blessing in heavenly things, for the whole of those seven years; but I stepped out on my way to the university that morning with a new song in my heart. I was saying, 'Lord Jesus, I thank Thee, for the first time in my life, this is Thy day! I no longer have the burden of running my own life. At last, I have a governor capable of governing!'

"I can remember that on my way down to the university, I thought over the meeting that I was to take on the following Sunday. It was a boys' class, and I said, 'Well now Lord, Thou are going to speak to that boys' class isn't it wonderful? I thank Thee, dear Lord, for the boys that Thou art going to save.' I did not know how many boys there were in that Bible class, but I began to dream dreams, and I thought, 'Well, maybe thirty will be converted.' Not bad for a start! 'For the first time in my life, I'll dare to invite boys, at the end of that meeting, to come and see me if they want to accept Jesus Christ as their Savior.' Now I had never done that in my life, and for very good reason—I had not expected them to come, and I did not want to look like a fool! Now, I thought, 'Lord Jesus this is different!' the following Sunday, up I went, and found there about ninety boys in the class. I just spoke simply about the Lord Jesus Christ, and at the end, I said, 'If any of you chaps want to receive Jesus Christ as your Savior this afternoon, I am going to be here. Just come and talk to me afterward.' Thirty boys came and talked to me afterward! I hardly knew what to do with them, but I just did the best I could, and I believe God honored the desire of their hearts in spite of my clumsiness!

"Of course, that was a tremendous joy to me; and this happened day after day, day after day. It did not matter what the meeting was. When I stepped out to the university that Thursday morning, I was stepping out into a new land. This was Canaan! I had had no memories of Canaan. I stepped out in blind faith. I was like the parachute, just pulling the cord and jumping into nothing! Now I had a memory! A memory that was going to reinforce my faith for the next step into Canaan!

"So, for the next meeting, I thought, 'Well, it worked last time, I wasn't quite sure that it would work, but it did, and so I will reckon upon Him again for this meeting.' I thanked the Lord again for the folk who were going to be saved, and I gave the invitation to meet me afterward, and others were converted. When I bumped into folk on the street, I seemed always to be bumping into the right people! 'This is an extraordinary thing,' I thought. For seven years I was always bumping into the wrong people, and now, I can't help bumping into the right people! For five weeks, almost every day, people were converted."

Christian friends began to notice that something was different in the life of God's young servant. He met Christians who were as weary and exhausted as he had been, and he was able to share with them the secret of the Life that vanishes depression and frustration. He and they were making the discovery that fullness of life in Christ Himself, and only in Him.

"At the end of five weeks God made it very plain to me He had something more to say. He had just begun to whet my appetite. He said, 'That is My life. You know perfectly well that it has nothing to do with you

because it happened overnight! It is not a new method. It is not a new technique that you have learned. It is simply My life; being what I am, doing the inevitable. This is now the thing you have got to realize, you cannot have My life for your program. You can only have My life for My program! That is the next issue you have got to face. In My program, you are not going to be a doctor, and you are not going to Africa as a missionary. I am not complaining, that plan was sincerely conceived;' but, God made this quite plain to me. He was very kind. 'You are going to leave the university now,' He said. 'This is such a precious truth that you have that I am going to send you up and down throughout the British Isles to tell folk about it. There are lots of hungry folks, just like you were amongst the Christians, and waiting to be "bumped into" are lots of unconverted folks.' "

Thus step-by-step the Most High led His trusting and obedient servant into paths that he did not foresee nor choose, but they were pathways of service eminently satisfying and always adventurous. Instead of medical school and the mission field, the ministry was evangelism throughout Great Britain, especially among young people. Before World War II broke out he had six wonderful years of ever-expanding ministry in sharing the secret of the Life that is Christ. Major Thomas testifies, "It was just His victory. It was just what He was. I found that the simpler I could make it, the more blessing He gave; and whenever I tried to be complicated or clever, He just closed down. Only as I related situations to Him, did I find that He undertook. As soon as I related a situation to myself, He retired into the background. So I soon learned to count upon Him, because then things happened! That is the secret; it is so simple! Just to relate everything to the Lord Jesus, and take our hands off—to stand back and say, 'I thank Thee, Lord, this is Thy situation!' "

What the Major learned that late November night when he fell to his knees and cried out to the Savior stayed with him his entire ministry and life can be summed up in his words, "It is not inactivity; it is simply His activity, and that is what makes the difference."[114]

WHAT ABOUT YOU?

2. Now, after having read Major Thomas' testimony, will you answer the following questions?

   a. As you look back over Major Thomas' testimony, do you clearly see the white flag of surrender?

   b. What caused Major Thomas to surrender?

   c. When he finally surrendered, what did that look like?

   d. Did you notice that he cried out to the Savior? When He did, what happened next?

   e. What did the Lord Jesus use to speak to the young Major Thomas?

114. V. Raymond Edman, *They Found the Secret* (Grand Rapids, MI: Zondervan, 1984), pp. 167-174.

f. When God's Spirit brought these verses to mind, what did Major Thomas do next? In other words, when God, by His grace, invited Major Thomas to respond in faith (surrender and obey), what did he do next? You can use his words if you like.

g. What part of the Major's testimony spoke the most to you? Why?

Note: If you go back to all that the Lord Jesus brought to the Major's mind that night of surrender, you will discover: Galatians 2:20; John 14:6; Romans 5:10; and Colossians 3:4. Do you see how the Spirit of God used the Word of God to speak to Major Thomas? That's exactly what He will do for you and me!

Do you see the radical difference in his life? Can you sense the costliness of obedience? Do you see how the Word of God was not just a head-knowledge for Major Thomas but actually became his life? Do you see how God's Spirit applied the Word He had given to direct the course of Major Thomas' life from that point forward? Do you think He would do that for you?

As I provided detail after detail of the Majors' testimony for this study, I could see many parallels with what the Lord Jesus did for me those twenty-five plus years ago. He radically changed my life with His Word!

Consider the words of Dr. Edman once again as he explains the parallel, stating,

> *The deep dealing of God and His children varies in detail but the general pattern seems much alike for individual cases. Into each life there arises an awareness of failure, a falling short of all that one should be in the Lord; then there is a definite meeting with the risen Savior in utter surrender of heart, which is indeed death to self. There follows an appropriation by faith of His resurrection life through the abiding presence of the Holy Spirit. As a result there is realized an overflow of life likened by the Lord Jesus to 'rivers of water' (John 7:37–39).*[115]

h. As you look over Dr. Edman's analogy, list the general steps to the pattern in the order they are given:

#1 - ____

#2 - ____

#3 - ____

#4 - ____

If I may, please allow me to add some additional comments to the pattern Dr. Edman submitted above.

First, Edman describes an awareness of failure and a falling short of what one should be in the Lord. I refer to this as the white flag of surrender. In my head, the white flag goes up. This is when I cry out in utter frustration and confess that I cannot live as He commanded. It's a cry of desperation as I cease striving in my flesh to be and to live what only He, in me, can be and do. It's a description of living out the first part of Psalm 34:6, which states, "*This poor man cried out,* and the LORD heard him, and saved him out of all his troubles" (Ps. 34:6; emphasis added).

115. Edman, 17.

Secondly, I have learned the moment I cry out, the LORD *always* does His part in the psalm, as His Spirit takes His Word and brings it to my mind. When this happens, rest assured, He is showing me the way out. With this step there is always a surrender of my will to His will (Word). Herein is the meaning of death to self. In essence, God's grace has just been extended as He is inviting me to surrender my will and follow Him.

Thirdly, as I respond in faith to His gracious invitation out of the trap I am in, He leads me out as I obey. The surrender of my will in obedience to His Word is the way out of the snare. When this happens, there is an exchange. My flesh is being put to death as I surrender and obey His Word in order for His Spirit to reign in that area of my heart.

Lastly, the result of the surrender of my will in obedience to His will always results in more of Him and less of me! The dominating influence of His Spirit always results in the fruit that the Spirit alone can give. I find that I am filled with love, joy, peace, patience, kindness, goodness, faithfulness, gentleness, and self-control (Gal. 5:22–23).

Do you see that although the pattern is the *same* in every life, the details will be as *different* as the individual who is following the pattern?

Can you identify with the general pattern just described? Maybe you are experiencing what he described right now. You sense, out of failure, your desperate need for a Savior. Will you cry out in surrender? I can assure you, the Savior is waiting. He is ever attentive to the cry of surrender. In fact, in His grace, He orchestrated the events leading to it. These events have led you once again, to Him, your Savior. He is waiting to make the exchange—your failure for His victory, your sin for His forgiveness, your weakness, for His strength. The white flag of surrender will lead you to the One, who alone can make the exchange.

Just recently, while viewing a series about the life of the late missionary, Hudson Taylor, he described his surrender and obedience (faith) as *radical* and *ridiculed*.[116] Can you identify? Are you willing to be called, radical? Are you willing to face ridicule, even from those closest to you for His great name? Is it worth the risk? Is He worthy?

Maybe as you are reading this now, Major Thomas' testimony has defined your Christian life. Perhaps this too is your providential encounter with the Major. Maybe this is your divine appointment with the Savior. Will you see this as His grace? Will you respond in faith?

3. Now, as we return to Galatians, let's continue in Chapter 5 by looking at verse 17. What are we told about the flesh and the Spirit in their regard to one another?

a. ______________________________

Note: In this verse, the word, "desire" (*epithumeo*) is used as a verb, with particular emphasis on the mind. In other words, the mind is intensely set on something, and in this case, because the source is the flesh, it is used in an evil sense and virtually means to lust.

b. With that in mind, what would the mind set on the Spirit desire?

____

c. With the Spirit and the flesh in opposition to one another, what purpose does that serve for the believer (v. 17)?

____

116. Tim Keesee, *Dispatches From The Front*, "Episode 8: No Regrets, No Retreat," (Taylors, SC: Frontline Missions International), available at https:www.DISPATCHESFROMTHEFRONT.ORG.

Note: The Greek word translated "please" (*thelo*), means to will, active volition and purpose, to have in mind, to intend, to choose.[117]

4. To better understand Galatians 5:16–17, let's look at Romans 8:5–16 and answer the following questions:

a. What are the two kinds of men God sees and what are their mindsets (v. 5)?

1) Those who are ____

Mindset - ____

2) Those who are ____

Mindset - ____

Note: When Paul uses the words "mindset" or "mind" in Romans 5, he is using the Greek word, *phroneo*. The activity represented by this word involves not only the mind, but the will, the affections (emotions), and the conscience."[118]

Now, consider the definition of man's soul/heart:

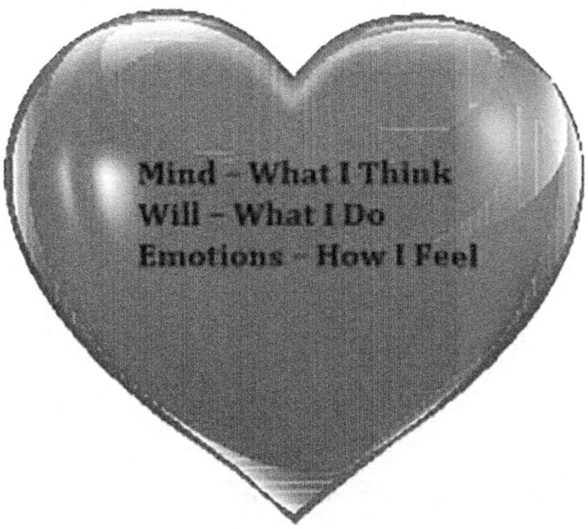

Doesn't that look just like the definition for mindset (*phroneo*)?

Note: Personally, one of the most helpful definitions of the word "mind" comes from *Baker's Dictionary of Theology*, which states,

> *The English versions of the Bible express a variety of emotional, volitional and intellectual movements by the one word—mind... If controlled by the Holy Spirit, the mind displays the right attitude to God and one's fellows (Luke 10:27; Rom. 12:2; 1 Cor. 1:10) and the mind thus bent on the service of God is contrasted with the flesh (Rom. 7:23, 25), the fallen nature still contending within the regenerate man. The mind even of the believer may be controlled by 'the flesh' (Col. 2:18), but such perversion of the mind is ascribed more to the unregenerate (Rom. 1:28; 2 Cor. 3:14, 4:4; 2 Tim. 3:8).*
>
> **The mind, therefore, is in itself neutral, and its moral quality is determined by the power to which it is subject** *(emphasis added).*[119]

117. Spiros Zodhiates, *The Complete Word Study New Testament Dictionary* (Chattanooga,TN: AMG Pub.,1993),727.
118. *Ibid.,* 1454.
119. Everett F. Harrison, Geoffrey W. Bromiley and Carl F. H. Henry, *Bakers Dictionary of Theology* (Grand Rapids, MI: Baker Book House, 1988), 355.

Keep this definition tucked away as you proceed through the lesson.

b. Now, look at verse 6. What do you learn about the contrast of mindsets (a.k.a., the heart/soul) between the flesh and the Spirit?

1) The mind (heart) set on the flesh = ____________________________

2) The mind (heart) set on the Spirit = ____________________________

and

____

c. What else do you learn about the mindset (heart) on the flesh according to verse 7?

Why? (v. 7) ____,

for it is not even ____.

d. What do you learn about those in the flesh from verse 8?

e. Now, look at what Paul says to the believers in Rome in verse 9?

You are _____________ in the _____________________ but in the ____________________,

If indeed ____.

f. What is true about the man or woman who does not have God's Spirit (v. 9)?

Do you see the contrast in verse 9? Who is the difference maker in the heart/soul of mankind?

g. Now, look at verse 10. The word "if" can better be translated "since." Notice to whom the subject shifts?

Since ______________________ is _______ you, what is true of your spirit and why?

Now, look at verse 11. Again, the word "if" is better translated "since."

h. What do you learn about the Spirit of Him (the Father) regarding Jesus Christ in verse 11?

i. What will the Spirit of Him who raised Jesus from the dead, who dwells in you do for your mortal bodies (v. 11)?

j. What is Paul's summary statement to the believers in Rome (v. 12)?

k. What must happen to those who are living according to their flesh (v. 13)?

They ______________________________.

l. Whose responsibility is it to put the flesh to death (v. 13)? Note the order.

By the ______________________________

______________ are putting to death the ________________ of the _________________.

m. What will the result be (v. 13)? You will __________________________.

n. What are those who are being led by the Spirit of God called (v. 14)?

o. Now, read verse 15. Notice the contrast. Record your insights below.

1) How is the spirit described for those who have *not* been adopted as sons of God?

2) To what does the spirit of slavery lead? ____________________________

3) What spirit have the sons of God received?

p. What will the Spirit of God do within us according to verses 15–16?

Did you notice that Paul here tells the believers in Galatia the same thing he told the believers in Rome? And if he were here today, he would tell us the same thing too. In fact, through the unchanging and eternal Word of God, He just did.

5. Before we move on, let's compare Galatians 5:16 with Romans 8:13b. As you examine these two passages, what do you see? Be specific.

6. Now, let's compare Galatians 5:16 and Romans 8:13b with Ephesians 2:8, and in particular, "For by grace you have been saved through faith..." What do you see?

7. Do you see that Galatians 5:16 is the *how-to* when it comes to the Spirit putting the flesh to death? What might that look like in the life of a believer?

Now, let's look at the summary statement Paul makes to the Galatians about the works of the Law (human effort) versus God's Spirit in verse 18.

Note: Again, a better translation for "if" would be "since." Additionally, the word "led" is a present indicative passive verb. The present tense signifies continuous action; the indicative mood indicates a statement of fact, and the passive voice means that the subject is being acted upon by an outside Source.

8. With this information in mind, what is Paul's summary statement to the Galatians in verse 18?

9. Now, we've come to the part in the letter where Paul contrasts the deeds of the flesh (vv. 19–21) with the fruit of the Spirit (vv. 22–23). First, we will look briefly at the deeds of the flesh. We will cover the details more thoroughly in the next lesson. For now, we will do a general overview of both.

Before we look at the list, let's set the context. For example, when we speak of the *deeds* of the *flesh*, remember this is the state of being of the life that says, "I will be god," with the motivating factor being love for self above God and others.

a. First, what does Paul tell us about the deeds of the flesh in verse 19a?

They are ____________________________.

b. With that stated, what will the "deeds" (*ergon*) of the "flesh" (*sarx*), which, by the way are both nouns indicating a state of being, look like?

1) ________________________________ 9) ________________________________

2) ________________________________ 10) ________________________________

3) ________________________________ 11) ________________________________

4) ________________________________ 12) ________________________________

5) ________________________________ 13) ________________________________

6) ________________________________ 14) ________________________________

7) ________________________________ 15) ________________________________

8) ________________________________ 16) ________________________________

Would it surprise you to know that all the deeds listed are nouns?

c. Now, what does Paul forewarn in verse 21b?

Keep in mind that these are all connected with the flesh that says, "I will be god!"

Because...

I love myself!

Therefore, all the deeds will be toward self!

10. Now, let's look at the exact opposite in Galatians 5:22–23. In fact, the person with God's Spirit indwelling knows that there is only one God (Father, Son, and Spirit) because God's Spirit has revealed that truth to their hearts. Furthermore, the Spirit of God within is the cause of the believer's love for God and others rather than for himself. With that context in mind, answer the following questions from verses 22–23.

    a. What, in verse 22, is contrasted with the deeds of the flesh (vv. 19–21)?

Note: Did you notice the word "fruit" is singular and not plural? The word is used metaphorically to mean deeds or works.[120]

b. Notice, who is the One working? ________________________

Quite a contrast with the one working in verses 19–21, right?

c. List the nine-fold fruit of the Spirit below.

1) ________________________ 6) ________________________

2) ________________________ 7) ________________________

3) ________________________ 8) ________________________

4) ________________________ 9) ________________________

5) ________________________

Would it surprise you to know that all the fruit listed are nouns as well?

Keep in mind that these are all connected with God's Spirit who says, "There is One God!" and His love is expressed toward God and others.

Now, let's look at Galatians 5:24. What are we told about those who belong to Christ? In other words, what will be true of those who are His?

We will look at this in more depth in our next lesson. For now, soak in the truths His Spirit has revealed in His Word. Thank Him for the grace He has bestowed upon you by revealing these truths to your heart. Ask Him what it would look like for you to respond to His invitation of grace by faith? And then do what He says! He will always lead you to Himself and others.

120. Spiros Zodhiates, *The Complete Word Study New Testament Dictionary* (Chattanooga,TN: AMG Pub.,1993), 821.

One final question for thought:

Do you see how your manner of walk (whether by the Spirit or by the flesh) is determined by who you love? If so, explain your answer.

Whom do you love most?

Is this true in all areas of your heart as far as you know right now?

Lesson 11

THE FLESH Versus THE SPIRIT (Part Two)

GALATIANS 5:21–26

In the last lesson, we did a general overview of the deeds of the flesh and the direct opposite, the fruit of the Spirit. We discovered that fundamentally, the deeds of the flesh are driven by our desire to be god because we love ourselves more than God and others. Even a glance at the deeds of the flesh will corroborate this truth because all the deeds listed are rooted in self. We also learned that lurking behind this inherent desire to be god and love for self is really the Enemy. In essence, the man or woman without Christ's indwelling Spirit is in the Enemy's trap of deception (see 2 Tim 2:25b-26).

The exact opposite is true concerning the fruit of the Spirit. God's Spirit residing within is the *cause* of any knowledge or thought of God. Only God's Spirit can *cause* us to see and know that there is only one God and that we are not anything like Him. Similarly, only His Spirit can love God and others as we have been commanded.

Furthermore, if we are truly honest with ourselves, we will quickly admit that without God in us, we cannot and will not *bear* this type of fruit. Notice that I did not say *produce*, as is often misquoted, but *bear* the fruit, for only the Spirit of God can *produce* the fruit of God. A believer is merely the *bearer* of the fruit God alone produces.

In this lesson, we will slow down and take a more detailed look at each of the deeds and fruit explicitly listed. Let's get started.

1. First, let's begin with the deeds of the flesh, which are listed in Galatians 5:19-22. You will notice that I have listed each deed along with a brief definition from the late theologian and New Testament Greek scholar, Spiros Zodhiates. You will also discover that after each definition, I have listed antonyms. Sometimes, the most helpful way to understand a word is to look at the antonyms. Keep in mind, the deeds listed are not an exhaustive list, which is evidenced by the phrase, "and things like these," located in verse 21. Feel free to consult any other Greek language aids to help you gain insight into the meaning of these words.

Immorality (*moicheia*) – the sexual sin that involves at least one married person. The general word used for sexual sin is *porneia*, which encompasses all kinds of sexual sins.[121] It is where the English word "pornography" is derived.

The antonyms of immorality are "purity," "cleansed," "holy."

Impurity (*akatharisia*) – without moral cleanness: any unnatural pollution whether acted out by oneself or on others.[122] This sin may be hidden or done in secret.

Some antonyms are "purity," "clean," or "holy."

---

121. Spiros Zodhiates, *The Complete Word Study New Testament Dictionary* (Chattanooga, TN: AMG Publishers, 1993), 994.
122. *Ibid.,* 108.

Sensuality (*aselgeia*) – a wantonness, lustfulness, excessive pleasure, the absence of restraint, an insatiable desire for pleasure (Mark 7:22).[123] This sin is done openly.

An antonym is "self-control."

Idolatry (*eidololatreia*) – a servant worshiper of idols (idolater), the act of worshiping and serving any created thing rather than the Creator.[124]

An obvious antonym is to worship and serve the Creator.

Sorcery (*pharmakeia*) – the use of drugs or medication often used with spells, a trance, or magical incantations. A synonym would be "magic."[125] Our English word *pharmacy* is derived from this Greek word. MacArthur, commenting on this word, qualified the use of the mood and mind-altering drugs specifically.[126]

An antonym is possessing a sound mind.

Enmities (*echthra*) – hatred, hostility, to be enemies.[127]

Brotherly love is an antonym.

Strife (*eris*) – contention, wrangling, metaphorically used for the love of strife

(Rom. 1:29). [128]

An obvious antonym is peace.

Jealousy (*zelos*) – envy, anger, to grieve not because another has good, but that he himself does not have it and seeks to supply the deficiency in himself.[129]

Antonyms to jealousy are gratitude and contentment.

Outburst of anger (*thumos*) – a violent motion of passion of the mind. *Thumos* is the outburst of *orge*, which is seething anger in the mind.[130]

An antonym is peace.

Disputes (*eritheia*) – to strive with words with the motive of self-interest, to scheme or canvass for public office, to work for hire in a bad sense, selfish ambition with the aim of profit/power.[131]

An antonym is humility.

Dissensions (*dichostasia*) a separate faction or division.[132]

The antonym is unity.

---

123. *Ibid.,* 270.
124. *Ibid.,* 510.
125. *Ibid.,* 1437.
126. John MacArthur, Jr., *The John MacArthur New Testament Commentary Galatians* (Chicago: Moody Press, 1987), 161.
127. Spiros Zodhiates, *The Complete Word Study New Testament Dictionary* (Chattanooga, TN: AMG Publishers, 1993), 692.
128. *Ibid.,* 654.
129. *Ibid.,* 699.
130. Spiros Zodhiates, *The Complete Word Study New Testament Dictionary* (Chattanooga, TN: AMG Publishers, 1993), 744.
131. *Ibid.*, 654.
132. *Ibid.*, 473.

Factions (*hairesis*) – a "heresy, a form of religious worship, discipline, or opinion. In contrast to *schisma*, schism, which is an actual tearing apart, *hairesis* may represent a divergent opinion but still be part of the whole. One can hold different views than the majority and remain in the same body, but he is a heretic. However, when he tears himself away, then he is schismatic. Heresy may lead to schism."[133]

The antonym is unity.

Envying (*phthonos*) – pain felt and malignity conceived at the sight of excellence or happiness. Differs from *jealousy* (*zelos*) in that it is never used in a good sense but always evil.[134]

An antonym is joy.

Drunkenness (*methe*) – to drink milled wine in excess. Often, associated with orgies, loud and lewd behavior.[135]

An antonym is self-control.

Carousing (*komos*) feasting with riotous conduct, reveling, festivities in honor of several gods, especially Bacchus, the god of wine, hence feastings and drunkenness with impurity and obscenity of the grossest kind.[136]

Antonyms are self-control and a sound mind.

Things like these (*Homoios*) – one and the same, like, similar in externals.[137]

Note: The King James Version adds the word, *murder*, to the list. However, it is not included in most manuscripts. Certainly, it would be included in the list of *things like these*.

2. As you look at the definitions, what do you see?

Do you see that they are all self-focused and involve the heart, and in particular, the mind?

3. When you look at all the antonyms, what do you see?

I see the fruit of the Spirit.

4. Now let's look at verse 21b and answer the following questions:

a. What has Paul done about these things listed?

133. *Ibid.*, 98.
134. Spiros Zodhiates, *The Complete Word Study New Testament Dictionary* (Chattanooga, TN: AMG Publishers, 1993), 1443.
135. *Ibid.*, 954.
136. *Ibid.*, 903.
137. *Ibid.*, 1041.

b. Is this his first warning to the Galatians (how do you know)?

c. What are we told about those who practice such things?

Note: The word "practice" (*prasso*), is a present participle active verb. The present tense signifies continuous action, and the active voice means that the subject is performing the action.

5. With that stated, what is Paul telling us about the people who are doing such things?

Because the deeds of the flesh are nouns, they represent a person's state of being. Therefore, out from their state of being these things become actions. In other words, you do what you do because you are what you are, right? Their actions, therefore, represent the habit of their lives.

6. Now, let's cross-reference Galatians 5:19–21 with 1 Corinthians 6:9–11 and answer the following questions:

a. Why do you think Paul begins verse 9 by asking, "Or do you not know..."

b. What are we told about the unrighteous in verse 9?

Note: If Christ is our righteousness, and He is, who is missing in the life of the unrighteous? ____________________

c. Again, why do you think Paul states, "Do not be deceived," in verse 9? Think about the definition of deception, which is *saying* one thing but *doing* another.

d. Who does Paul include in his list of the unrighteous in verses 9–10?

1) ________________________________ 6) ________________________________

2) ________________________________ 7) ________________________________

3) ________________________________ 8) ________________________________

4) ________________________________ 9) ________________________________

5) ________________________________ 10) ________________________________

Note: The word "effeminate" is used for male prostitutes.

Would it surprise you to discover that all the things listed above were nouns and not verbs?

7. What are we told about the people in this list according to verse 10b? What is their end?

Personal Note: As I looked over this list, I could not help but think how deceived we are today. Countless people around us are dying, whose very lives are the definitions of the things listed above; and yet, when you attend their funerals, everyone around you, even professing believers, are placing them in heaven. But as you consider God's Word, is that where they really are? Oh, that the Church would have the courage to say what God is saying.

Some may read this and think, *That's a little harsh, isn't it?* I would answer, "No, that's called speaking the truth in love." Read Luke 16:27–28. In this passage, Jesus speaks of the rich man who went to Hell. Notice the only concern on the heart of the rich man. What do you see?

---

8. Now, look at what Paul says to the Corinthian church in verse 11. What does he remind them?

"Such were ________________ of _____________

But You were ____________________________

You were ____________________________

You were ____________________________

Note: The Greek words translated "sanctified" and "justified" are in the passive voice, meaning that the subject is acted upon by an outside Source.

9. As you read verse 11, who is the outside Source who *justified* and *sanctified* the believers in Corinth?

a. ____________________________

b. ____________________________

10. One more similar list before we proceed. Look at Revelation 22:15. Who is in this list?

a. ____________________________

b. ____________________________

c. ____________________________

d. ____________________________

e. ____________________________

f ____________________________

Note: For a better understanding of the term "dogs," see the cross-reference in Deuteronomy 23:18.

Again, the things listed above are all nouns.

11. Where are these people (v. 15) regarding the tree of life and the gates that lead into the city of God (v. 14)?

12. Now, as you consider Galatians 5:19–21, 1 Corinthians 6:9–10, and Revelation 22:15, what do these verses have in common?

13. Now, let's look at the antithesis of the deeds of the flesh. Read Galatians 5:22–23 and list the fruit of the Spirit below:

a. ______________________________

b. ______________________________

c. ______________________________

d. ______________________________

e. ______________________________

f. ______________________________

g. ______________________________

h. ______________________________

i. ______________________________

Note: The Greek word translated "fruit," is the noun *karpos*, which is used metaphorically to describe deeds and works. Each listed are nouns which comprise the whole, designated as fruit.

Look closely. Who is the One doing the deeds and works? ______________________________

Oftentimes, if we are not careful, we can be misled into thinking the fruit is our deed or work. I know I have believed this deception. When contrasting the deeds of the flesh with the fruit of the Spirit, MacArthur notes that the deeds of the flesh are done by a person's own efforts, whether saved or unsaved. However, the fruit of the Spirit is produced by God's Spirit alone and only in the lives of those who belong to Him through faith in Jesus Christ.

14. What would be the mindset of a believer who thinks it is their job to produce the deeds or works (fruit) of the Spirit? What might that look like?

In noting the contrast between the words "works" and "fruit," I found the late pastor, Bible teacher, and author, Warren Wiersbe's thoughts most helpful. He states,

> *A machine in a factory works, and turns out a product, but it could never manufacture fruit. Fruit must grow out of life, and, in the case of the believer, it is the life of the Spirit. When you think of "works" you think of effort, labor, strain, and toil; when you think of "fruit" you think of beauty,*

quietness, the unfolding of life. The flesh produces "dead works" (Heb 9:14), but the Spirit produces living fruit.[138]

Quite a contrast wouldn't you say?

15. As we consider the part that the believer plays relating to the fruit of the Spirit, we must consider the words of Jesus in John 15. Read John 15:1–16 and answer the following questions:

    a. Let's begin by identifying the root. Who is the true vine? ___________________

    b. Look closely at verses 2, 4, 5, 8, and 16. What are we to do in terms of the fruit?

    c. When you compare the root with the branch, what is the difference in relation to the fruit?

Note: Where there is no root, there is no fruit.

Do you see the difference between fruit production and fruit bearing? If we are not careful, we can confuse our role with His. When this occurs, we have taken on the position of striving to produce something that at best is artificial, will not nourish, nor last.

16. Now, as we examine the fruit listed in Galatians 5:22–23, let's look at the specific characteristics. Again, I will be relying on the work of Dr. Zodhiates for help.

Love (*agape*) – With reference to God's love, it is God's willful direction toward man. It involves God doing what He knows is best for man and not necessarily what man desires. This love is derived from God.[139]

The antonyms are hatred, enmity.

Joy (*chara*) – to rejoice, gladness.[140] Notably, joy is different than *happiness*, which is closely associated with one's external circumstances. Paul, for example, wrote the Book of Philippians, wherein the theme could be entitled "How to Have Joy"—ironically while he was in prison. Circumstantially, there was no apparent cause for joy. However, because joy describes an internal state of being, one's external circumstances cannot alter the joy from within.

The antonyms are grief, sorrow, pain, and suffering.

Peace (*eirene*) – the opposite of war and dissension. Metaphorically, it speaks of peace of mind, tranquility arising from reconciliation with God and a sense of divine favor. God is said to be a God of peace, not as One who needs peace, but One who dispenses peace.[141] In other words, He is the Source. Therefore, the man without Christ cannot have peace with God; and therefore, can have no true peace with others.

Antonyms are war, conflict, anxiety, fear, confusion, and division.

---

138. Warrren W. Wiersbe, *The Bible Exposition Commentary Vol. One* (Wheaton, IL: Victor Books, 1989), 719.
139. Zodhiates *Word Study Dictionary*, pp. 66–67.
140. *Ibid.,* 1468.
141. *Ibid.*, pp. 519-520

Patience (*makrothumia*) – to be longsuffering in regard to people; a self-restraint before proceeding with the action. The quality of a person who can avenge himself yet refrains from doing so. It is closely associated with the mercy of God.[142]

Antonyms are wrath (*thumos*) and anger (*orgē*).

Note: There are two Greek words for our one English word "patience": *makrothumia*, as described above; and *hupomone*, which involves patience in reference to things and circumstances. *Hupomone* is the ability to bear up under immense pressure caused by difficult circumstances.

Kindness (*chrestotes*) – useful and profitable. It is the grace, which pervades the whole nature, mellowing all that would be harsh and severe. *Chrestotes* describes the harmlessness of the dove but not the wisdom of the serpent.[143]

The antonyms are callousness, hardness, bad character, depravity, and iniquity (*poneria*).

Goodness (*agathosunē*) – character energized, benevolent, active goodness. There is more activity in *agathosune* than in kindness (*chrestotes*). *Agathosune* does not spare sharpness and rebuke to cause good in others. A person may display his *agathosune*, his zeal for goodness and truth, in rebuking, correcting, or chastising. Christ's righteous indignation in the temple showed his *agathosune*, but not His *chrestotes*, gentleness.[144]

Antonyms are evil, malice (*kakos*) mischievousness, malignity, iniquity, and wickedness (*poneria*).

Faithfulness (*pistis*) – Objectively, it means that which is believed, doctrine, and the received articles of faith.[145] In other words, the object or foundation of faith is based upon the Father, Son, and Holy Spirit, as well as the revealed Scriptures.

Subjectively, it is comprised of three components, all which are necessary and in the order they are mentioned, namely:

A firm conviction of God's Word

(The conviction comes from God's Spirit using the Word of God.)

Personal surrender of the worshiper's will to God's will (Word).

Obedience to God's Word[146]

The antonym is unbelief, which is a refusal to surrender one's will and obey God's Word.

Gentleness (*praotes*) – meekness and forbearance. Primarily it does not denote the outward expression of feeling, but an inward grace of the soul. It is calmness toward God in particular, which involves the acceptance of God's dealings with us as we consider them as good because they enhance the closeness of our relationship with Him. However, *praotes* also includes His expression of wrath toward the sin of man as demonstrated by the Lord Jesus (who indeed was called meek but expressed His anger toward those who were chiding Him because He had done good on the Sabbath day [Mark 3:5]).[147] Antonyms are anger (*orgē*) and wrath (*thumos*).

---

142. Spiros Zodhiates, *The Complete Word Study New Testament Dictionary* (Chattanooga, TN: AMG Publishers, 1993), 939.
143. Zodhiates, *The Complete Word Study New Testament Dictionary*, 1482.
144. Ibid., 63.
145. Ibid., 1162.
146. Kenneth S. Wuest, *Wuest's Word Studies From the Greek New Testament: Galatians*, Volume One, (Grand Rapids: Wm. B. Eerdmans Publishing Co., 1972), 71.
147. Spiros Zodhiates, *The Complete Word Study New Testament Dictionary* (Chattanooga, TN: AMG Publishers, 1993), 1208.

Self-Control (*egkrates*) – an inward power, dominion, strength, and government. Having power over or being master of fleshly desires and appetites.[148]

Antonyms are fleshly, carnal, given over to, and powerless.

17. As you look at the definitions, what do you see?

Do you see that the man or woman without the Spirit of God residing within cannot bear this kind of fruit? In fact, since the Source of this fruit is God's Spirit, the only thing that an unbeliever can bear is artificial fruit.

18. When you look at all the antonyms, what do you see?

Do you see the deeds of the flesh?

Look again at the fruit of the Spirit and think of each in light of them being toward God and others instead of self. What a contrast!

Now, consider the phrase, "*...against such things there is no law* (Gal. 5:23b)." Isn't Paul reiterating that for the believer, these virtues rise from within—from God's Spirit; therefore, no external law can produce them? In other words, any attempt to externally follow and keep these virtues is futile and frustrating. For no person can accomplish what only God can do, as He is the Source of each virtue required. Furthermore, He will only require of His people what He alone can do and has made available in them.

19. Now, let's look at Paul's conclusive statement regarding the flesh and its desires in verse 24. Fill in the appropriate blanks:

Now those

who ________________ to __________________ have ________________________

↓

the ________________

with

its __________________

and

____________________.

a. Notice the qualifier. Who alone can crucify the flesh according to verse 24?

148. *Ibid.*, 500.

b. What does that tell you about the unbeliever regarding his flesh with its passions and desires?

Note: Just like their English counterparts, the Greek words translated "flesh," "passions," and "desires" are all nouns. The word flesh (*sarx*) is a reference to the residual flesh of a believer. [Remember, at justification, the flesh was not eradicated.] Therefore, the word, *passions* (*pathema*) denotes evil passions, as an equivalent to *desires* (*epithumia*), which remain an issue for even the believer.

c. What do you learn about the residual flesh of a believer?

d. What must the believer do about the residual flesh with its passions and desires?

Note: The word translated "crucified" is an aorist indicative active verb. The aorist tense signifies a punctiliar action, at a moment in time. The indicative voice is a statement of fact, while the active voice means that the subject is performing the action.

e. With that in mind, how does the one who belongs to Christ, crucify the residual flesh with its passions and desires? Think back to Galatians 5:16.

Now, carefully consider the words of Dr. Wuest as he comments on verse 24, stating,

> *The Christian's identification with Christ in His death, resulted in the breaking of the power of the sinful nature over the life. This victory over sin, which the Lord Jesus procured for us at the Cross, is made actual and operative in our lives as we yield (surrender and obey) to the Holy Spirit and trust Him for that victory. It is the Holy Spirit's ministry that applies the salvation from the power of the sinful nature, which God the Son procured at the Cross—for us. Thus the Holy Spirit has a two-fold ministry in the saint, that of making actually operative in the life of the Christian, the victory over sin, and that of producing in the Christian's experience, His fruit. But this He is only able to do in a full and rich measure as the saint puts himself definitely under subjection to the Spirit (parenthesis added).*[149]

WHAT ABOUT YOU?

Is there anything in you that needs to be crucified? Is there some deed of the flesh that is having power over your heart right now? Has God's Spirit placed His finger (so to speak) on an area of your heart?

If so, confess it to Him now. Ask the Lord Jesus to save you from its power. Ask the Lord Jesus if He will grant you repentance. And then ask Him what repentance might look like in your life. Listen, as the Spirit of God will bring the Word of God to your mind. And then ask Him to *cause* you to surrender your will in that area and obey what He has just brought to mind. This is the manner whereby we are in the process of being sanctified by His

149. Wuest, *Word Studies in the Greek New Testament*, 161.

Word as noted in His High-Priestly prayer just hours before the cross (John 17:17).

Once again, will you let Him save you?

Now, as we continue to look at the command to *walk in the Spirit* (Gal 5:16), let's take a closer look at verses 25-26.

Note: First, we must establish that the English word "if," at the beginning of verse 25, would be better explained, "since.' Technically, when the word "if" (*ei*), is used with an *indicative* verb, the word is better translated "since." In this case, the Greek verb translated "live," is present indicative active; therefore, Paul is making a statement of fact, wherein there is no doubt.

20. With the information provided above, what is Paul saying about the Galatians in verse 25a?

21. Now, having established that the Spirit indwells the believer and is the very life-giving source within the believer, what is the instruction that follows in verse 25b?

Note: The term "walk" (*stoicheo*), means "to walk in an orderly manner, to walk in a straight line."[150] Fittingly, the antonym is to miss the mark, to deviate, to transgress.[151]

Furthermore, the verb used is present subjunctive active. Present tense indicates continuous action, while the subjunctive mood is the mood of probability and is used to express an action, which may or should happen. In other words, the action is thought of as possible or potential. The active voice indicates that the subject is doing the action.

By using the subjunctive mood, Paul is saying that it is possible to walk by the Spirit as we yield to the Spirit and God's Word, because God's Spirit makes it possible, but there is also the potential to choose not to surrender and obey when we say, "No" to the Spirit, and "Yes" to our flesh.

22. Using the information above, along with 2 Timothy 3:16, what might the Spirit of God apply to help the believer walk in a straight line, so as not to deviate or transgress? Explain your answer below.

Note: God's Spirit (*pneuma*), or breath, is the literal definition of the word, "inspired" (*theopneustos*) used in 2 Timothy 3:16. Notice that He uses God's Word to *reprove* and *correct* the believer. The word "reprove," shows that the believer can get off track. Whereas the word "correct" indicates how the believer can get back on track. Both are necessary for the Christian walk. Both require that the believer willingly surrender her will in obedience to God's Word. With that being stated, do you see that the believer is being saved by *grace* through *faith*?

a. Where is God's *grace* visible? ____

b. How is *faith* demonstrated? ____

150. Kenneth S. Wuest, *Wuest's Word Studies From the Greek New Testament: Galatians, Volume One*, (Grand Rapids: Wm. B. Eerdmans Publishing Co., 1972), 162.

151. Spiros Zodhiates, *The Complete Word Study New Testament Dictionary* (Chattanooga, TN: AMG Publishers, 1993), 856.

Do you see that *grace* is demonstrated as *God's Spirit uses God's Word*? In essence, grace is God extending an *invitation* for the believer to respond correctly in *faith* by the surrender of his will and in obedience to God's Word. When we follow God's Spirit in surrender and obedience, we are walking in the Spirit, which, in turn, is not only how to crucify the deeds of the flesh with its passions and desires, but also how His creation can rightfully glorify Him as God (Isa. 43:7).

23. Now, let's look at the opposite of glorifying God in verse 26.

a. What is Paul's first warning? Let us not become ______________________________

We would do well to pause here for a moment for clarity. The word "boastful" (*kenodoxos*) is derived from two Greek words. Note, the word, *kenos*, means empty or vain; and *doxa* means glory. Dr. Zodhiates explains that the boastful person (*kenodoxos*) is a person who is void of real worth but who wants to be admired by others. The antonym is to be humble.[152]

b. By stating the warning this way, what is Paul implying?

We would all do well to heed this warning. No one, no matter how spiritual, is above becoming boastful. At least not while the residual flesh remains.

c. What happens when we become boastful according to verse 26?

We ___________________________________ one another.

Note: The word "challenge" means to call someone forward. The middle voice is used here, which means that the subject, *the boastful one*, is calling another believer before himself to provoke or irritate.[153] In effect, the other believer is now answering to you, the boastful one.

d. If you look closely at verse 26, you will see why? What is in the heart of the boastful one?

Do you remember that the word "envy" is listed as one of the deeds of the flesh? In other words, the believer who has become *boastful* (and we all can) is no longer walking in the Spirit but rather the flesh.

24. Now, let's compare Galatians 5:26 with Isaiah 66:2b. What do you see?

Note: The Hebrew word translated "trembles," literally means to *obey*.

152. Zodhiates, *The Complete Word Study New Testament Dictionary*, 856.
153. *Ibid.*

25. Now look at the exact opposite of Isaiah 66:2. What do you see?

While listening to one of my favorite Bible teachers, pastor, and author, Alistair Begg, I heard him say something that caught my attention and I think, bears repeating. He stated, "Our conduct toward other people is governed by our opinion of ourselves."[154]

26. As you ponder Dr. Begg's statement and consider the opposite of Isaiah 66:2, what do you see regarding Galatians 5:25–26?

Let this statement be a barometer, so to speak, as you evaluate yourself. How are you doing?

27. Now, as you continue to Galatians 5:25 with Galatians 5:26, what do you see involving glory?

WHAT ABOUT YOU?

How would you describe your conduct toward others lately? More importantly, how would God's Spirit?

What do we do when we sense a boastful spirit that manifests itself by challenging others to answer to us, with a heart that is filled with envy toward another believer? It can happen to us all. What then?

As you look over the lesson, what would the Spirit's counsel be to you?

Remember, walking by the Spirit will manifest itself in a love for God and others, while the deeds of the flesh are rooted in a love for self above everyone and everything else—including the God who made us.

Whose *glory* do you actively seek?

Lord Jesus save us from ourselves! Will you let Him? *Grace* is inviting you now to respond in faith.

---

154. Alistair Begg, "Let Me Carry That For You," {on-line]; accessed March 26, 2019; available at http://tflmedia.s3.amazonaws.com/free_downloads/1424-letmecarrythatforyou.mp3; Internet.

Summary Review of Galatians 5

"It was for freedom that Christ set us free; therefore keep standing firm and do not be subject ***again*** to a yoke of slavery." (Galatians 5:1, emphasis added)

What yoke of slavery?

Look back at Galatians 2:16; 3:2, 3, 5. Do you see the repeated contrast between the works of the Law and faith in Christ?

Prior to salvation, we were all yoked to sin!

We were enslaved by the Enemy, under the dominion of the world, and in bondage to our fleshly desires.

Man's attempt to keep God's Law by the works of our flesh was futile. We were in a snare.

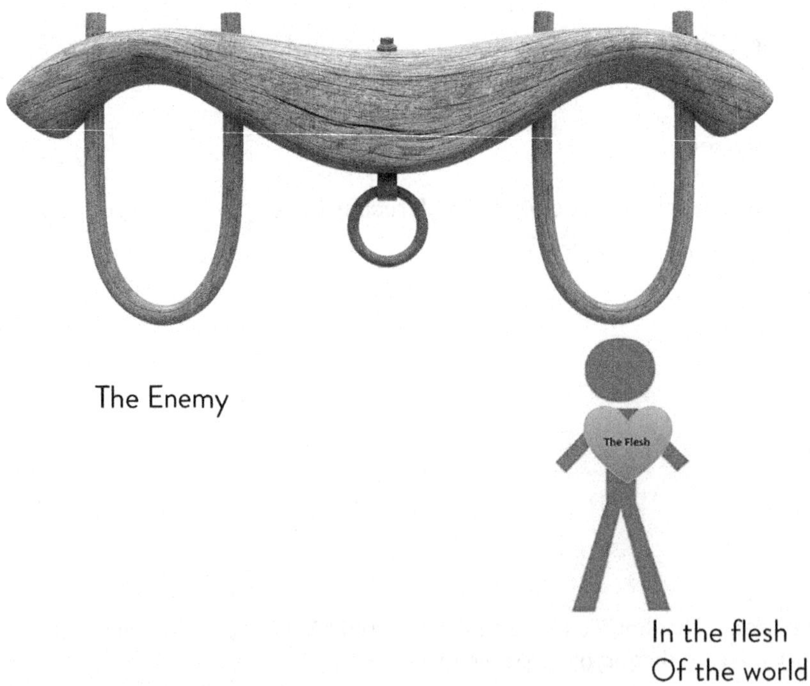

But God, who is rich in mercy, sent His Son, Jesus Christ to set us free (Eph. 2:4).

Now, because Jesus Christ set us free, we have a new Master. Jesus Christ resides within our hearts by His indwelling Spirit. We are now yoked to Him.

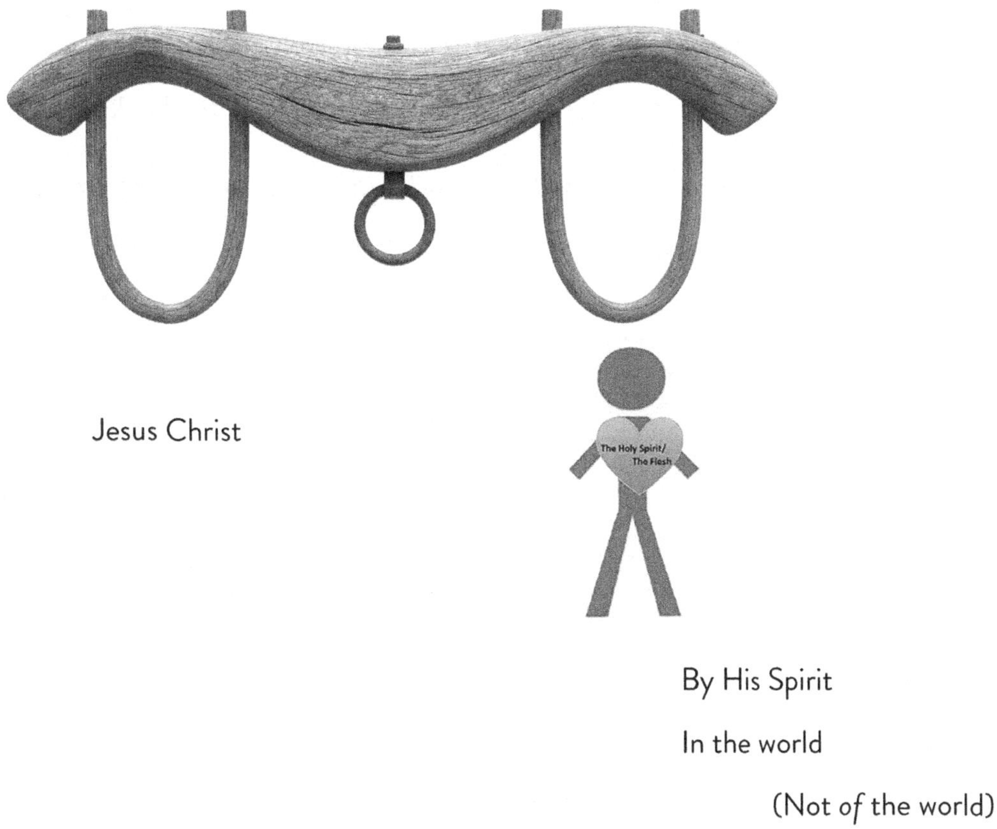

Christ lives in us to do for us what He requires. All the commands in Galatians 5–6 are possible because of the finished work of Christ on the cross.

Sadly, the false teachers had deceived the Galatian believers into thinking they needed to come back up under the works of the flesh, as if, somehow, their flesh could please God. Therefore, Paul's questions to the Galatian believers make sense. Let's review his questions from Galatians 3:

1) This is the only thing I want to find out from you: did you receive the Spirit by works of the Law, or by hearing with faith? (3:2).

2) Are you so foolish? Having begun by the Spirit, are you now being perfected by the flesh? (3:3).

3) Did you suffer so many things in vain—if indeed it was in vain? (3:4)

4) Does He then, who provides you with the Spirit and works miracles in you, do it by the works of the Law, or by hearing with faith? (3:5).

Do you see the distortion of the gospel is clearly stated in these questions?

Paul is contrasting the works of the Law with hearing with faith. The false brethren are teaching a "different gospel" (1:6). This "gospel" includes human works as a means of salvation. To add anything to the work of Christ on the cross "nullifies the grace of God," and implies that "Christ died needlessly" (2:21).

Christ's death on the cross is a finished work that covers sin's penalty (justification), sin's power (sanctification), and someday, sin's presence (glorification). Humans add nothing to Christ's atoning work on the cross, but the sin that placed Him there.

And now, in Galatians 5:1, Paul reminds the Galatian believers of the fact (indicative) that since "Christ set us free," His indwelling Spirit enables us to keep His commands. Man's ability or power to keep God's commands is possible only because His Spirit indwells us. In other words, it takes God in us to obey God.

Herein, we see the shift in the letter. From Galatians 5 until the end of the book, Paul will charge the Galatian believers with twelve imperatives (commands). The believers will not be able to accomplish even one of these commands without God's Spirit. Sadly, this will not stop them (or us) from trying on their own.

Therefore, in view of the stick figures, let's review the imperatives in Galatians 5:

1) Keep standing firm (5:1).

2) Do not be subject ***again*** to the yoke of slavery (5:1).

3) Through love, serve one another (5:13).

4) Take care lest you be consumed by one another (5:15b)

5) Walk by the Spirit (5:16)

> How are these commands possible?
>
> Will they be accomplished by the works of our residual flesh or by His Spirit?

Do you see that every command is possible **<u>because</u>** His Spirit resides within? Only God can keep God's requirements, which is why Christ had to die!

Do you also see how the Enemy can tempt the believer into relying on his residual flesh and the world to accomplish what God requires? Our residual flesh is a magnet to works—our works!

Works of the Law versus Faith in Christ

↓ ↓

Our residual flesh/ God's Spirit

The ways of the world

Every time you and I try to keep His commands by striving in our flesh, or by relying on the world, we are guilty of nullifying the grace of God, and, in essence, saying that Christ's death was needless (2:21). God forbid!

As you look at the command to walk by the Spirit in Galatians 5:16, do you see that this is the *how-to*, in terms of not fulfilling the desires of the flesh?

As I thought about Galatians 5:16, I could not help but think about the believer's three enemies, as stated in Ephesians 2:1-3, namely: 1) the world, 2) Satan, and 3) the flesh.

Would it surprise you to discover that the way to overcome all three enemies is the exact same? For example, let's look at what Scriptures say regarding the believer's three enemies:

1) The world – Look at 1 John 5:4 and record how the believer overcomes the world. What do you see? How do we overcome the world?

____

Keep in mind that faith has three components, specifically:

a) A firm conviction of God's Word. Remember, our conviction begins with God's Spirit, who is the one who convicts and, He uses God's Word. Therefore, the first component of faith is God's Spirit, using God's Word.

b) A personal surrender of the will to God's Word.

c) Obedience to God's Word.

All three are necessary for saving faith. Therefore, to be saved from the world, the believer surrenders and obeys God's Spirit, and He illumines God's Word.

2) **Satan** - Look at James 4:7 and list the three parts of this verse in the order Scripture records them. Note, the order matters greatly!

a) ____________________ to God.

b) ____________________ the devil

c) and He will ________________________ from ________________.

Note: To submit to God is precisely the same thing we see in the three components of faith, as listed above in the definition. When we submit to God, we are surrendering our will and obeying His Word as His Spirit illumines the Word to our hearts.

3) **The flesh** - Look again at Galatians 5:16. What are we commanded?

________________ by the Spirit, and you will not carry out the desire of the flesh.

Do you see the order? Walking by the Spirit is *how* the desires of the flesh are put to death. What does it mean then to walk by the Spirit? What will He use?

Every time we surrender our will and obey God's Word by the illuminating work of God's Spirit, the world, Satan, and our flesh are defeated!

To attempt to gain victory over any (or all) of these three enemies is futile in our flesh. Only by God's Spirit do we overcome. Praise God for the finished work of the cross of Jesus Christ and His indwelling Spirit!

Do you see that whether we *have been saved* from the **penalty** of sin (justification), or we *are being saved* from the **power** of sin (sanctification), or we *will be saved* from the **presence** of sin (glorification) is by *faith* alone *in Christ* alone?

How foolish and deceptive to think that we could ever be justified, sanctified, or glorified by the works of the Law! Salvation is by grace through faith alone! Therein lies Paul's point.

As we have summarized Galatians 5, let's continue to examine the imperatives given in Galatians 6.

LESSON 12

RESTORING A BROTHER OR SISTER IN CHRIST

GALATIANS 6:1

It's something we all shudder to think about; and yet, it is a reality all believers face—the propensity to sin and even worse, the potential to fall. Although saved by the grace of God, we have been left with residual flesh that opposes the Spirit of God, and we are all daily vulnerable to the lure of sin. Sadly, the believer who does not think it could happen to him or her is the one in most danger. While we remain on this earth, no believer is immune. Why else would Jesus, while teaching His disciples how to pray, include the phrase, "And lead us not into temptation but deliver us from evil" (Mt. 6: 13)? He knew we would need to be delivered. Why else would Jude conclude his letter with the statement, "Now to Him who is able to keep you from stumbling, and to make you stand in the presence of His glory blameless with great joy," if it were not possible to stumble? Why do you think Peter called Jesus the Shepherd and Guardian of our souls if our souls did not require being daily shepherded and guarded (1 Pet. 2:25)? Wouldn't Peter of all people know this fact? We are no different than Peter.

So, according to Galatians 6:1, what are we to do when we find that we have stumbled into a trap because we love ourselves more than God and others? What if we discover that our brother or sister has also fallen in the same trap and needs restoration? The likelihood is high, for in the words of Paul David Tripp, "No one is a grace graduate."[155]

As we continue in the practical application portion of the Book of Galatians, keep in mind that everything the Lord commands His children to do is not only possible, but it is evidence that He reigns in you. Jesus came to die for us so that He could live in us by His Spirit and do for us what we could never do if left to ourselves. What an amazing God! Let's see what that might look like in our lives today.

You will recall from former lessons that the context of walking in the Spirit rather than in the flesh is love. Not the mushy-gushy love that men and women have the ability to muster within themselves, especially when they are the recipients of the love, but that deep love that requires the very Source of love within. Not the love of feelings alone but a volitional love, which involves the direction of the will. It is based upon what God deems best and not necessarily what we want. And because He is God and knows all things, this love trusts the Source to act in a manner that brings Him glory and our highest good. This love (because He is the Source) understands that He alone is God and that we are not!

As we begin this lesson, consider the words of Dr. MacArthur, as he so aptly sets up this portion of Galatians, stating,

> *The most important pursuit for all Christians, individually and corporately, is holiness. The first mission of the church is to honor and glorify God, and He can be honored and glorified by His children only as they grow to be like Him in character. Although evangelism is the cutting edge of the church's ministry, holiness is the only foundation on which effective evangelism or any other ministry can be built. The supreme priority of the church is holiness, purity of inward life. God can*

155. Paul David Tripp, *New Morning Mercies* (Wheaton, IL: Crossway, 2014), March 30 excerpt.

> *accomplish whatever He desires through a believer or a church that is holy, but He can do little through one that is not.*
>
> *Positively, holiness involves growing in Christlikeness, in knowledge of and obedience to God's Word, and in submission to His Spirit. Negatively, it involves correcting that which is impure, first in a believer's own life and then also in the lives of other believers.*[156]

Did you notice that there is a positive and negative aspect of holiness? A person can lose sight of the holiness (set-apartness) of God when he or she believes that they are god. Our flesh's desire to be god competes with the holiness of God for He alone is God. He alone is Creator of all things. Nothing created (whether heavenly or earthly) can remotely compare.

In addition, there is a positive and negative aspect of God's love as well. Think about Paul's admonition which states, "Let love be without hypocrisy. Abhor what is evil; cling to what is good" (Rom. 12:9). Positively, we are to love. Therefore, the negative aspect of loving God is to hate the things He hates, which is evil, and when necessary, will incur the discipline of the Lord.

If you think about hypocrisy, rather than loving God and others, you actually just love yourself. Your love for God and others is just a disguise or mask for your love for self. Tragically, the love a person has for self can cause them to miss the true scope of their life, which is to know, love and glorify Him forever. Self-love competes with the love He alone deserves and it's in all of us!

Therefore, in this portion of Galatians, we will look at the negative side of His holiness and love. We will examine the need for reproof and correction when we veer from either because we can veer so easily (2 Tim. 3:16). Remember, the propensity of our residual flesh is to wander away from God's holiness (set-apartness) because our flesh yearns to be god and to stray from the love of God and others because we are prone to love ourselves more. And for these reasons, thankfully, we have been given His Spirit and His Word to keep us on the right path.

As we proceed, let's do so cautiously and prayerfully, for this message is to every believer since the potential to fall lurks within our residual flesh. Let's get started.

1. First, notice to whom Paul is addressing in this section of Scripture. Whom do you see?______________________

2. Without trying to be redundant, and by process of elimination, whom is he not addressing? _________________

The purpose of noting to whom Paul is addressing is important. Too often, we (believers) are holding unbelievers to the same standard of conduct. We can easily get frustrated when an unbeliever is trapped in sin. We can become exasperated when they just don't seem to get it or worse when we realize that they do not even want out of the trap. We tend to forget that it is God's indwelling Spirit who gives us the desire to hate and escape sin and provides the power necessary to get out of its snare.

Furthermore, we must establish that in verse one, Paul is addressing a *hypothetical* situation because the word "if" used here with the verb, *caught*, is in the subjunctive mood, which makes the action a possibility or a potential deed. Paul could be talking about any believer because, as we have noted, no man or woman is above the situation Paul is describing.

3. In what specifically is the man *caught* (v. 1)? _____________________________________

---

156. John MacArthur, Jr., *The John MacArthur New Testament Commentary Galatians*, (Chicago: Moody Press, 1987), pp. 174-175.

As we begin to examine Galatians 6:1, we must first take into consideration that there are two potential viewpoints to be deliberated, namely:

1) Was the man caught in the act of sin?

or

2) Was the man caught up in a sin?

Dr. Zodhiates explains the two options concisely, by stating,

> *If the preposition* by (en) *is taken to mean the instrument, then the idea is that the* fault (paraptoma) *catches the individual by surprise, suddenly, without notice, i.e., before he is aware of what has happened.*
>
> *However, the concessive phrase "even if," seems to introduce an exceptional case, implying a scandalous or flagrant sin. The preposition could, therefore, be taken as a locative (a grammatical case indicating place or direction) and have reference to someone being caught in the act of a particular sin (definition included in parenthesis added for clarity).*[157]

The latter example would be a case such as the woman caught in the act of adultery in John 8:2–10.

Because of these two competing views, we must look at the context, the specific verbs used (as well as the one not used), and the verb's tense, mood and voice for help.

Note: First, the word "caught" (*prolambano*), in its most basic definition, means to be overtaken.[158] In Galatians 6:1, it is in the aorist tense, which indicates at a point in time (rather than the present tense), which would suggest that this is not the habit of the individual's life. In other words, Paul is referring to a believer who is caught in any given trespass. The passive voice is used, which signifies that the subject has been acted upon by an outside source.

4. As you consider that the word "caught" means to be overtaken at a point in time and that it is in the passive voice, what comes to mind?

Also noteworthy is the specific word Paul chose for sin, as well as the one he did not choose. For example, he used the Greek noun *paraptoma*, translated "trespass," which means to fall by the wayside into error and wrongdoing as opposed to the word *parabasis*, which would have been a stronger word that involves a willful sin and includes guilt.[159]

5. As you consider the things mentioned, and the context of the previous verses of study, which is it? Is Paul addressing the man caught in the act of a sin, or is he addressing the man caught up in a particular sin? What are your thoughts?

When I think of the verb "caught" in the passive voice, I cannot help but think about the trap of the Enemy. Can you see why a boastful person from our previous verse (Galatians 5:26), has the propensity to set himself up for an

157. *Ibid.*
158. Spiros Zodhiates, *The Complete Word Study New Testament Dictionary* (Chattanooga: AMG Pub.,1993), 1222.
159. *Ibid.,* 1113.

outside trap from the enemy? Pride, which is rooted in a desire to be god, and is motivated by self-love, becomes the lure that the Enemy can use to put you and me in his trap. Even worse, when this happens, we are deceived and have no idea that we have just stepped into his trap.

Furthermore, the word Paul used for "sin" (*paraptoma*), which means to fall by the wayside into error, makes me think how the Spirit of God uses the Word of God to reprove and correct (2 Tim. 3:16). Since every believer has the propensity within to get off track, aren't you grateful that the Holy Spirit uses God's Word to help us get back on track?

In either case, whether the man is caught in the act of sin or finds himself caught up in a sin, the main issue is that this man needs restoration.

So, what are we to do with the one caught in a trap of sin?

6. First, let's note to whom Paul appeals on behalf of the one caught in a trespass (v. 1)?

Note: The word "spiritual" (*pneumatikos*) is defined as, "a body dominated by the Spirit in contrast to an unbeliever (natural) soulish, which obeys one's natural instincts."[160]

7. As you look at the definition of the word, *spiritual*, what do you see? Who can help in the restoration of another brother or sister in need? Any thoughts?

8. What is the goal of the one who is *spiritual*? In other words, what is his purpose in this verse?

To ____________________________________

Note: The word "restore" (*katartizo*) is used metaphorically, of a person in error, to set one right.[161] In the physical realm, this exact word is used in Mark 1:19 in reference to the *mending* of fishing nets. Similarly, this same word might also be used in reference to an orthopedic doctor who *sets* a bone after it has been broken.

If you think of the word "restore" as it was literally used pertaining to fishing nets and the setting of bones, why would the fisherman need to repair his nets, or why would the doctor need to reset a bone? How are these literal uses helpful in interpreting Galatians 6:1? What do you see?

Note: Aren't both rendered useless without repair?

9. In addition, the word "restore" is a present imperative active verb. Remember, the present tense signifies a continual action, and the imperative mood is a command that the subject performs (active voice). With this added information, what do you see?

160. *Ibid.,* 1185.
161. *Ibid.,* 842.

10. Now, record *how* the spiritual one is commanded to restore another?

Would it surprise you that the *how-to* involves the fruit of the Spirit? The word "gentleness" (*praotes*) can be deceiving if not properly defined. It is primarily not an outward expression but an inward grace of the soul. Look back at the previous lesson where this word is specifically identified as a fruit of the Spirit. What do you see?

As I thought about the word "restore," I could not help but think about the pain involved when a bone needs to be reset and who I would want to perform that task. Wouldn't you want someone trained and gentle to restore your bone to its former usefulness? Don't you see that restoration of a bone is not optional if that limb is ever going to be functional again to the body? These thoughts then bring us to the next part of the restoration process.

11. What must the one who is restoring another do first and why (v. 1b)?

Caution: Before going to another, first take a look at yourself. Ask the Lord what the motive of your heart is in going. Keep in mind that you do not know your own heart (Jer. 17:9-10).

On a personal note, I am always leery of someone who is quick to correct and confront others. In fact, confronting the sin of another should be done only when the Spirit of God has given you a clear Word, and then, sent you. In other words, you would only go to another if not to go would result in disobedience.

Note: Be warned; if you have not allowed God's Spirit to apply His Word and restore you first then you have no business trying to restore another. Can you imagine going to a physician who, with an injured and debilitated hand, was attempting to mend yours? How *useful* would he be to you?

12. For additional biblical support, look at Matthew 7:3-5 to discover what Jesus said about this issue. What do you see? Notice carefully what Jesus calls such a person.

Keep in mind that Galatians 6:1, due to the verb used as well as the tense, mood, and voice, is about restoring a brother or sister who has been caught in the trap of a sin. Remember, the "trespass" (*paraptoma*), which is mentioned in Galatians 6:1, is not the stronger word, *parabasis*, which is both willful and guilt-ridden. And the aorist tense is used, meaning a punctiliar action and not the continuous habit of their life (present tense).

You may be thinking, *So what if the sin of a "brother" or "sister" is willful and habitual? What if they know the truth and they are deliberately choosing to remain in the sin?* A good example of how to biblically deal with *parabasis* can be found in 1 Corinthians 5. Let's take some time to examine this passage about restoration.

Note: Before we consider 1 Corinthians 5, we must first put the chapter in context. First, it has been reported to Paul that a man in the Corinthian church, who has professed to be a Christian, is having an immoral relationship with "his father's wife" (1 Cor. 5:1). Whether it is his mother or his stepmother, we are not told. We are told, however, that the sin being addressed is immorality within the church. We will pick up in verse two, where Paul addresses the church on the issue.

13. Answer the following questions using 1 Corinthians 5:

a. Notice how Paul addresses the church. What word does he use to describe them in verse 2?

____

b. What two things have they not done (v. 2)? 1) ___________________________________

2) ___________________________________

Note: You may rest assured that God's Spirit was grieved and mourning.

c. Now read verses 3–5. Note that even though the church had not chosen to handle the situation correctly, Paul (although not physically present with them) had made a choice. What did he decide to do in response to this man's sin (v. 5)?

d. Why had Paul made this choice according to verse 5?

Consider the following illustration of 1 Corinthians 5:5, in light of the stick figures we have been using throughout the workbook.

"I have decided to deliver such a one to Satan" (1 Cor 5:5).

The Umbrella of the Church

Protected

In Christ

The Umbrella of the World

Exposed

In the world (god of this world)

If God's Spirit resides within, when removed, God's Spirit is grieved, and the believer would be miserable and repent.

If God's Spirit does not reside within, when removed, they are more comfortable in the world.

e. Now read verse 6. Of what sin does Paul accuse the church? ________________________

What do they obviously not know (v. 6)?

____

____

f. Now, let's pause for a moment to address the boasting to which Paul accuses the church. What is boastful or prideful about not addressing known sin in the church? (**Hint:** Go back to the root issue.)

____

____

____

g. What was the solution to the leaven that had crept into the church according to verse 7?

Note: The word "clean" (*ekkathairo*), is used metaphorically meaning to purge, to make clean, to cleanse thoroughly. In this case, it means to put away.[162]

What if I told you that the word translated "clean out" is a command? When commands like this are given, don't we all have a tendency to want to *pick and choose* the ones we want to obey? Are we ever given that liberty?

h. What does Paul remind the believers in Corinth about themselves in verse 7?

Note: Since "leaven" in Scripture represents sin, the word "unleavened" is a reference to "no sin." It doesn't mean sinless but blameless. In other words, no man is sinless (save Christ), but we are commanded to be blameless. Blamelessness indicates that what sin has been committed has been biblically dealt with and forgiven.

i. What does Paul say about Christ (the sinless Lamb of God), and why does He bring this to their attention at this point?

Dr. MacArthur's comments on this verse are helpful. He explains,

> *As pictured in the Passover in Egypt, the sacrifice of Jesus Christ, God's perfect Passover Lamb, and the placing of His blood over us, completely separates us from the dominion of sin and the penalty of judgment. We, too, are to remove everything from the old life that would taint and permeate the new. As Israel was set free from Egypt as a result of the Passover and was to make a clean break with that oppressor, so the believer is to be totally separated from his old life, with its sinful attitudes, standards and habits. Christ died to separate us from bondage to sin and give us a new bondage to righteousness (Rom 6:19), which is the only true freedom.*[163]

Now, read verse 8. Notice that Paul references the celebration of the feast. This is a reference to the Lord's Supper, which is an ordinance commemorating Christ's death and all that it accomplished for the believer.

j. According to Paul in verse 8, there is an incorrect and correct way to observe the Lord's Supper (feast).

What is an incorrect manner? a) ____

nor

b) ____

nor

c) ____

What, then, is the correct manner?

162. *Ibid.,* 540.

163. John MacArthur, Jr., *The John MacArthur New Testament Commentary: 1 Corinthians* (Chicago: Moody Press, 1984), 129.

The unleavened bread of ____________________________________

and

____________________________________.

Now, as we look at verses 9–13, Paul reiterates what he had already written to the Corinthians in a previous letter. Let's look at what he said.

k. What had Paul stated specifically in his previous letter according to verse 9?

____

l. Now watch as Paul qualifies the immoral.

1) First, who was Paul not addressing (10)? ______________________________

Who does he add to the list with the immoral of the world (v. 10)?

____

____________________________________ Note: These are all nouns.

____

2) Second, to whom is Paul addressing (v. 11)? ______________________________

if he should be a) ______________________________________

b) ______________________________________

c) ______________________________________

All Nouns.

d) ______________________________________

e) ______________________________________

f) ______________________________________

not even to ____ (v. 11).

Note: The word "if" is a hypothetical situation because the Greek verb translated "should be," is present subjunctive active. The present tense indicates a continuous action or habit of life, while the subjunctive mood is used when the action is thought of as possible or potential. The active voice indicates that the subject is the one performing the action.

Moreover, all the descriptions mentioned in verse 11 are nouns, which represent their state of being. When you add the subject, "so-called brother" with these specific nouns, you can easily understand why Paul doubts their claim to Christ. In other words, their profession does not coincide with their state of being, which would become manifest in their habitual actions. When what someone says does not match what they do, this is a clear indication of deception on the part of the "so-called" brother. Heartbreakingly, not only is this person deceived, more than likely, he is not saved.

And finally, to eat with one another, in Scripture, was a demonstration of close fellowship. In fact, it is a reference to communion (the Lord's Supper) as referenced earlier in verse 8. Just as sin breaks fellowship with God, it also causes a break in fellowship with one another. When I am not in fellowship with the Lord, then I typically find myself at odds with others as well.

By refusing to eat with the one who is living in sin, yet professes to be a believer, you are demonstrating what is really happening between that person and the Lord. In other words, you are His living instrument pointing another to the weight and consequence of their sin. This action demonstrates God's love and your love for the one who is living apart from God. Keep in mind, however the refusal to eat is with the "so-called" brother in Christ who is living in sin.

m. What does Paul ask in verse 12 about outsiders (also known as unbelievers)?

n. Now, look closely what he asks in verse 12 regarding believers?

o. Who is to judge those outside the church according to verse 13? ___________________

p. Now, notice what Paul says about the wicked within the church (v. 13)?

Note: Again, Paul quotes from the Old Testament to make his argument. This time, he quotes several places in Deuteronomy (13:5; 17:7 and 12; 21:21 and 22).

At this point in the lesson, you might be thinking, "What might the restoration of a brother look like?" How is that command to be lived out in my life? Of course, the answer is in God's Word. In fact, Jesus addresses this issue in Matthew 18 specifically.

14. Let's begin by reading Matthew 18:15–17. Do you see that Jesus is outlining how to handle the sin of a brother (or sister) in Christ? Let's look at the steps Jesus instructs us to take in the order they are given.

a. What is the first step to take if a brother (or sister) sins (v. 15)?

Note: The word translated "sin" (*hamartano*) means to miss the mark, to do evil or wrong against another.[164] It is in the aorist tense indicating a particular point in time (as opposed to present tense, which would be continuous in action).

1) ________________________________

and

________________________________ in ______________________________;

b. If he listens, you have ___________________ your brother.

1) What is the second step if he refuses to listen (v. 16)?

so that (purpose)

164. Spiros Zodhiates, *The Complete Word Study New Testament Dictionary* (Chattanooga: AMG Publishers,1993), 129.

2) BY THE MOUTH OF TWO OR THREE WITNESSES EVERY ______________ MAY BE CONFIRMED.

Note: Jesus quoted Deuteronomy 19:15 in His instruction.

c. Now, if he still refuses to listen to them, what are you to do (v. 17)?

1)

d. What if he (or she) refuses to listen to the church?

1) Let him (or her) be to you as a ______________________________

and

____

15. Now that we have observed the text, let's take a moment to consider the specifics in Matthew 18:15–17. Answer the following question using the information you gathered in the question above:

Do you see compassion and wisdom in the order the steps were given? If so, what do you see?

Did you notice in verse 15, the specific word "sin"? Why is the word "sin" important in this entire situation? In other words, someone may do something to you that you do not like or agree with, but that does not give you the biblical right to confront in this manner. What do you see by the specific word used in view of these steps?

What might you use to *reprove* another? Hint: See 2 Timothy 3:16 for help.

How do you know when to move to the next step? What is the key repeated phrase?

Note: The word "listen" (*akouo*) literally means to hear with understanding so as to obey.[165]

What does it mean, then, for the one being confronted? Is hearing with the ear enough? What might it look like for the one who has sinned?

165. *Ibid.*, 113.

Did you notice what needed to be confirmed in verse 16? Why do you think He added the word "fact" in regard to confronting with witnesses?

What did it mean in Jesus' day for the Jew to treat someone as a Gentile and a tax-gatherer?

Do you see the progression in each step, namely: First in private, and then with two or three others, and lastly, in a very public arena? What do you see with this type of progression and why would it be important not to miss one of the steps?

And finally, what is the end goal of each step?

In Matthew 18:15-17, restoration with one-another is the focus. How we treat others in God's economy matters greatly. Ever since the Fall, restoration with God and others has been the goal. To think that you can be in fellowship with God and yet, out of fellowship with your brother or sister in Christ is sheer deception.

Also, never forget that it is the kindness of God that leads us to repentance (Rom. 2:4), even if it doesn't feel or look kind to others or us.

16. And now, since restoration with God and others is always the end goal, let's look at a few cross-references and answer the specific questions regarding each reference:

a. Psalm 19:7 – What is in need of restoration? ______________________________

What does He use to restore? ______________________________

b. Psalm 23:3 - What is in need of restoration? ______________________________

c. Psalm 51:12 – What is in need of restoration? ______________________________

Note: Although joy is explicitly mentioned, do you see that the underlying issue is the turmoil in David's soul?

1) As you read Psalm 51, what has caused David to lose the joy of His salvation?

Note: Joy is affected when our sin has grieved the Holy Spirit, because it is one of the nine-fold fruit of the Spirit.

2) Do you think joy is the only aspect affected? How might the other aspects of fruit be affected as well? What would that look like? Be specific.

3) Did you notice that David did not say, "my salvation"? What do you see here?

Did you notice that all the cross-references I used come from the Psalms? That's because I once heard Alistair Begg refer to the Psalms as the "medicine chest for the soul." Aptly spoken, don't you think?

Where do you turn to medicate your soul?

Is reading the Psalms enough or are we called to be doers of the Word (James 1:22)?

Wouldn't being a doer of the Word require surrender and obedience?

WHAT ABOUT YOU?

What if while reading this you find a description of your life? What should you do? According to Galatians 6:1, you should go to a brother or sister who has matured in their walk to help in time of the need for restoration.

If you are walking with the Lord Jesus, and God in His mercy and kindness, has sent someone your way to ask for help, will you be a vessel to point them to Jesus, the Savior, and His life-restoring Word?

Take care not to point them to yourself. You never want someone depending upon you as if you are the Savior. There is only one Savior, and we are not Him! We are merely pointers!

So where do you point others?

Has the Lord entrusted someone in your life for restoration? I can assure you He will not send another your way if you need restoration or if you have been unwilling to bow the knee. You cannot lead anyone farther than where you are. Dead people are not up tending the living, nor can sick people nurse those who are sick.

However, when you have allowed the Lord Jesus to heal your heart, you will find yourself a compassionate listener and pointer instead of a critical and self-righteous judge.

On a personal note: ashamedly, there was a time in my life when I had a very critical and judgmental spirit. In all honesty, as I look back, it was just fear disguised in self-righteousness. It was easier to see the sin of another rather than deal with my own hidden sin, guilt, and shame.

But when I allowed the Great Physician to take the scalpel of His Word to those areas of my heart I thought I had kept hidden, He used His Word to heal me. In His grace, the Spirit of God took the Word of God to open my eyes, and I cried out for my Savior. As I surrendered and obeyed what He had revealed to my heart, He used His Word to sanctify my heart and set me free from the *power*, which that hidden sin had had over me. In essence, all that was left was a scar of remembrance.

As I continued to walk in the freedom His Son had purchased with His blood, He began to send others to me. Not for me to heal anyone, but to show them my scar and tell them of a time when that scar represented a pus-filled infected wound that I had been trying to hide, cover, or blame on others.

As I began to share with others how the Lord Jesus healed my heart by allowing His Spirit to take His Word and heal me, I began to see Him transform others as well. As I reflect back, I see that He was entrusting other people to me so that I would point them to Him. You see, scars don't hurt. They are simply reminders of a time of great pain and suffering. They serve as a testimony of a great Savior who rescued, delivered, and healed a person who was in desperate need!

As this continued to happen, I found such a softening in my heart for others. There was absolutely no way I was going to criticize or judge them for the same things of which I had been forgiven. And if I had not participated in the same things, I had either thought of doing them or had not done them solely by the grace of God. It's amazing when you let the Holy Spirit deal with your heart how compassionate you can be to others. It's actually His compassion dominating my critical residual flesh, and I find myself so grateful that I have a Savior who is still rescuing me from me!

WHAT ABOUT YOU?

Will you let Him restore to you the joy of His salvation (Ps. 51:12)?

Will you allow Him to use you as He restores another?

Summary of Galatians 6:1

In keeping with the stick figures, let's visualize the sixth imperative (out of the twelve listed in Galatians 5—6. Keep in mind; the imperatives are written to believers because only the believer has God's indwelling Spirit. Christ in you by His Spirit is the enabling power, which causes us to keep God's commands.

"Brethren, even if a man is caught in any trespass, you who are spiritual, restore such a one in a spirit of gentleness; *each one* looking to yourself, lest you too be tempted." (Gal. 6:1)

Who is Paul addressing? Brethren: The Believer

What is the situation being addressed? Caught in any trespass

You will recall that the word "caught" means to be overtaken or overcome by sin's power, and the word "trespass" means to fall by the wayside into error.

WHAT MIGHT THAT LOOK LIKE?

How can a believer get caught in the trespass of sin if he belongs to the Lord Jesus?

Remember, the believer still has three enemies, namely: Satan (The Enemy), The World, and Man's Residual Flesh.

What in the heart of the believer makes us prone to sin? Look at the contrast below:

Trespass of Sin	versus	**Freedom in Christ**
↓		↓
Works of the Flesh		Surrender & Obedience
Ways of the World		
↓		↓
Temptation of the Enemy		God's Spirit & God's Word

Our residual flesh

Vices of the Enemy's temptation

Ways of the world

Anytime the believer succumbs to the Enemy's temptation via the residual flesh or the ways of the world, our relationship remains intact; however, our fellowship with the Lord and other believers becomes broken, rendering us useless to the Master.

Note: When I say *useless*, I mean in terms of service. Rather than serving the Lord and others, we serve ourselves!

WHO IS COMMANDED TO HELP? You who are spiritual

Note: The word "spiritual" means those with God's Spirit. Therefore, Paul is exhorting the believer.

WHAT ARE WE COMMANDED TO DO IN THIS SITUATION? Restore such a one

Note: Remember, the word "restore" is an orthopedic term used when a doctor sets a bone that has been broken. If not correctly set, the limb is rendered useless. Although this is a painful procedure, when properly applied, it can heal and restore the body to its proper use.

As you consider the stick figure below, how useful is the one with the broken bone?

Do you see how the entire body can be affected when one part requires restoration?

HOW IS THE ONE TO BE RESTORED (BONE SET)? In a spirit of gentleness

Note: Gentleness is an inward grace of the soul. Grace comes from God alone. It is a fruit of God's Spirit (Galatians 5:23), as He uses God's Word.

THE HUMAN INSTRUMENT GOD USES: *Each one* looking to yourself, lest you too be tempted.

Would the Lord use another who is equally in need of restoration to restore another?

Only one who is submitting to God's Spirit by surrendering their will and obeying God's Word can help another who needs restoration. In other words, only someone who is spiritually well can be a useful instrument in the Master's hand to help another who is in need.

WHAT IS HIS ULTIMATE PURPOSE? RESTORATION

As I thought about this lesson, my mind went back to when my son was in the tenth grade. While at baseball practice, he dove to catch a ball and landed with full body weight on his elbow—OUCH! When we took him into the Emergency Room, the x-ray revealed a severely dislocated elbow. The nurse gave him a little dose of a medication to produce amnesia before the doctor came into the room to reset his elbow, so that he would not remember the pain.

His arm healed, but I will never forget the pain and suffering he endured while his elbow was reset. I am grateful that he has no memory of the pulling and yanking that went on that day in the ER. However, without the skill of the ER professionals that day, my son would have no use of his arm today. Can you imagine how ineffective the doctor and nurse would have been had their arms been injured? Neither would have been able to restore my son's arm. Thankfully, they were both knowledgeable and useful, and my son's arm, although in a sling for weeks, was wholly restored that day.

NOTES

Lesson 13

Bear One Another's Burdens

GALATIANS 6:2–5

We have been looking at the imperative (command) portion of Paul's letter to the Galatian churches (Galatians 5—6). Nothing could be more practical or necessary than biblical restoration. We need it, and other believers need it too. Let's face it; every believer needs the reproof and correction from God's Word, or 2 Timothy 3:16–17 is not true. And we know every word uttered in Scripture is true!

I once heard a seminary professor say, "Conflict is normal." At first, his statement offended me because I hate conflict so much. In fact, I try to avoid it at all costs. My initial response after hearing this statement, although nonverbal, was strong. In my head I said, *Are you kidding me, conflict is anything but normal!*

But as I listened to my professor, he explained that conflict, which entered at the Fall, involves separation from God and others. Even the life of a believer can be filled with internal strife as our residual flesh wars with God's residing Spirit. Sadly, when we refuse to surrender and obey God's Spirit, the flesh wins out, and the conflict within manifests itself externally as we can become separated from the joy and fellowship with God and others.

In the last lesson, we examined in some detail the command to biblically restore a brother (or sister) caught in the trap of sin. In this lesson, we will pick up on the theme of restoration because verses 2–5 are vitally connected with restoration (Gal. 6:1) and what it means to walk by the Spirit (Gal. 5:25).

In Galatians 6:2–5, we will continue to look at two imperatives (commands) to discover what it means to be useful vessels for the Master as He brings about restoration. If you are like me, you may be surprised at what you see. Let's begin.

1. What are we commanded to do in Galatians 6:2a?

At first glance, what does it mean to "Bear one another's burdens?"

If you are like me, you may have immediately thought of taking dinner to someone sick, helping a sister in a time of need, or praying for a sister in a time of trouble. Don't get me wrong, helping another physically or spiritually through prayer is only fitting and proper as the Spirit of God leads you. But as I studied, I was a bit taken back, for

Galatians 6:2 is set in the context of the restoration of a brother or sister trapped under a load of sin. Somehow, this changes things, don't you think? Allow me to explain.

Note: The word "bear" comes from the Greek word, *bastazo*, and in its literal sense, it means to take up and hold; to carry in the hands or on the shoulders, which is the duty of every servant.[166] The verb used is present imperative active. You will recall the present tense signifies a continuous action. The imperative mood indicates a command to be followed, and the active voice means that the subject is performing the action.

The word "burdens" (*baros*) means "weight," specifically in reference to its pressure. When used purposely in Galatians 6:2, it indicates sinful conduct and its consequences, resulting in trouble and sorrow.[167]

2. As you look at the information provided, what does it mean to "Bear one another's burdens"?

3. What will be the result of bearing another's burden, according to 2b?

4. To better understand the phrase, *the law of Christ*, let's look at a few cross-references. What do you see?

1) John 13:34–35

2) John 15:12

3) 1 John 3:23

4) Romans 13:8–10

What, then, is *the law of Christ*? ____

166. Spiros Zodhiates, *The Complete Word Study New Testament Dictionary* (Chattanooga, TN: AMG Publishers, 1993), 328.
167. Ibid., 323

5) Romans 5:5 – From where does the love of Christ come?

____

____

Clearly, the one without Christ cannot love God or others, right?

If you think about it, isn't this exactly what Jesus did for us? Didn't He come to *restore* what we lost in the Garden the day we chose to be like god, demonstrating a deeper love for self than Him? Was it not our *burden* He bore in His body on that tree? Wasn't the motivating factor the love He had for the Father and the love God had for us?

5. Now, let's go back and re-read Galatians 5. As we look at each imperative (command), you will discover a common theme. Let's begin.

   a. There are two imperatives in Galatians 5:1, and as you fill in the blanks, you will see them.

      "It was for freedom that Christ set us free; therefore, ____________________

      ______________________ ___________________ and __________ __________________

      be subject again to a yoke of slavery."

Do you see the two imperatives (commands) in this verse?

Remember, the liberty to which we have been set free in Christ is the freedom from the lie that we are God, which manifests itself as a love for self above God and others. In other words, we have been set free to become who and what we were created to be and do before the Fall.

Who were we created to be? People in need of God.

What were we created to do? Love God and others.

Christ, the God-Man, came to live as a human in total dependence upon the Father, completely filled with God's Spirit (Is 11:1-2). He did so to set us free so that we can be restored back to our rightful place as people in need of God so that we can love God, as He deserves, and one another.

As we have discovered, the believer still has residual flesh. Therefore, there is a propensity within every believer to be subject again to a yoke of slavery when we try to be god because we love ourselves more than God and others.

   b. The next imperative in Galatians 5 can be found in verse 13.

      "For you were called to freedom, brethren; (an indicative statement of fact),

      only *do* not *turn* your freedom into an opportunity for the flesh,

      but through ______________ ______________ one another."

Note: The words in *italics* were added by translators for grammatical clarity.

Do you see the imperative (command)? Do you see how you are to carry out the command?

   c. The next imperative is in verse 15.

      "But if you bite and devour one another, _______________ _______________ lest you be consumed by one another."

Do you see that this statement is just the negative way of stating the positive in verse 13?

d. In Galatians 5:16 you will see the next imperative.

"But I say, ________________ ______________ ______________ _________________, and

you will not carry out the desire of the flesh."

Note: If you walk in the Spirit, what might that look like? Look at the first characteristic of the fruit of the Spirit in verse 22? What do you see? ________________

e. Now, in Galatians 6:1, we find the next imperative (command).

"Brethren, even if a man is caught in any trespass, you who are spiritual,

______________________ such a one in a spirit of _____________________________ ..."

What is the motive behind the restoration of a brother (or sister) trapped in sin? ____________________________

f. Now let's connect Galatians 6:1–2 because when you are willing to restore another, you are essentially,

"______________ one another's _________________

and

thus

____________________ the law of Christ."

Do you see the two imperatives in Galatians 6:2? Again, what is the underlying motive for each?

---

5. Do you see the resounding theme? As you survey all the imperatives we've seen so far in Galatians 5—6, do you see the package in which each is wrapped?

_______________________ for ____________________

and

_______________________ for ____________________

Similarly, Jesus, when questioned by the lawyer in Matthew's Gospel, states that love for God and love for others <u>are</u> the fulfillment of the Law? See Matthew 22:35–40.

6. And who alone is the Source of that kind of love? ______________________

You see the liberty, which is found *only* in Christ Jesus, is the freedom to be restored back to our original created and designated place, to need and love God, which will result in loving others rather than ourselves.

While writing this, my heart burst into song, as the next thought that came to mind was the chorus from the hymn entitled, *And Can It Be?* Carefully consider the words of this great hymn by the late evangelist and pastor, Charles Wesley, as it captures God's amazing love and immense grace as He purchased our freedom. Wesley penned,

And can it be that I should gain

An interest in the Savior's blood?

Died He for me, who caused His pain?

For me, who Him to death pursued?

Amazing love! How can it be
That Thou, my God, should die for me!

He left His Father's throne above,

So free, so infinite His grace;

Emptied Himself to show His love,

And bled for Adam's helpless race.

Tis mercy all, immense and free;

For O my God it found out me.

Amazing love! How can it be
That Thou, my God, should die for me!

Long my imprisoned spirit lay

Fast bound in sin and nature's night;

Thine eye diffused a quickening ray,

I woke, the dungeon flamed with light.

My chains fell off, my heart was free;

I rose, went forth and followed Thee.

Amazing love! How can it be
That Thou, my God, should die for me!

No condemnation now I dread;

Jesus and all in Him is mine!

Alive in Him, my living Head,

And clothed in righteousness divine;

Bold I approach the eternal throne

And claim the crown, through Christ, my own.

Amazing love! How can it be
That Thou, my God, should die for me![168]

Precious and costly freedom. Amazing love!

---

168. The Master's Seminary, "And Can It Be?" (Los Angeles,CA: The Master's Seminary Press, 2015), 180.

7. One final thought before we leave the topic of liberty. Turn to John 18:12 and record what Jesus allowed both Jew and Gentile authorities to do to Him. What do you see?

_____________________ and _____________________

Now, look at John 18:24. What do you see? ____

Now, look at John 19:17. What is Jesus bearing in this verse? ________________________

How do the facts (indicatives) in John's Gospel make the commands (imperatives) in Galatians possible? What do you see? Any thoughts?

Note: When you read that Jesus allowed Himself to be bound so that we could be free and that He bore *His own cross*, which was for the sin of the world because He was sinless, can you see amazing love? Can you see why He would command us to stand firm in the liberty He purchased on our behalf? Can you imagine how it grieves His Spirit when we do not? Do you know that Christ died not just so that we could get out of hell and into heaven, but so that He could get out of heaven and into us? Hallelujah! What a Savior!

8. Now, as we continue in Galatians 6, and specifically at verse three, notice that Paul begins the verse with the word, "For" (*gar*), which means *because*, thereby connecting verse 3 with bearing one another's burdens (v. 2). Let's examine the connection a little closer.

Fill in the appropriate blanks:

For

If anyone _______________ he is _________________________

when he is _________________________

he _________________________ himself.

Note: The word "thinks" (*dokeo*), means to consider, to imagine, or to appear. The word is a present indicative active verb. The present tense indicates this is a continuous mindset. The indicative mood signifies a statement of fact, while the active voice means that the subject is performing the action.

In addition, the word "nothing" is used as a metaphor here, meaning, "of no account, no weight of character." While the word "deceives" comes from two Greek words: *phren*, the mind, and *apatao*, to deceive. In other words, the mind is ensnared and led astray. By the way, all three verbs used are in the present tense (continuous) and the active voice (meaning the subject is performing the action).

9. Now, as you look at the definitions and verbs used, how does Galatians 6:3 correlate with bearing another's burdens (v. 2)?

Consider the following commentary on Galatians 6:3, as Dr. John MacArthur explains,

> *One of the chief reasons many Christians do not bother to help fellow Christians is that they feel superior to sinners and wrongly consider themselves to be spiritually* **something** *when the truth is they are really* **nothing**. *Like the Pharisees, their concern is not for the true righteousness that God gives and that comes only through humility (see Matt. 5:3–8) but for their own self-righteousness, which has no part in God's kingdom or its work. Their desire is not to help a stumbling brother but to judge and condemn him.*[169]

MacArthur further warns, "Conceit can coexist with outward morality, but it cannot coexist with spirituality. In fact, conceit (pride) is the ultimate sin, first on the list of things God hates (Prov. 6:16–17). The Christian who **thinks he is something when he is nothing** needs help in facing his own sin before he can be qualified to help anyone else out of a sin."[170]

Do you see that the overarching propensity of man's flesh, whether the residual flesh of a believer or the dominating power in the unbeliever, is always toward conceit? So, what are we to do? The answer can be found in Galatians 6:4–5.

10. What does Paul urge the Galatian brethren to do in verse 4a?

Note: The word "examine" (*dokimazo*) means to put to the test, to try. It has the notion of proving a thing whether it is worthy or not.[171] The verb used is present imperative active. Again, we see an imperative (command), which is possible since the Source is the One accomplishing the action required. In this case, the Spirit is the indwelling examiner of our work.

Moreover, the word "work" is a noun. Dr. Zodhiates explains, stating, "Good works acceptable unto God are only possible through ***God's grace*** active in one's heart. They are always the result of salvation and not the means of salvation (emphasis added).[172]

a. If you consider the active grace of God (His Spirit and His Word), what is the proper work of every believer? [**Hint:** Think in terms of the believer's appropriate response to God's grace.]

b. So, according to Galatians 6:4a, when the believer allows God's Spirit and His Word to examine his own work (surrender and obedience), what will he then have reason to do (4b)?

c. What might it look like to boast in regard to yourself as you examine your own work? Any thoughts?

169. John MacArthur, Jr., *The John MacArthur New Testament Commentary Galatians* (Chicago, IL: Moody Press, 1987), 181.
170. *Ibid.*
171. Spiros Zodhiates, *The Complete Word Study New Testament Dictionary* (Chattanooga, TN: AMG Publishers, 1993), 475.
172. *Ibid.*, 651.

On a personal note, as I contemplated Galatians 6:4, I couldn't help but think when I allow God's Spirit to take God's Word to examine my work (whether I have submitted and obeyed), the *only* One in which I can boast is Jesus Christ! It is His residing Spirit that is the *cause* of my surrender and obedience (Ezk. 36:26–27). Therefore, my only boast is in Him! Isn't that what Paul is saying here?

d. If this is true, then, according to Galatians 6:4b, in what will we not have a reason for boasting?

e. Do you see that in Galatians 6:4b, we are not to compare ourselves with another? In fact, what reason would a believer ever have to boast? What does Paul say in 2 Corinthians 12:9? In what did he boast?

f. What would boasting in weakness accomplish? In other words, when we are weak, what does that make Christ?

11. Now, let's add Galatians 6:5 for clarity's sake. What is Paul sharing in verse 5?

At first glance, it seems as if Paul contradicts himself when you compare Galatians 6:2 with 6:5. Why would Paul command the brethren to bear another's burdens and then tell each one to bear his own load?

The answer is in the word "load" (*phortion*), which, in a literal sense, is a reference to the goods or merchandise carried by a ship, freight. However, in the New Testament, the word is used only figuratively as the burden of one's own responsibilities and failures. In other words, Christians are told that each person must assume responsibility for his duties in life. They have no right to shirk their responsibilities to expect others to perform them.[173] Notice that the emphasis in Galatians 6:5 is on one's own responsibilities.

12. Now, as you take the information provided in Galatians 6:4–5 regarding "each one," what do you see? Record your insights.

Do you see that when *each one* is looking to God's Spirit and God's Word in surrender and obedience, there is no competition or judgment of another? In fact, there is little to no time or energy left as we discover that we are a full-time project of God's amazing grace.

WHAT ABOUT YOU?

Are you a useful instrument in the Master's hands as you restore and bear one another's burdens?

Are you willing to examine your own work in the light of His Spirit and Word?

173. Ibid., 1452.

Are you bearing your own load or are you shirking your spiritual responsibilities so that another is burdened?

You see, restoring a brother (or sister) caught in the trap of sin (v. 1), bearing one another's burdens (v.2), and examining our own work (v. 4) are all imperatives (commands) made possible to the one surrendered and obedient because of the One who resides within.

Will you let Him do for you what you cannot do?

May our only boast be in Him!

To God *alone* be all glory!

Notes

Lesson 14

Sowing and Reaping

GALATIANS 6:6–10

In this lesson, we will look at one of the most known truths in all of Scripture, the law of sowing and reaping. The principle is universal in that it is relevant to both believer and unbeliever. The concept is true both physically and spiritually. Even a child can understand the simple truth that when you plant corn, you reap a harvest of corn and not wheat. Only a person who is deceived would expect otherwise. And that, my friend, is what can happen to us all, whether the unbeliever (who is controlled by the dominating flesh) or the believer (who will remain at war with the residual flesh until glorification). We can all become deceived in sowing and reaping; hence, the warning by Paul to the Galatians (and us).

Keep in mind that we are looking at the imperative portion (commands) in the Book of Galatians. In this section of Scripture, there are two imperatives. Let's look at each and see how all can be connected to the command to walk by the Spirit (Gal. 5:16, 25).

Let's get started by examining the first imperative (command) in this lesson, which can be found in verse 6.

1. Answer the following questions from Galatians 6:6:

   a. What is the command?

   ____

   b. Who is to obey this command? ______________________________

Note: The word "taught" is in present tense and passive voice, meaning that the subject is being acted upon by an outside source continually. In this case, the outside source would be those teachers who are teaching the gospel *of grace* alone *through faith* alone *in Christ* alone.

   c. What is to be shared? ______________________________

Note: The word "good" is *agathos*, which means something useful, profitable, beneficial. When you see the word *agathos*, you need to think God-good.

      1) Jesus defined the word "good" (*agathos*) in Mark 10:17–18. Read these verses and record His definition of good.

   ____

   d. With whom is it to be shared? ______________________________

      1) Let's look at one cross-reference in 1 Corinthians 9:14. What do you see?

   ____

2. With the information provided so far, how would you interpret Galatians 6:6?

Now, before we proceed, let's do a little more digging because as you know, every word in Scripture matters! Did you notice the word "share"? I think the meaning of this word will further help us in our attempt to interpret the passage accurately.

Note: First, the word "share"is translated from the Greek word *koinoneo*, which is better translated *fellowship*, *participation*, in keeping with a sharing in common with one another.[174] To better understand *koinoneo*, look at some of the cross-references of the noun, *koinonia*, to gain further insight.

3. Look up the following verses and record what you see about "fellowship" (*koinonia*)":

a. 1 John 1:3-

Do you see that for John to have *fellowship* (*koinonia*) with the recipients of the letter, they must first have *fellowship* with God the Father and His Son, Jesus Christ?

Think about the meaning of *fellowship*, which means *to share in common*. What do you and I have in common with God the Father?

Do you see that without Jesus Christ, there is no fellowship with God the Father and no true fellowship with one another?

b. 1 John 1:6 -

Do you see the deception in this verse regarding *fellowship*?

c. 1 John 1:7 -

174. Spiros Zodhiates, *The Complete Word Study New Testament Dictionary* (Chattanooga, TN: AMG Publishers, 1993), 873.

Do you see the way to true *fellowship* is also the way to avoid or escape deception in 1 John 1:7?

Note: We typically think of *good* things as material in nature, which is only part of the message being communicated here, but there is more at stake than just the physical provision. Even more importantly, by altering the gospel message, their spiritual fellowship had been compromised.

Rather than having fellowship with Paul and the true teachers of the gospel of grace, their fellowship with one another had been disturbed by the false teachers and their message of Christ plus the works of the law.

Consider the following comments from Dr. Wuest, as he explains, stating,

> *In neither the act of deserting grace for the law and that of committing an act of sin, could Spirit-filled Galatians hold fellowship with the Judaizers, for the latter were not teaching the Word of God nor were they ministering good things to them.*
>
> *Now the Judaizers had precipitated a situation in the Galatians churches in which those who followed their teaching broke fellowship with the true teachers of the Word. Paul resumes fellowship with teachers of the Word.*[175]

Make no mistake, as sad and harmful as the disruption of fellowship between Paul, and his spiritual children had been, there was an even more significant disturbance.

d. Look back at Galatians 1:6 and record the more significant issue. What do you see?

Now, as we return to Galatians 6, let's examine the next imperative (command) found at the beginning of Galatians 6:7.

4. Paul states, "Do not be ____.

   Again, what does that imply? ____

5. Because deception is a very real possibility for the believer, and the unbeliever lives continually with deception, let's see what Scripture has to say about it. Although not exhaustive, let's look at a few cross-references to discover the source, the target, the instruments, the cause, and the result of deception.

I. **The Source of Deception**:

a. Genesis 3:1 - ____

   Genesis 3:13 - ____

b. Revelation 12:9 - ____

   Who has he deceived? ____

c. Revelation 20:10 - ____

d. 2 Corinthians 11:3 - ____

e. John 8:44 – He is the father of ____

   What does "father" imply? ____

---

175. Kenneth S. Wuest, *Wuest's Word Studies From the Greek New Testament*: *Galatians*, Volume One (Grand Rapids, MI: Wm. B. Eerdmans Publishing Co., 1972), 170.

II. **The Targeted Place of Deception**:

a. Deuteronomy 11:16 – Note where deception occurs? ________________________________

and causes you to

____

and

____

b. Isaiah 44:20 – Note again, where the deception occurs? ________________________________

What has deception caused? ________________________________

c. Proverbs 12:20 - Where is deceit found? ________________________________

In whom is deceit found? ________________________________

d. Jeremiah 23:26 – Notice where the deception is occurring? ________________________________

Hebrews 3:10 – Note the place of deception. ________________________________

III. **The Vessels of Deception**:

a. Matthew 13:22 - ________________________________

Notice what is choked? ________________________________

Is money the issue, or does it bring out the real problem? What do you think?

____

b. Hebrews 3:13 - ________________________________

c, Again, Jeremiah 23:26 - ________________________________

Isn't that who Paul is targeting in the Book of Galatians?

d. Obadiah 1:3 - ________________________________

e. Ephesians 5:6 - ________________________________

f. 1 Corinthians 15:33 - ________________________________

g. 1 John 1:8 - ________________________________

h. 1 John 3:7-8 ________________________________

i. 2 John 7 - ________________________________

Notice how the many are explicitly described in reference to Jesus?

____

What does John equate in this verse? The ____________________________

and

The ____________________________

IV. The Cause of Deception:

a. Mark 12:24 – Jesus, answering the Sadducees, who had questioned Jesus, asked, "Is this not the reason you are *mistaken*? The word, *mistaken*, is better translated, *deceived* (*planao*). Why did Jesus say they were deceived? What was the cause?

1) ____________________________

2) ____________________________

Note: Do you see the Spirit of God and the Word of God in Jesus' answer? Wouldn't the cause of all deception Jesus described be true of all false religions?

b. Look down a few verses to Mark 12:27 where Jesus warns that they were greatly "mistaken" (*deceived*). Record the reason.

____

c. Do you see that not knowing God was the cause of their deception?

1 John 1:8 - ____________________________

James 1:22 - ____________________________

d. What is the anecdote for deception in James 1:21?

____

____

e. What is the Word implanted able to do? ____________________________

V. The Result of Deception:

a. Deuteronomy 11:16 - ____________________________

and

____

and

____

b. 1 Timothy 2:14 - ____________________________

c. Hebrews 3:13 - ____________________________

The ultimate result of deception –

d. Matthew 7:21-23 - ____________________________

e. 1 Corinthians 6:9-10 – ____

Although we did not cover every Scripture involving deception, the passages above paint a good picture of the very real state in which an unbeliever dwells, as well as the potential in which every believer may succumb and fall.

5. Now, looking back at Galatians 6:7, what do you learn about God?

Note: The term "mocked" (*mukterizo*), is interesting. It means, "to turn up one's nose in scorn."[176] The verb is present indicative passive. In other words, no one can continue to turn his or her nose up at God!

You might be thinking, "I know someone right now who is mocking God." That may be true right now, but look at the following cross-references and record what will happen at the end of all things. What do you see?

a. Philippians 2:10 -

b. Romans 14:11 -

c. Isaiah 45:23 -

Do you see that a person may mock and reject Him in *time*, but for all *eternity* he or she will confess that He is Lord!

6. Now, look at the entire phrase, "Do not be deceived, God is not mocked..." How do these two concepts fit together? We could add this to our information on deception, right? Any insight?

7. Now, let's look at Galatians 6:7–8 to discover ***how*** man is deceived. Through diagramming the verses on the next page, learn more about the result of a heart that is deceived. Fill in the blanks using Scripture.

176. Spiros Zodhiates, *The Complete Word Study New Testament Dictionary* (Chattanooga, TN: AMG Publishers, 1993), 999.

Galatians 6:7–8

6:7 [you]

do not be ________________________, **God** is not ________________________;

↓

for whatever a man _____________,

↓

this he will also ________________.

↓

↙ ↘

6:8 For the one BUT the one

who sows to _________ own __________ | who sows to the ____________________

↓ ↓

shall from the __________________ | shall from the _________________

↓ ↓

reap _____________________, | reap ___________________ _____________

Did you notice that there are only two modes from which to sow and two completely different outcomes?

Notice that the unbeliever can only sow from one field. The believer, on the other hand, can sow from both.

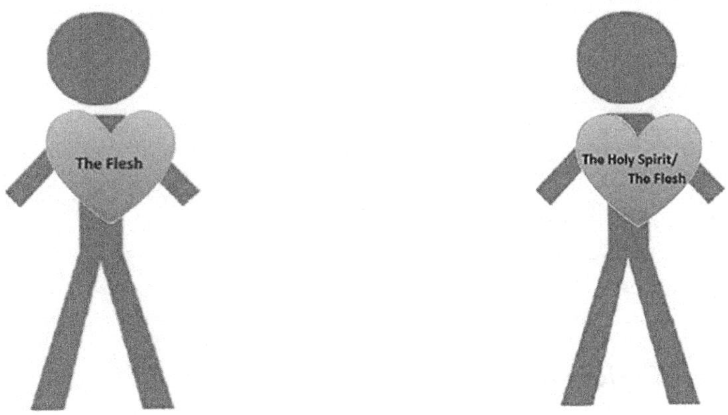

To help with the diagram, consider the following information:

Paul's use of an agricultural example brought simplicity and clarity to the point he was driving home. By offering the only two choices with subsequent consequences, there could be no misunderstanding the analogy.

Note: The word "corruption" (*phthora*) means to spoil, ruin, decay, ending in destruction. It is degenerative, making it progressively worse with time, allowing for much spoiling, ruin, decay, and destruction along the way until ultimately ending in death (Rom. 6:23).

8. Look at Hosea 8:7a and record what the prophet Hosea warns

Note: Do you see the point Hosea is making here? When we sow to the wind, we reap the whirlwind. In other words, what you sow may seem small, like a seed, but what you get in return is always much bigger than expected. In fact, it may even have the capacity to destroy.

9. As you look at the *results* of one who sows to the flesh while considering John 10:10, what do you see? Who is behind this corruption and death?

10. Now, let's look at the exact opposite result, eternal life. Look at 1 John 1:1–2 and list the facts concerning eternal life. Fill in the blanks.

1:1 What was from the beginning,

What we have __________________,

What we have __________________ with our eyes,

what we ________________________

and

our hands ________________

↓

concerning **the Word of** ________________

1:2 and

the __________________ was manifested,

and we have ___________________

and

bear ___________________ } to you

and

____

the ________________ ______________,

which was _____________ the ____________________

and

was ________________________ to ___________

11. Now, as you look at the facts from 1 John 1:1–2, what do you see about eternal life?

Doesn't it just make perfect sense that if you sow to God's Spirit, *from God's Spirit,* you will reap the Son? Do you see that the source from which a person sows can make all the difference?

12. Now, think with me:

 a. To which "field" would a salvation-by-works person be attracted? ________________________

 1) Who would be glorified? ________________________

In commenting on the religious person who seeks to sow to the flesh, Dr. Wuest points out that, "Man can go on in sin while seeking to buy the favor of God with his so-called good works."[177] Doesn't that sound like every religion apart from Christ? Can you see how this mindset could lead to corruption?

 b. To which "field" would a "saved by grace through faith" person be attracted? ________________________

 1) Who would receive all of the glory? ___________________________

13. As you look at verses 7–8, what were the Galatians deceived about? In other words, if deception means to say one thing and do the opposite, what was happening in the church at Galatia?

14. What does it mean to sow to the flesh? (Think back to the deeds of the flesh in Chapter 5.)

177. Kenneth S. Wuest, *Wuest's Word Studies From the Greek New Testament: Galatians, Volume One* (Grand Rapids, MI: Wm. B. Eerdmans Publishing Co., 1972),173.

15. Likewise, what does it mean to sow to the Spirit?

16. What sort of corruption might a believer experience if she should choose to sow to the flesh? Any thoughts?

17. What might it look like to reap eternal life for the believer who chooses to sow to the Spirit?

18. Now let's look at Paul's words of encouragement to the Galatians in verses 9–10.

a. What is Paul's admonition in verse 9a?

b. Why should they *not lose heart in doing good* (v. 9)?

Note: The English words "lose heart" derive from one Greek word, *ekkakeo*, which was used of a farmer tempted to slacken his exertions due to weariness caused by prolonged effort. Similarly, the word "weary" (*ekluo*) was used of "reapers overcome by heat and toil."[178]

You should also know that *ekkakeo* is a present subjunctive active verb. The subjunctive mood indicates that the action is thought to be probable or potential. However, *ekluo* is a present participle passive, meaning that the subject is being acted upon.

Furthermore, in the Greek language, there are two words used for *time*, namely: (1) *kairos*, which has to do with fixed seasons and distinct periods or opportune times, and (2) *chronos*, which is where our English word chronology is derived, and has to do with the succession of minutes.[179] In both Galatians 6:9–10, the word *kairos* is used.

And last, you will recall the word "good" from page one of this lesson. Both verses (9–10) use the word *agathos*, which qualify the *doing* Paul commends. Consider the following explanation, once again, from Dr. Wuest, as he describes the word as "not merely what may be good in character as judged by anybody's standards, but the good which is the product of the Holy Spirit through the saint."[180]

c. Now, as you consider all the information given, what might cause a believer to lose heart and grow weary?

178. Ibid.
179. Spiros Zodhiates, *The Complete Word Study New Testament Dictionary* (Chattanooga, TN: AMG Publishers, 1993), 805.
180. Kenneth S. Wuest, *Wuest's Word Studies From the Greek New Testament: Galatians*, Volume One (Grand Rapids, MI: Wm. B. Eerdmans Publishing Co., 1972)174.

(Think back to the "field" from which one sows to help with the answer.) What do you see?

d. What is the exhortation in verse 10? ____

When? ____

To whom? to ____________________________________

and

especially

to ____.

e. As you look at the recipients of the *good*, what do you see?

f. Look at 1 John 4:20–21 as a cross-reference to Galatians 6:10. What do you see?

g. As to the message in Galatians 6:9–10 in reference to *opportunity* and *due time* (*kairos*), look at 1 Peter 1:17b. What do you see?

Note: To *conduct yourself in the fear of the Lord* is just another way of saying, walk in the Spirit. Notice the time of stay on earth for each is different. In other words, before the foundation of the world, each of us has been given a time of stay on earth. All our days are numbered before one of them came into being (Ps. 139:16). Each will give an account of our own time of stay. Will the Lord say, on that day, "Well done, you conducted yourself in the fear of the Lord during the time of your stay on earth"? Isn't that what you want most to hear?

WHAT ABOUT YOU?

As you reflect on the truths in Galatians 6:6–10, think about the following questions and allow the Holy Spirit to do what only He can do—know and reveal your heart.

Is there any area of your heart where you are saying one thing but doing another?

Is there any part of your heart where you have turned your nose up at God (to mock)?

Into what "field" or "soil" are you sowing? Remember, there are only two.

Is your heart lacking the fruit of the Spirit in some area? Keep in mind that you cannot sow to the flesh while hoping to reap a harvest of fruit from the Spirit? If you find yourself lacking, you may be deceived.

What about the believer who has come again under the yoke of slavery to sin by listening to the lies of the enemy?

Have you found yourself burdened by the weight of trying to live the Christian life in your residual flesh or by the world's methods?

19. If this describes you, read Matthew 11:28–30 and answer the following questions:

a. What does Jesus instruct? ________________________ to Me

b. How does Jesus describe the ones He is inviting to Himself? ________________________

and

___________ ____________

c. What does He promise to give to those who come? ________________________

d. Now, look at the end of verse 29. What, in man, needs the rest? ________________

Note: Keep in mind this is our mind, will, and emotion. Furthermore, the word translated "rest" means, "inner tranquility while one performs necessary labor."[181]

In other words, the *rest* Jesus extends is not a seat upon which to sit or a bed upon which to lie. The *rest* Jesus is offering is Himself. He is our rest! His finished work on the cross is what we rest in. The difference is in *whom* we labor. Are we laboring in the works of our flesh or in Him by His Spirit and His Word?

Consider the following visual for help:

"It was for freedom that Christ set us free; therefore keep standing firm and do not be subject again to a yoke of slavery" (Galatians 5:1).

Works of the Law versus The Finished Work of Christ

Do you see that when a believer succumbs to the lies of the enemy and attempts to obey God's commands in the flesh, it is like coming back up under the old yoke of sin? The burden becomes too heavy to carry and it is impossible to do in the flesh.

As you read Matthew 11:29, do you see an exchange of yokes?

181. Spiros Zodhiates, *The Complete Word Study New Testament Dictionary* (Chattanooga, TN: AMG Publishers, 1993), 156.

Who, in me, is bearing the yoke of His work?

Am I yoked to Him and following His lead, or have I come back up *again* under the yoke of my residual flesh?

So, how will I know? Look at verse 30. How does Jesus describe His yoke and load?

My yoke is ________________________, My load is ________________________.

Keep in mind that Christ's work on the cross was anything but easy and light. And yet, because of His finished work, the yoke He offers us is easy, and the load is light.

Anytime the yoke seems too heavy and the load is burdensome, be assured, you have come *again* under a yoke of slavery.

Would you like to trade your yoke and load for His? He's waiting to make the exchange. Will you let Him? Will you come?

My prayer is that as the Spirit of God has taken the Word of God (specifically Matthew 11:28–30), that you will see this as His invitation of grace and respond in faith (surrender and obedience to His Word). Keep in mind that it is by grace through faith that we are saved! Will you be saved from whatever has power over your heart today?

Remember, only *doers of the Word* and not merely hearers are kept from deception (James 1:22). Do not be deceived!

Notes

Lesson 15

In Whom Do You Boast?

GALATIANS 6:11–18

In this final lesson, Paul will close the letter by revisiting the theme of the entire epistle, which is the grace of God. Watch closely as he equates the grace of God with the cross of Jesus Christ. Pay close attention to the one who boasts and in whom he boasts, for we will either proclaim Christ or ourselves. Either we boast in the flesh, or our only boast is in the cross of our Lord and Savior, Jesus Christ. Paul addresses the contrasting two options as he brings the letter to a close.

As we have seen repeatedly throughout the letter, grace is wholly and completely from God and we as humans have no merit. In fact, when it comes to the salvation of humanity, the only thing we can bring to the table is our sin and utter inability to save ourselves.

No one knew this truth more than the apostle Paul. As Saul, he had been the living definition of boasting and striving in the flesh. If you recall, in the first chapter of the letter, Paul summarizes his entire identity before Christ as being *in Judaism* (Gal. 1:13, 14). Under the disguise and deception of religion, Paul relied upon his flesh in an effort to please God. In truth, he was actually just striving to be god because he did not know the true God, Jesus Christ.

But when grace literally entered the picture as he encountered the living Lord Jesus Christ on that road to Damascus, one look at the glorified Christ changed everything, forever! Now, Paul's only boast was *in Christ*. His years of striving to be God ceased when he met Christ. You see, striving separates us from grace every bit as much as sin separates us from Him. Striving puts emphasis on the flesh, and our flesh loves religion. Christ is our only hope of salvation. Indeed, there is salvation in no one else; "for there is no other name under heaven that has been given among men, by which we must be saved" (Acts 4:12).

Salvation is *by grace* alone *through faith* alone *in Christ* alone! It is totally a work of God, whether it is from the *penalty* of sin (justification), or the *power* of sin (sanctification), or someday, when we see Him face-to-face (glorification), we will be saved from the *presence* of sin forever. Hallelujah!

Paul's influence among the Jews, specifically the Judaizers, had a lasting effect. He became the Judaizer's arch-enemy while on earth. They tenaciously followed him every step. His message, *in Christ*, revealed the lie and trap of being *in Judaism*. The Judaizers hated the message of the cross of Jesus Christ; therefore, they hated Paul.

As Paul closes his letter let's look at his comparison of two types and sources of boasters. A close examination will reveal in whom you boast. Watch as Paul ends the letter by exposing the one who boasts in the flesh, even if that flesh looks religious. Let's get started.

1. What does Paul want the Galatians to know in verse 11?

For us, this verse may seem a little strange. Therefore, to gain insight into what Paul said and why he said it, consider the following information.

Note: Typically, Paul would have used an *amanuensis* (scribe or recorder), like he did when writing the letter to the Romans. Tertius was Paul's amanuensis according to Romans 16:22. However, even with the use of a scribe, Paul would typically conclude his letter in his own handwriting and with his signature, as evidence that he indeed was the author (see 1 Cor. 16:21; 2 Thess. 3:17; and Col. 4:18). The personal authentication proved necessary because a counterfeit letter, supposedly from Paul, had been sent to the Thessalonian church stating that the day of the Lord (judgment) was upon them, causing them great distress (see 2 Thess. 2:1-2).[182]

Equally helpful, Dr. Wuest explains that there were two styles of Greek writing during Paul's time, namely: 1) "the literary uncial," which consisted of inch-high letters formed singly and with no connection with other letters, and 2) the cursive, which uses smaller letters in a running hand, joined together.[183]

Quoting from Sir Frederic Kenyon, Dr. Wuest further explains that there were four classes of workmanship in the style of the manuscripts of the first century. (Sir Frederic Kenyon was a British paleographer [an expert on ancient handwriting and historical manuscripts], as well as a classical biblical scholar in the early 1900's.)

The four categories of writing included:

- *The work of a thoroughly good professional scribe.*
- *The work of a good ordinary professional hand.*
- *The work of an educated man (not a professional scribe), writing a careful copy of a literary hand.*
- *The running hand of common everyday writing.*[184]

According to Dr. Wuest, "Paul dictated his epistles (letters) to Tertius, Sosthenes, Timothy, and Silvanus. These were educated men, but not professional scribes. Therefore, their writing would fall under the category of educated amateur.[185]

Biblical scholars debate as to whether Paul wrote the entire letter or just the final portion (Galatians 6:11). Many attribute the large letters to a possible ophthalmic condition that had caused his eyesight to be affected (mentioned in a previous lesson). However, when you consider the type of message he sent, and the personal connection regarding his spiritual children, you are left with the impression that Paul penned this entire letter himself. For Paul, it was personal.

2. Now, for the next portion of the lesson, I think it would benefit you to see the contrast for yourself. Fill in the following blanks on the next page.

182. Kenneth S. Wuest, *Wuest's Word Studies From the Greek New Testament: Galatians*, Volume One,(Grand Rapids: Wm. B. Eerdmans Publishing Co., 1972), 174.
183. *Ibid.,* 175.
184. *Ibid.*
185. *Ibid.*

6:12 Those

who ________________ to make a ______________ _________________

↓

in the _________________

try to ________________________ you

↓

to be ___________________________,

simply

that

they may ___________ _________ _________________________

↓

for the ________________ _______ ______________.

6:13

For those

who are ____________________________

↓

do not even ________________ the Law themselves,

but they desire to have ________________ circumcised,

that they may __________________________

↓

in _________________ ____________________.

6:14 But

may it never be

that ↓

______ should ____________________,

↓

except in the ____________ of our __________ __________ __________

↓

through

which

↓

_____________ ____________ has been ___________________

↓

to ___________,

and

______ to the _____________.

3. Now, answer the following questions using the diagram you just completed.

a. First, let's begin by identifying *who* is contrasted.

_________________________ (vv. 12-13)

_________________________ (v. 14)

Note: You will recall that Paul has been warning the Galatians about the Judaizers this entire letter. Who better, than a man who once proudly identified himself as being *in Judaism*?

b. Did you notice that each mentioned are boasting? Record below in what they boast:

<u>Whom?</u> **<u>In?</u>**

1) ______________________________ ______________________________________ (v. 13)

2) _____________________________ ______________________________________(v. 14)

Do you see that **all** people are boasters? In fact, boasting is just the verbal or outward *expression* of an inward heart of pride!

Note: The word "boast" is interesting. It comes from the Greek word *kauchaomai*, which means "the neck, which vain persons are apt to carry in a proud manner."[186] It can be used in a good and bad sense.

When I read the definition above, I could not help but think of how the Lord repeatedly described the Israelites in the Old Testament.

c. Now, let's look at the following cross-references and record what He said about them.

1) Read Exodus 32:1-9.

a) Note what the LORD calls the Israelites in verse 9? ___________________ (**Hint:** The Hebrew word translated "obstinate" in this verse can also be translated, *stiff-necked*.)

Did you notice that Exodus 32:9 is in the context of Moses' delay, as the Israelites await his return from the mountain where he had received the Ten Commandments from God?

Tired of waiting, the Israelites approach Aaron to "make a god who will go before us; as for this Moses, the man who brought us up from the land of Egypt, we do not know what has become of him" (Ex. 32:1).

b) What is the first indication of their stiff necks in Exodus 32:1? Record what they wanted and to whom they gave credit (boast) for their salvation from Egypt.

---

186. Spiros Zodhiates, *The Complete Word Study New Testament Dictionary* (Chattanooga, TN: AMG Publishers, 1993), 855.

Next, you will notice that after Aaron instructs the people to bring their gold rings to him, he fashions a molten calf for them to worship. Sadly, the very gold that had been a gift from the Lord for all their years of hard labor under the Egyptians was what they used to craft their image. Isn't that true with us? We use the very things God has given as His gifts to construct our idols today. Truly the heart of *all* flesh would rather worship and serve the created rather than our Creator (Rom. 1:25). Only the Truth can set us free from this lie!

c) What do the Israelites proclaim when he presented the molten calf to the people (v. 4)?

d) What does Aaron do and proclaim next in verse 5? ___________________________

Note: Do you see the spiritual deception of Aaron's heart? Describe his deception in words.

Do you see that by making an idol with his own hands and saying it was to the LORD, he was saying one thing but actually doing another?

e) Now, look at what follows their idolatry in verse 6. What do you see?

Note: The English word "play" does not quite paint the picture that the Hebrew language portrays, because the Hebrew verb *sahaq* means "to laugh, to make jokes, to mock."[187] Specifically, in Exodus 32:6, it has sexual, licentious overtones.[188]

Note: Two sins are like twins in Scripture, namely: idolatry and immorality. In other words, where you see one, you will *always* see the other.

f) Now, let's look at this situation from the LORD'S perspective:

Note what He says they have done in verse 7?

Now, record what they have done in verse 8.

"They have ________________ ________________ ______________ from the way

which ____________ ______________________________ them.

They have _________________ __________ _____________________ a molten calf,

and

have ___________________________ it,

187. Warren Baker and Eugene Carpenter, *The Complete Word Study Dictionary Old Testament* (Chattanooga, TN: AMG Publishers, 2003), 946.

188. Ibid.

and

have __________________________ to it,

and

said, '____

____.' "

g) Now, as you think about what the LORD said concerning the stiff-necked Israelites, what do you see in relation to the flesh? Remember, the root issue of our flesh and the underlying motive as you answer. What do you see?

Do you see that our flesh's desire to be god causes us to corrupt ourselves? Our love for self, rather than God, is openly displayed in our disobedience to God's commands. Little did they realize that the idol that had "made for themselves" was just a substitute for themself. In fact, they became the god they were worshiping.

2) Read what happened years later, as Israel continued to rebel against the LORD God in 2 Chronicles 30:7–9.

a) What warning is given in verse 7?

b) What had their fathers and brothers been regarding the LORD God? _______________

c) Read verse 8 and record what is contrasted:

"Now do not _________________ your _____________________ like your fathers,

but

________________________ to the ___________________________

and

____ which He consecrated forever,

and

____." (emphasis added)

Why? ____

Note: A stiff-necked person is under the wrath of God.

d) Notice, if they will turn from themselves (which is really turning from the Enemy) and return to the LORD, what will they find (v. 9)?

e) What do you learn about the LORD God in verse 9?

He is ________________________________

and

____

and

____

if you ______________________________________

Did you notice that the compassion they *needed* could only be found in a Person? Proving once again, that our greatest *need* is a Savior!

f) What does the Scripture imply if they will *not* return to the LORD God?

If you think about it, isn't this a description of hell—separation from God? Notice also, it's the *face* of God they *needed* most rather than the *hand* of God, which we typically *want*.

And now, although there are so many more references to the stiff-necked Israelites in the Old Testament, let's look at the cure for their stiff-necked condition. You may be surprised to discover that it is the same remedy for the Galatians and us today.

3) Read Deuteronomy 10:15–16 and answer the following questions:

a) Now, since grace *always* precedes faith, let's begin with grace by recording what you learn about the LORD God in verse 15.

1) ____

and

2) ____

Notice the motivating factor and the order in which these two facts occur. Did you see that love preceded being chosen?

b) Now, record how Israel was to respond to God's invitation of grace in verse 16?

____

and

____

c) As you look at the responses, do you see that there are only two ways to respond to grace? Record your insights?

4) One last look at the stiff-necked Israelites, except this time, we will look in the New Testament. Turn to Acts 7:51, where you will pick up in the middle of Stephen's defense of the gospel of Jesus Christ as he faces the "brethren and fathers" of Israel one final time before he is stoned to death. Keep in mind that Saul (Paul) is in the crowd that day. He has heard the message from Stephen and yet refuses to bow his stiff-neck, which results in his consent to allow Stephen to be killed, as those who stone Stephen lay their robes at his feet (Acts 7:58).

a) How does Stephen describe the religious leaders who brought him in for questioning in Acts 7:51?

1) ______________________________________

and

2) ______________________________________ in __________________________

and

____

b) What are they doing about the Holy Spirit? ____________________________

c) Who else has *resisted* Him? ____

Do you see that the issue is not about external circumcision but internally, within the heart? Do you see that first and foremost, it is a sin against God's Spirit?

5) What does it mean to circumcise your heart? How is that possible? Look at the opposite of Acts 7:51 to discover the answer. What do you see?

Think about it. The opposite of stiff-necked is humility. The heart is one's mind, will, and emotion. When the Spirit of God takes the Word of God to reveal our heart, He has just extended grace. You will recall that grace is an invitation from God to surrender and obey His Word, which in turn, is how our hearts are circumcised. In other words, surrender and obedience to God's Word is how the Spirit of God crucifies our flesh!

Now, if you think about it, wouldn't it just be easier and more beneficial to boast in the flesh by promoting external circumcision than to die to one's flesh? Doesn't that sound like the Judaizer's message? Isn't this exactly what Paul is warning the churches in Galatia about the Judaizers?

4. Let's look back in Galatians 6, specifically regarding the Judaizers, and record what they are doing in verses 12–13. There are four things explicitly mentioned.

a. Let's begin with their desire in verse 12. What do you see?

Note: The English words "good showing" come from one Greek word, *euprosopeo*, which means, "to present a good face."[189] By using this word in particular, Paul is showing the difference between appearance and reality.

189. Spiros Zodhiates, *The Complete Word Study New Testament Dictionary* (Chattanooga, TN: AMG Publishers, 1993), 681.

1) Notice, in what they desire to make a good showing?

2) How are they attempting to do this (v. 12)?

3) Notice, who is going to benefit from the Galatian's circumcision?

Who is this about? ___________________________

b. What is their concern (v. 12b)? ____

Note: The word "persecuted" (*dioko*), means to repeatedly pursue with the act of enmity.[190]

1) Why would they be persecuted? ____

2) Again, who is this about? _________________________

c. Now read verse 13 and record what you learn about the Judaizers (those who are circumcised) regarding the Law?

d. Again, what is their desire (v. 13)?

1) Why? ____

2) One last time, who is this about? _____________________

When you look back at the diagram of Galatians 6:12–13, do you see that the repeated focus is on the Judaizers? Truly, it's all about them!

5. Now, let's look at the exact opposite—Paul. What does he say about boasting in verse 14?

a. In what would Paul *not* boast? ____

In fact, the English translation, "May it never be," comes from the Greek words, *me genito*, which carries the strongest negative possible, making it virtually impossible when used.[191]

What would make it impossible for Paul to think about boasting in his flesh? How could he be so certain? Wouldn't the answer include the fact that he had seen the Lord (Acts 9:3–4)? You see, when you and I boast in our flesh, one thing is sure, in whatever area of boasting, we obviously have not seen the Lord! In fact, these areas of our life would be considered blind spots. A blind spot occurs when we are not able to see ourselves as we should. Blind spots are areas of our heart where we have not seen Him, causing our view of self to be skewed. For once you see Him, you will never ever doubt that He is God, and you are not!

So does that mean that Paul stopped boasting? As he would say, *may it never be*!

b. In what did Paul boast? ____

190. *Ibid.*, 474.
191. John MacArthur, Jr., *The John MacArthur New Testament Commentary Galatians* (Chicago, IL: Moody Press, 1987), 204.

6. Did you notice the *centrality* of the cross of Jesus Christ in both the Judaizers (v. 12) and Paul (v. 14)? What do you see?

Quite the opposite, don't you think?

Look at the following visual for help in understanding the centrality of the cross:

Only the God-Man can extend the Love of God:

Vertically – Toward God

Horizontally – Toward humanity

When your boast is in the cross of Jesus Christ, you know that He alone is God, and, because of the cross, you can now love the Lord your God with all of your heart and love others as yourself.

But, when your boast is in the flesh, you despise the cross of Jesus Christ because you are usurped, as God, and you can only love yourself.

The cross represents the symbol of Divine Accomplishment with no room for Human Achievement. In fact, all that humanity can bring to the cross is sin, guilt, and shame. In other words, there would be no reason to ever boast in the flesh!

7. Now, let's look at the cross of Jesus Christ regarding the world and Paul specifically. What do you see in verse 14b?

Note: The word "crucified" (*stauroo*) is used "metaphorically, to crucify the flesh with the affections and lusts . . . to mortify them through the faith and love of Christ crucified."[192] Explaining the verse specifically, Zodhiates states,

> *When Paul says, "The world is crucified to me, and I unto the world," he means that his regard for his crucified Savior was so great that the world had no more charm for him than a corpse of a crucified malefactor would have had, nor did he take any more delight in worldly things than a person expiring on the cross would do in the objects around him.*[193]

192. Spiros Zodhiates, *The Complete Word Study New Testament Dictionary* (Chattanooga, TN: AMG Publishers, 1993), 1309.
193. *Ibid.*

Also noteworthy, the word "crucified" is a perfect indicative passive verb. The perfect tense indicates a completed action in the past with present and future results. The indicative mood signifies a statement of fact, and the passive voice means that the subject (in this case, *the world*) has been acted upon by an outside source.

8. To help understand what Paul is saying, look at 1 John 5:4. What do you see? Can you explain what this verse means using the definition of faith?

One final time, allow me to share the definition of faith from the late Bible scholar and theologian, W. E. Vine. He defines faith in three components, namely:

- A firm conviction of God's Word
- Personal surrender of the will to God's Word
- Obedience to God's Word[194]

In other words, a firm conviction of God's Word occurs when the Spirit of God takes the Word of God and illumines our hearts. This is God's invitation of grace! We will either respond in surrender and obedience, which is faith, or in unbelief.

With the definition of faith in mind, what does 1 John 5:4 mean?

9. Now, how does 1 John 5:4 correlate with Galatians 6:14b?

Aren't these two verses essentially saying the same thing?

10. Now, look at Paul's final statement about circumcision in Galatians 6:15. What is he saying?

What matters most according to verse 15? BUT ____

Do you see that Paul is contrasting the outward physical act of circumcision with the spiritual, inward circumcision of the heart? No amount of outward change or mutilation of our flesh can change the inward soul of man.

Note: The word "new" (*kainos*) means never before known. It is qualitatively new as contrasted with *neos*, which is temporarily new.[195]

194. W. E. Vine, *Vine's Expository Dictionary of Old and New Testament Words* (Grand Rapids, MI: Fleming H. Revell, 1981), 71.
195. Spiros Zodhiates, *The Complete Word Study New Testament Dictionary* (Chattanooga, TN: AMG Publishers, 1993), 804.

11. Now, look at 2 Corinthians 5:11–17 and record how these verses help explain Galatians 6:12–15. What do you see?

12. Look at Galatians 6:16. What does it mean to *walk by this rule*? Keep in mind that he has just referenced the *new creation*, which is in Christ.

13. What is the result of the one who walks by this rule? ______________________________

and

____

Note: The word "rule" (*kanon*), means measuring rod. It was a straight rod used to examine other things. In the New Testament, it refers to the rule of conduct and behavior.[196]

It might interest you to know that the Scriptures are called the Canon (*kanon*) of Scriptures. The Word of God is the measuring rod. It is the standard by which we are to measure our conduct and behavior.

14. Now, compare Galatians 6:16 with Galatians 5:16 and Galatians 5:25. What do you see?

15. Now, look again at Galatians 6:16. Upon whom will the peace and mercy of God be?

1) ____________________________________

2)____________________________________

Now, look at Galatians 3:7. Who is the *Israel of God*? ________________________________

Do you see it is those who are of the faith?

16. In closing, what does Paul request of the Galatians in verse 17?

Do you see that what troubled Paul most was that his spiritual children were under attack? Although taking the gospel to the Galatians had been costly to Paul, the pain and suffering were well worth it. Read 3 John 4.

196. *Ibid.*, 818.

17. What does Paul mean by brand-marks of Jesus (Gal. 6:17)? To understand this portion, look at the following cross-references to get a glimpse into the life of Paul. Record what was physically happening to Paul.

a. Acts 14:19 -

Note: Keep in mind that the events described in Acts 14 followed the gospel going to Galatia (Acts 13). God's invitation of grace through His instrument, Paul, was costly to Paul, and he had the scars to prove it.

b. Read 2 Corinthians 11:12–30. You will notice that this entire portion of Scripture is set against the backdrop of false teachers. List the hardships Paul faced primarily due to the Judaizers who followed him every place he went. What do you see?

Now what is Paul's conclusion in verse 30? ______________________________________

____

Think about it. *In Judaism*, Paul boasts in his person and his works (*i.e.* circumcision, his ancestral heritage, his ability to keep the Law... Phil. 3:4-6), but *in Christ*, Paul's only boast is in his weakness (need) and the cross of Jesus Christ (his Savior). Do you see that's how Paul's weakness results in God's glory?

WHAT ABOUT YOU?

In whom or what do you boast?

Do you sense the boaster that lives within your flesh? I know I sure do. It makes me sick just to think about it.

What about you? *When* you boast, and we all do, is it in your weakness? Or do you hide, cover, and blame others for your weakness? One type of boasting brings Him glory. The other grieves His Spirit. Since there are only two ways in which we boast, which one describes you? The next time you have the urge to boast, remember what the Scripture says about it!

And finally, just as Paul's scars gave the Lord glory, our scars do the same. We must be willing to allow His Spirit to take the scalpel of His Word and cut out those areas that have gained power over us. At first, those pus-filled pockets of sin seem unbearable. However, once we have surrendered and obeyed what the Spirit has illuminated from His Word regarding sin, those excruciatingly painful areas become scars, and scars don't hurt. They are just reminders of our sin, and how a loving Savior is rescuing us from the world, our flesh, and the Enemy of our souls. When this happens, although you may be weak, He is glorified. He is mighty to save (Zeph. 3:17)!

Will you let Him?

18. And finally, we see Paul ending this letter the way he began it, with the grace of our Lord Jesus Christ. What have you learned about the grace of God? Can you end this study with a prayer of gratitude and thanksgiving to the only one who deserves your praise? How would He lead you to respond to His invitation of grace? Share your thoughts in the space below.

Are you tired of striving to be God? Do you experientially know that He alone is God?

Listen to the words of the late American Baptist Bible scholar, pastor, and founder of the Gordon-Conwell Theology Seminary in the late 1800s, Adoniram Judson Gordon. Named after the late missionary to Burma, Adoniram Judson, in his spiritual autobiography, *How Christ Came to Church*, he referred to the growing drudgery and desperation of spirit that was his experience in the ministry. The record of this deep exercise of spirit is familiar to many of us. He writes:

> *Well do we remember those days when drudgery was pushed to the point of desperation. The hearers must be moved to repentance and confession of Christ; therefore more effort must be devoted to the sermon, more ours to elaborating its periods, more pungency put into its sentences, more study bestowed on its delivery. And then came the disappointment that few, if any, were converted by all this which had cost a week of solid toil. And now attention was turned to the prayer meeting as the possible seat of difficulty—so few attending it and so little readiness to participate in its services. A pulpit scourging must be laid on next Sunday, and the sharpest sting which words can effect put into the lash. Alas, there is no increase in attendance, and instead of spontaneity in prayer, and witnessing there is a silence, which seems almost like sullenness! Then the administration goes wrong and, opposition is encountered among officials, so that caucusing must be undertaken to get the members to vote as they should. Thus the burdens of anxiety increase while we are trying to lighten them, and should-be helpers become hinderers, till discouragement comes and sleepless nights ensue; these hot boxes on the train of our activities necessitating a stop and a visit of the doctor, with the verdict overwork and the remedy absolute rest.*
>
> *It was after much of all this, of which even the most intimate friends knew nothing, that there came one day a still voice of admonition, saying, "There stands One among you whom you know not" (John 1:26). And perhaps I answered, "Who is He, Lord, that I might know Him?" I had known the Holy Spirit as a heavenly influence to be invoked, but somehow I had not grasped the truth that He is a Person of the Godhead who came down to earth at a definite time and who has been in the church ever since, just as real as Jesus was here during the thirty and three years of His earthly life. . . .*
>
> *With lightening heart came the climax: "...how many true Christians toil on, bearing burdens and assuming responsibilities far too great for their natural strength, utterly forgetful that the mighty burden-bearer of the world is with them to do for them and through them that which they have undertaken to accomplish alone! Happy also for these if some weary day the blessed Paraclete, the invisible Christ, shall say to them, 'Have I been so long with you, and yet you have not come to know Me?' (John 14:9). So it happened to this writer. The strong Son of God revealed Himself as being evermore in His church, and I knew Him, not through a sudden burst of revelation, not through some thrilling experience of instantaneous sanctification, but a quiet, sure, and steady*

> *discovery, increasing unto more and more. Jesus in the Spirit stood with me in a kind of spiritual epiphany and just as definitely and irrevocably as I once took Christ crucified as my sin-bearer I now took the Holy Spirit for my burden-bearer."*[197]

What about you? Isn't it time for you to cease striving and know Him as God (Ps. 46:10)?

And now my prayer for you as we close, is that you will continue to *grow in the grace and knowledge of our Lord and Savior Jesus Christ. To Him be the glory, both now and to the day of eternity* (2 Peter 3:18).

Some Concluding Thoughts:

As we bring our study in Galatians to a conclusion, what has the mirror of God's Word shown you about your heart about striving?

The presenting issue in Galatians was the external act of circumcision. But we all know that the presenting problem is never the real issue. The root issue is always our flesh competing for His place as God. We have discovered that our flesh is nothing more than our desire and attempt to be *like god*. Deep down, we think very highly of ourselves. We genuinely love ourselves the most.

We all have our theology, which is based upon what we think is right. It's how we would carry out God's plan to save mankind but with a slightly different twist. Things would be done *our* way.

We would have done things differently if we had been God in that situation.

Deep down, if we are willing to be honest with ourselves, we think:

- we have a better plan.
- we would make a better Savior.
- we have merit.
- we have something to bring to the table before a holy a righteous God.

Do you see the repeated word, *we*?

But the theme of Galatians is all about grace, and grace is all about *HIM*, right.

Herein lies the issue.

Cease striving, the Scripture tells us. Striving for what? Do you see it? We want to be god! But what does the end of that verse instruct us? Cease striving and *know that I am God* (Ps. 46:10).

Know that I am God! There it is.

- He has the plan!
- He is the perfect Savior!
- He is the only one with merit, for He alone is God.
- Christ Jesus presented Himself before a holy and righteous God.

Why? Because He alone is the holy and righteous God!

---

197. V. Raymond Edman, They Found the Secret (Grand Rapids, MI: Zondervan, 1984), pp. 72-73.

Do you see the order? Do you see that you and I will never know that He is God if we persist on striving in our flesh to be Him?

Only God can know God! Without God's Spirit, we will never truly know God. And if we spend our lives competing in our flesh with His Spirit, we will spend our entire lives striving. Is that any way to live?

Any external thing we might add to Christ changes the entire gospel of Jesus Christ, making it a different gospel (Gal. 1:6). There is only One Gospel!

Will you cease striving to add yourself to Christ and His finished work on the cross? Will you allow Him to be God?

What would that look like right now in your life? Where are you striving with God for His place? Will you pray, *Lord Jesus, save me*?

You see, either salvation is a work of grace by God the Father, Son, and Spirit, or it involves our work as well. But what do the Scriptures teach? God's Word emphatically states, "Salvation belongs to the LORD" (Psa. 3:8; 62:2, 6; Jonah 2:9; Eph. 2:8, etc.). Furthermore, the psalmist repeatedly warns, "Vain is the salvation of man" (Psalm 60:11; 108:12, 146:3). So, in whom have you placed your trust?

Thankfully, the grace of our loving God included the Father's plan from before the foundation of the world. That plan is the Father's work of grace through the Son's redeeming work. The Son executed the Father's plan perfectly and completely in His work of grace, and now, the work of grace is being extended through God's Spirit as He applies the finished work of Jesus Christ in the lives of those who are His.

Truly salvation is totally and completely a work of God's grace!

Praise the Father, Son, and Spirit!

To God alone be the glory!

AMG INTERNATIONAL
MEETING THE DEEPEST NEEDS

WE BELIEVE THE GOSPEL IS TRANSFORMATIVE

And you can change the world one child at a time.

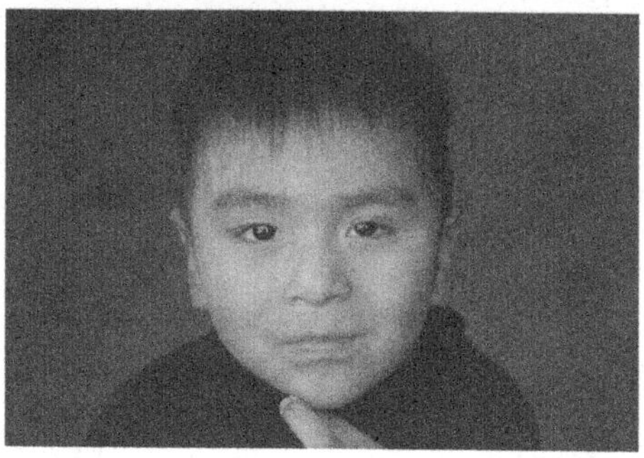

Thousands of children in the world are born into a cycle of poverty that has been around for generations, leaving them without hope for a safe and secure future. For a little more than $1 a day you can provide the tools a child needs to break the cycle in the name of Jesus.

OUR CONTACT

423-894-6060
info@amginternational.org
@amgintl
6815 Shallowford Rd. Chattanooga, TN 37421

Made in the USA
Middletown, DE
05 February 2022

59727166R00124